SAINT ALOYSIUS GONZAGA, S.J.

Silas S. Henderson

SAINT ALOYSIUS GONZAGA, S.J.

With an Undivided Heart

IGNATIUS PRESS   SAN FRANCISCO

Unless otherwise noted, Scripture quotations (except those within citations) have been taken from the Revised Standard Version of the Holy Bible, Second Catholic Edition, © 2006 by the Division of Christian Education of the National Council of the Churches of Christ in the United States of America.

Author's note: While respecting the integrity of the translations of the writings and letters of Saint Aloysius and others included in the earlier biographies of Cepari, Meschler, and Martindale, some minor changes were made to some of the texts to facilitate ease of reading by modern readers and to include translations of foreign-language texts. Adapted texts are acknowledged in the footnotes.

Cover art:
Gianni Dagli Orti / The Art Archive at Art Resource, N.Y.

Cover design by Riz Marsella

This book is dedicated to my grandparents,
Harry and Marianne Henderson,
without whose support and guidance
I would never have discovered the
treasures of the Catholic Faith nor
Saint Aloysius nor all those saints who have
been my guides and inspiration for so many years.

Who shall ascend the hill of the LORD?
    And who shall stand in his holy place?
He who has clean hands and a pure heart,
    who does not lift up his soul to what is false,
    and does not swear deceitfully.
He will receive blessing from the LORD,
    and vindication from the God of his salvation.
Such is the generation of those who seek him,
    who seek the face of the God of Jacob.

—Psalm 24:3–6

CONTENTS

ACKNOWLEDGMENTS

No one ever truly accomplishes anything on his own. In the research and writing of this life of Saint Aloysius Gonzaga, I am indebted to many men and women who, over the years, have encouraged, challenged, and inspired me to keep working. In a particular way, I want to thank members of the Benedictine community at Saint Meinrad Archabbey, especially Father Harry Hagan; the late Fathers Cyprian Davis and Gavin Barnes; and Father Christian Raab for the interest they have shown in this project. I would also like to acknowledge the late Father Simeon Daly, O.S.B., for graciously agreeing to read early drafts of the manuscript and for his discerning suggestions and comments. Special acknowledgment goes to Father Vincent Tobin, O.S.B., for his thoughtful translations of certain Latin and Italian texts. My good friend Brother Martin Erspamer, O.S.B., has offered unparalleled support and encouragement and deserves credit for the title for this book.

Beyond the cloister walls of Saint Meinrad, I want to thank Bear Waters; Dr. Melanie Prejean-Sullivan; Dr. Patricia J. Hughes; Father James Martin, S.J.; Carrie Williamson; Linus Mundy; Jon Sweeney; Phil Etienne, my friend and supervisor at Abbey Press; and my family, along with so many others, for their support and contributions for the success of this project, as well as for their suggestions and critiques.

INTRODUCTION

The great fourth-century Desert Father Anthony the Abbot (d. 356) encouraged his followers to "repeat by heart the commandments of the Scriptures, and to remember the deeds of the saints, that by their example the soul may train itself under the guidance of the commandments".[1] While Saint Anthony would have been speaking specifically of the early martyrs, his words may easily be applied to the many individuals throughout salvation history who lived lives of charity and simplicity, confessing their faith through the witness of their lives, just as the martyrs bore witness to their faith by the manner of their deaths.

Remembering the "deeds of the saints" is one of the foundational elements of our Christian faith. Although devotion to many saints is confined to a specific time or place, there are those who seem to have captured the imagination of the whole world. We need only think of Saint Christopher (d. ca. 250), Saint Francis of Assisi (d. 1226), Saint Thérèse of Lisieux (d. 1897), or Saint Teresa of Calcutta (d. 1997) to recognize that within the heart of every believer is an attraction to those who have lived their faith in a heroic manner.

Our contemporary culture places before us many types and images of success that reflect a worldview that is often at odds with Christian values. Even within the Catholic Church, the period immediately following the reforms of the Second Vatican Council witnessed an almost complete turning away from traditional devotions, including interest in the saints. Advances in historiography and changes in scholarship dismissed the often spectacular tales of miracles and martyrdoms that characterized the vitae (lives) of the saints for nearly two millennia. The saints more often than not appeared to be larger than life, mere caricatures, exhibiting a holiness that could never be matched by the "normal" person of faith. Yet their stories (and

---

[1] Athanasius of Alexandria, *The Life of Saint Anthony the Great* (Willits, Calif.: Eastern Orthodox Books, 1989), 76.

adventures) have inspired countless men, women, and children of faith to strive to lead lives that were more pleasing to God, more holy, and more perfect.

Although the early Church initially limited the cult of the saints to martyrs, local churches soon expanded their vision of the "friends of God" to include the "white martyrs": the desert hermits and ascetics. Later, holy bishops, virgins, and widows were recognized as saints because of the witness of their lives. As Kenneth Woodward notes, "The cult of the saints brought the dead to life, breathed life into legend, and provided the community of Christians with their own heavenly patrons."[2] With the development of the canonization process, first by the local bishop and later by the pope, the image of holiness presented by the Church began to shift officially from the heroic witness of the martyrs and ascetics to the lives of poverty, chastity, and obedience lived by the flourishing mendicant orders of the later Middle Ages. In point of fact, no martyrs at all were canonized between 1254 and 1481.[3] The papacy sought to promote candidates for canonization whose lives were worthy of imitation by the faithful, reflecting a concern with virtues rather than miracles. Pope Innocent IV (1243–1259) declared that sanctity required a life of "continuous, uninterrupted virtue", which, as Woodward notes, was essentially perfection.[4] For a cause for canonization to be successful, the proof of virtue was not enough unless it was also heroic.

Because of this shift, the written lives of the saints and blesseds became more stylized. Flaws disappeared while the individual's virtues were enhanced by stories of supernatural graces and gifts and by superhuman discipline. This new style of vitae emphasized contemplation over action, detachment over engagement with the world. Biographers (or, more appropriately, hagiographers) often looked to the vitae of earlier saints, seeking precedents for their efforts.[5]

---

[2] Kenneth Woodward, *Making Saints: How the Catholic Church Determines Who Becomes a Saint, Who Doesn't, and Why* (New York: Touchstone, 1990), 60.

[3] Ibid., 69.

[4] Ibid., 71.

[5] Jodi Bilinkoff notes that the life of Saint Catherine of Siena written by Blessed Raymond of Capua acted as a model for the biographers of later women saints. Jodi Bilinkoff, *Related Lives: Confessors and Their Female Penitents, 1450–1750* (Ithaca, N.Y.: Cornell University Press, 2005), 40. See also Woodward, *Making Saints*, 72–73.

Aloysius Gonzaga was one of those saints who lived in the decades immediately following the Council of Trent and whose life and virtues were "enhanced" by his religious community (the Society of Jesus) and his admiring biographers. In a way that was typical of the hagiographical writings of the time, this young nobleman was portrayed as possessing superhuman virtue at an early age, as practicing the most severe penances, and as eschewing the company of his noble counterparts, particularly women. The first vita of Aloysius was actually compiled during his lifetime by Jerome Piatti, S.J., the priest charged with the care of the Jesuit novices sent to study at Sant'Andrea in Rome. He had first met Aloysius when the young man arrived in Rome, and Piatti began making a record of his words and actions almost immediately. These notes were later handed over to Virgil Cepari, S.J., who continued to keep a record of Aloysius' actions. Following Aloysius' death in 1591, Saint Robert Cardinal Bellarmine (d. 1621), the young man's spiritual director, asked Cepari to complete his work. Cepari was initially unable to fulfill Bellarmine's request, so he turned all of his notes over to other Jesuit writers. A short time later, a rather brief biography was printed, but it became clear that a more complete account of Aloysius' life needed to be compiled. Twelve years after Aloysius' death, Claudio Aquaviva, the general of the Society of Jesus, asked Father Cepari to compose a proper vita. This first official biography (which was published in 1606) was examined and approved by representatives of the Jesuits, the Dominicans, the Capuchin Franciscans, the Benedictines, and finally, the pontifical censors.

The stylized portrait of this saintly prince presented in Cepari's *Life of Saint Aloysius Gonzaga* would capture the imaginations of artists and composers, adding further appeal to his story and cult. Italian-born Johann Simon "Progetto" Mayr (d. 1845) composed an oratorio, *San Luigi Gonzaga* (1822), based on the young prince's struggle to obtain his father's permission to enter the Jesuits. French composer Joseph-Guy-Marie Ropartz (d. 1955) dedicated his *Missa Te Deum Laudamus* (1925–1926) to Saint Aloysius. While numerous painters and sculptors have made their own contributions to Aloysius' cult, these pious works of art have done little to support his cause in our own day.[6] Many of the historic devotional images of him are

---

[6] James Martin, *My Life with the Saints* (Chicago: Loyola Press, 2006), 331.

extremely sentimental, portraying an effeminate youth yearning for Heaven. Unfortunately, this is the image of Aloysius Gonzaga that has endured. As one of my own Benedictine confreres exclaimed, "Why do they always make him look like a little girl?"

In the wake of the Second Vatican Council, Aloysius was easily dismissed as being "exceedingly scrupulous in prayer, almost masochistic in the exercise of self-mortification, frightened of women ... obsessing with the idea and hope of an early death".[7] Even the most recent edition of *Butler's Lives of the Saints* declares that Aloysius' behavior suggested "religiosity rather than true religion", allowing that he has been described as "priggish", "naïve", "angular", and "unattractive".[8] And yet, in spite of these criticisms, Aloysius remains a fixture in the life of the Church. His memorial on June 21 is obligatory for celebration by the universal Church. He was proclaimed the patron of Catholic youth in 1729 (three years after his canonization); this title was confirmed by Pius XI (1922–1939) in 1926 in his Apostolic Letter *Singulare Illud*. A more recent popular devotion honors Aloysius as the patron of those suffering from HIV/AIDS and their caregivers.

Contemporary historiography recognizes the value of placing historic figures within the context of their time and place in history. Saints were individuals with faults and failings who were responding by grace to the challenges of their times. Kenneth Woodward notes that, when they are considered from this perspective, the saints "were in the depths of the Spirit, wholly new creations, initiators in the life of faith, hope, and charity, traditional in the—best—sense that they reinterpreted the meaning of Christ for their own age".[9] As they reinterpreted Christ for their particular time and place, each left an enduring mark on the life of the Church, helping to shape the traditions that come down to us today. Aloysius Gonzaga was certainly no exception.

As we explore the world in which he lived—from his family's estates and holdings in Castiglione; to the court of King Philip II

---

[7] Richard P. McBrien, *Lives of the Saints: From Mary and Saint Francis of Assisi to John XXIII and Mother Teresa* (New York: HarperCollins, 2001), 248. See also Francis Corley and Robert Willmes, *Wings of Eagles* (Milwaukee, Wis.: Bruce Publishing, 1941), 50.

[8] Paul Burns and Kathleen Jones, eds., *Butler's Lives of the Saints: New Full Edition; June* (Collegeville, Minn.: Liturgical Press, 1997), 152.

[9] Woodward, *Making Saints*, 95.

of Spain, where he was a page; to Sant'Andrea in Rome, where he received his Jesuit formation—we will certainly see that, in many respects, Aloysius was a product of his time and circumstances. As the first son and heir of the Marquis of Castiglione, Aloysius was, from the moment of his birth, immersed in the intrigue, scandal, and politics of his day. The reforms of Trent were reshaping the Church as the threat of Protestantism and the spread of Islam cast a shadow over the lives of nearly every man, woman, and child in Europe. Fierce plagues continued to ravage the land, while ecstatic seers offered their visions of both Heaven and Hell to the uneducated masses.

As the heir of the Marquis of Castiglione and a prince of the Holy Roman Empire, Aloysius' future was effectively decided for him before he was born. Although the tenor and manner of his rule would be left up to him when the time came, it was expected that he would inherit the family's holdings and take his place among the elite of the age—it was for this that he was formed from his earliest days. But Aloysius recognized a call to become more than his family or peers could imagine. He recognized that in order truly to embrace the vocation he had wisely and patiently discerned, he would have to become truly free. For this young prince, Christ's admonition to "take up your cross and follow" was more than a mere platitude (see Mt 10:38; 16:24; Lk 14:27). In those words lay the secret to a happiness and freedom that could never be his in his given state of life. It was only over the course of several years that Aloysius came to understand his vocation, and this actually remains both his glory and one of the tragedies of his life. In his pursuit of this ideal, he had little to no guidance from a spiritual director or mentor, and his zeal all too often took the form of excessive penance and self-denial, ascetical practices for which he is strongly criticized today. Although it is true that the types of penance embraced by this saint should not necessarily be imitated by those of our own day, the spirit of self-awareness, contrition, and compunction that motivated his actions is just as valuable for us today as it was for him four centuries ago.

In order for Aloysius to achieve the freedom he desired, a freedom that he hoped would one day take him to the Jesuit missions in Asia, he recognized that he must be freed from the burdens imposed upon him by his rank and title. He also realized that he must free himself from those inner drives and tendencies that threatened to lead him away from his goal of union with God. Embracing the same ascetical values that animated the lives of the Desert Fathers and Mothers, he set out on his way, following his thorn-crowned King.

Therein lies the heart of Aloysius' message for today. In many ways, our world differs little from that of this sixteenth-century Italian prince. Ambition, sensuality, and greed, as well as a false sense of entitlement and lust for power and possessions, are as real in the twenty-first century as they were in Renaissance Italy. Aloysius was born with everything but walked away from wealth and prestige to embrace a life of poverty, chastity, and obedience that bespeaks an absolute trust in and abandonment to Divine Providence. It is this trust and abandonment, manifest from his earliest days, which make him a worthy guide and patron of old and young alike.

Chapter 1

The Family Gonzaga

Northern Italy is a rich land of lofty mountains and fertile valleys. The heights of the Alps dissolve into rolling, vine-covered hills and lush plains. This picturesque landscape has changed little over the centuries. It was here, centuries ago, that one of the most influential families in sixteenth-century Europe ruled with the force and vigor of the lords of that age. For centuries, the House of Gonzaga had increased its holdings in land, while its sphere of influence, political and family ties, and power came to extend far beyond the family holdings centered at Mantua, Italy, spreading north to Lorraine, Württemberg, Bavaria, Brandenburg, and Austria. Daughters of the dukes of Mantua became empresses, and emperors' daughters became duchesses of Mantua. The nobles of the Gonzaga family were prominent figures in the all-too-frequent wars of fifteenth- and sixteenth-century Italy, and they were to be found commanding the armies of Venice, the Holy Roman Empire, and the Papal States. The family also played a prominent role in the life of the Church, boasting no fewer than ten cardinals, including Ercole Cardinal Gonzaga, who, in 1562, presided over the proceedings of the Council of Trent. Prince Luigi Alessandro Gonzaga of Solferino supported Saint Angela Merici (d. 1540), as she worked to found her Company of Saint Ursula.[1] Another member of the Gonzaga family, Osanna Andreasi of Mantua (d. 1505), is honored with the title of Blessed.[2]

---

[1] Philip Caraman, *Saint Angela: The Life of Angela Merici, Foundress of the Ursulines (1474–1540)* (New York: Farrar, Straus, 1963), 37–38, 69.

[2] Blessed Osanna of Mantua (1449–1505) was the daughter of Nicholas Andreasi and Louisa Gonzaga. From an early age, she experienced a wide array of mystical experiences, and she was said to have had the grace of sharing the pain of Christ's Passion. She often suffered because of her ecstasies and vision, but she received support from Duke Frederick Gonzaga of Mantua, who invited Osanna into his household, where she was both friend and advisor for

The advent of the sixteenth century saw the powerful Ducal House of Mantua divided into four separate lines: the families of counts of Novellara-Sabionetta, the princes of Bozzolo, the lords of Guastalla-Molfetta, and finally, the marquises of Castiglione.[3] The members of this branch derived their name from the town of Castiglione delle Stiviere, which was located on the high road between Brescia and Mantua in Lombardy and home of the infamous Castiglione delle Stiviere Castle. In the town square stood the collegiate church, dedicated to the martyrs Saints Celsus and Nazarius and claiming rights to a chapter governed by an archpriest.[4] Overlooking the town was the castle Rocca di Castiglione, the stronghold of the marquises.[5] Beyond the castle's high ramparts were the lodgings of various officials and the musketeers, the stables and riding ground, the mint, the mansion of the marquis, and the private Church of San Sebastian. Below the castle lay the town, and from the high walls one could see the man-made lake, on whose shores was the Franciscan friary of Santa Maria and one of the marquis' summer homes. In the distance,

---

Frederick and his son Francis II. At the age of thirty-seven, she took the vows of a Dominican Tertiary and is remembered for her charity and the simplicity of her life. Her many letters attest to her holy life and her unhappiness with the corruption in the Church of her day. Blessed Osanna died on June 20, 1505, and was beatified in 1514 by decree of Pope Leo X.

[3] Maurice Meschler, S.J., *St. Aloysius Gonzaga: Patron of Christian Youth* (Rockford, Ill.: TAN Books, 1985), 3.

[4] It was customary in the Middle Ages to join the priests serving in cathedrals and large urban churches into administrative groups who assisted the local bishop or the archpriest, who took the place of the bishop in civil affairs or public worship. Incidentally, in 1804, the remains of Aloysius' mother, Donna Marta, were transferred to this church, where they were interred in a vault immediately in front of the sanctuary on the spot where, according to tradition, she knelt before the image of her son when it was exposed for the first time for veneration on the high altar.

[5] The fortress of Castiglione that served as the home to Saint Aloysius' family no longer exists. On March 3, 1701, during the Spanish War of Succession, Castiglione came into the possession of the imperial party. Following a renewed attack by the French in 1702, the imperial forces were unable to retain control of the fortress and were forced to flee. In 1706, a fierce battle was fought at Guidizzolo in which the French successfully retained control of the fortress. The imperial forces, allied with the Austrians, acknowledging its strategic position, ordered the stronghold to be demolished.

Today, all that survives of the birthplace of Saint Aloysius is the gateway, the small Church of San Sebastiano, and the walls that surround the hill. All that remains of the castle itself are eighty stones taken from the floor of the room where Aloysius had been born. These were moved to the college belonging to the Virgins of Jesus at Castiglione.

one can still see forested hills and the blue waters of Lago di Garda, framed by the majestic heights of the Alps.

It was to this majestic setting that the Marquis of Castiglione, Ferrante Gonzaga, had brought his young bride, Donna Marta, Countess of Tana di Santena, on March 19, 1567. Ferrante was a man of culture and a gifted soldier. A loyal and practical Catholic, he had refused to accept the post of commander in chief of the cavalry of King Henry VIII of England. A perfect courtier, he was determined to uphold the honor of his distinguished family. And like so many other Italian princes, he had served the king of Spain, Philip II (d. 1598), who awarded him the Grand Cross of the Order of Alcántara, for his bravery in the battle against the sultan of Barbary at Oran.

It was with King Philip's blessing and endorsement that Ferrante sought the hand the queen's beloved maid of honor: the Lady Marta, daughter of Don Baldassare Tana di Santena of Chieri and Donna Anna della Rovere.[6] Donna Marta had become the favorite maid of honor of Elizabeth of Valois (d. 1568) during a visit to the court of King Henry II of France. She accompanied Elizabeth to Spain at the time of her marriage to King Philip II. Marta's many admirable traits, especially her gentle disposition and piety, caught the attention of Don Ferrante. When he proposed, she asked for time to reflect and requested a number of Masses to be offered in honor of the Most Holy Trinity, the Holy Spirit, the Sacred Passion, the Blessed Virgin, and the Holy Angels, asking that she be given the grace to decide correctly. She ultimately accepted Ferrante's proposal, and the two were betrothed on the Feast of the Birth of Saint John the Baptist, June 24, 1566. In accordance with the request of the queen, who was expecting her first child, the couple deferred their wedding until after the birth, which took place on August 11. The wedding was celebrated soon after in the splendor of the Royal Chapel; it was the first time the new Rite of Marriage, revised according to the regulations of the Council of Trent, was celebrated in Spain.

Before the couple left Spain in the first months of 1567, King Philip bestowed on Ferrante the title of grand chamberlain, granting

---

[6] The Roveres were another great Italian family known for their military exploits and their support of the arts. Their house had given the Church two popes—Sixtus IV (1471–1484) and Julius II (1503–1513)—and eleven cardinals.

him considerable revenues from possessions in Naples and Milan. He also appointed him commander of all the Italian infantry.

Following their arrival in Castiglione, the couple assumed their duties with a certain zeal and a spirit of prudence. Each Sunday and feast day, they attended the liturgies of the parish church rather than their private chapel, expecting their subjects to follow their example. Donna Marta prayed fervently that God would bless her with children, and she devoted herself to works of piety and charity in the service of the people of Castiglione. In her devotion, she resolved that, should God grant her a son, she would dedicate the child to his service in a religious order.

Within a year, she was pregnant with her first child. The pregnancy was not without complications, however, and when the time came for the birth, both mother and child were in grave danger. Having exhausted all human expertise, Donna Marta asked her husband's permission to make a vow that if the Blessed Virgin would protect her life and that of the child, she would take the child on a pilgrimage to the shrine of Our Lady of Loreto. While the danger soon passed, the child was, according to the custom of the time, baptized before the birthing process was completed. After several difficult hours, the infant was finally delivered around six o'clock in the evening on March 9, 1568. The exhausted mother asked that the child be placed in her arms; she made the sign of the cross on his forehead and embraced him. Because the newborn infant did not cry and lay quite still and motionless, the attendants did not know whether he would live or die. The baby did finally cry after an hour, and, according to pious biographers seeking to establish the child's "meekness and innate sweetness", this cry was the first and last of his entire infancy.[7]

The news of the boy's birth was proclaimed the following day to the people of Castiglione by the firing of the cannons from the Rocca di Castiglione, along with the reading of a solemn proclamation by Don Ferrante and the chanting of the Te Deum in the parish church. Bread and wine were distributed in the courtyard of the castle throughout the day, and the people were entertained by all sorts of popular sports, with the winners being awarded valuable prizes.

[7] See, for instance, Meschler, *St. Aloysius*, 8.

The other ceremonies of the Rite of Baptism were performed on April 20, in the Church of Saints Celsus and Nazarius. Duke William of Mantua, the child's godfather, was represented by Don Prosper Gonzaga, the son of a cousin of Don Ferrante. The wife of Don Alfonso of Castel Goffredo, the sister-in-law of Don Ferrante, was the godmother. The baby was given the name Aluigi (or, in Latin, Aloysius),[8] after his paternal grandfather and in honor of Saint Louis of Anjou.[9] After the archpriest John Baptist Pastorio entered the child's name in the baptismal registry, he added the following words: "Sit felix, carusque Deo, ter optimo terque maximo, et hominibus in æternum vivat."[10] When the rite was concluded, a young student from Padua offered an elaborate oration, and the party returned to the castle surrounded by a joyful crowd.[11]

The child became the object of much affection and care—he was the firstborn and therefore the heir apparent to all the feudal holdings of the Marquis of Castiglione. But beyond this, Aloysius was also a

---

[8] Aloysius' name was actually Ludovico or Lodovico, a name that is commonly changed to Luigi or Aluigi in the northern Italian vernacular; Aloysius, himself, generally signed his letters with "Aluigi". The name by which the saint is most commonly known, Aloysius, is the Latin form of Luigi. See Virgil Cepari, S.J., *Life of Saint Aloysius Gonzaga*, ed. Francis Goldie, S.J. (New York: Benziger Brothers, 1891), 335–36n6. Although Jesuit historian Francesco Sacchini objected to the name and tried to introduce the regular Latin form of Ludovicus (Louis) in 1612, he was strongly opposed by Aloysius' brother Francis, who had succeeded in having the name "Aloysius" used by Pope Paul V in his beatification in 1605.

[9] Born Louis d'Angio (1274–1297), Saint Louis of Anjou was the second son of Charles II, king of Naples and Sicily, and Mary, daughter of Stephen V of Hungary. Despite his noble status, Louis was noted for his modesty and his cheerful spirit. It was recorded that he shunned the company of women, including his mother. In 1295, Louis renounced his royal title and rights to the crown of Naples in favor of his brother Robert, proclaiming, "Jesus Christ is my kingdom. If he is all I have, I shall have everything. If I don't have him, I lose everything" (Paul Burns and Kathleen Jones, eds., *Butler's Lives of the Saints: New Full Edition; August* (Collegeville, Minn.: Liturgical Press, 1997), 188. Pope Boniface VIII appointed Louis as Bishop of Toulouse, granting him a dispensation so that he could be ordained a priest at age twenty-three. Louis hesitantly accepted the post, but before his ordination, he fulfilled his longtime desire to profess vows as a Franciscan friar. In his service as bishop, Louis was humble and modest. Finding episcopal duties too much for him, he soon asked to resign his post. Shortly after his resignation, he died on August 19, 1297, at the age of twenty-three. Saint Louis of Anjou was canonized in 1317.

[10] "May he be happy, beloved by the thrice holy and powerful God, and may he live forever in the memory of men." Cepari, *Life of Saint Aloysius*, 9.

[11] Father Cepari cites a certain doctor, Rudolph Petruccini, who was present at the ceremony and who recalled that the student was of the Rossi family of Padua. Ibid., 8.

prince of the Holy Roman Empire and the putative heir to the lands of Solferino and Castel Goffredo, the patrimony of uncles who had no sons.

During these early years, Aloysius' father was often away from Castiglione, fulfilling his obligations to the king of Spain. Through all of these absences, Donna Marta remained peacefully in Castiglione with Aloysius and her second and third sons: Rudolfo, who was born in 1569, and Ferrante, who was born in 1570, respectively.[12]

Many remembered the boy as having been calm and easily contented, showing signs of piety at an early age. His greatest influence was undoubtedly his mother, Donna Marta; his later letters reveal that it was with her alone that he felt free to express the sentiments of his heart.[13] She often encouraged him to make the sign of the cross and to say the names of Jesus and Mary; and he soon learned to recite the Our Father, the Hail Mary, and other prayers, which he often repeated. Donna Marta used to instruct those who were with him to encourage these devotions, and Aloysius' early biographers relate that even as a child, he would often be found in out-of-the-way corners, reciting these prayers.[14] In a certain sense, this type of behavior should not surprise us. Why would Aloysius, an intelligent, sensitive child, not respond in this way when religion held such a prominent place in his early education? But in addition to his piety, the boy soon manifested a spirit of compassion and charity, especially for the poor. From his earliest years, the virtues of piety and charity were further complemented by that spirit of purity and modesty that would come to characterize Aloysius in his later years. In reflecting on these attributes, Jesuit Father Maurice Meschler writes:

> Aloysius really was a favored child in quite a special sense. He owed his natural and supernatural life, one may say, to the intervention of

[12] C. C. Martindale, *The Vocation of Saint Aloysius* (New York: Sheed and Ward, 1946), 27; Margaret Monro, *A Book of Unlikely Saints* (Freeport, N.Y.: Books for Libraries, 1943), 27. Ferrante was to die in 1577, at the age of seven. Aloysius' other siblings included Carlo (1572–1574); Isabella (1571–1593); Francis (1577–1616), who inherited the marquisate after the murder of Rudolfo; Cristierno Vincenzo (1580–1635); and Diego (1582–1597), who was stabbed to death when he was fifteen.

[13] Martindale, *Vocation of Saint Aloysius*, 27; Monro, *Unlikely Saints*, 18.

[14] See for instance, Cepari, *Life of Saint Aloysius*, 9.

Our Blessed Lady. God wished to take possession of this little heart before it was sullied by the world—the heart in which Holy Baptism had deposited such wonderful graces, the plentitude of the Holy Ghost, and the germs of virtue which were afterwards to bring forth such marvelous fruit. At an age when these treasures of grace are still slumbering in the hearts of many of the baptized, they began in Aloysius to unfold and blossom.[15]

[15] Meschler, *St. Aloysius*, 11.

Chapter 2

The Church of the Counter-Reformation

Aloysius was born into a world of change, a time plagued by religious and civil wars. This was an age when the service of God, combined with the search for gold, built empires. The Council of Trent (1545–1563) brought back a sense of stability within the Roman Church, even as Europe's nobility sought to push back the Turkish armies threatening to overtake Christian Europe. Northern Germany suffered from the ravages of schism and apostasy, even as Protestantism was making inroads into Austria. France was being torn apart by the wars of Charles IX (d. 1574) and Henry III (d. 1589). In the Netherlands, the people were engaged in a bloody battle for spiritual independence from Rome and political independence from Spain. In England, Queen Elizabeth I (d. 1603) initiated a fierce persecution of her Catholic subjects, seeking to ensure the future of England's state church. Austria struggled to maintain its ties with Catholic Spain, which was then, under King Philip II, at the height of its power. Lombardy, the native province of Aloysius, was one of the points of contact between these two powers. The Duchy of Mantua, as well as most of the other states in northern Italy, was under the rule of the Holy Roman Empire.

In spite of the many political and spiritual threats facing the Church, the Spirit of God was at work and awoke in the Church a new life and strength. Earlier in the century, on December 13, 1545, a small group of churchmen had assembled in the Church of the Most Holy Trinity in the city of Trent to address the twin problems of reform and heresy facing the Roman Church. Three archbishops, twenty-one bishops, and the generals of five mendicant orders—the Conventual and Observant Franciscans, the Augustinians, the

Carmelites, and the Servites—represented the official delegates.[1] The reforms of the Augustinian monk Martin Luther (d. 1546) had swept through Germany, and only Bavaria remained loyal to the See of Peter. Under the banner of the Smalkaldic League, Protestant bishops and princes swore to defend their new faith in defiance of the pope and the emperor.[2]

Reformers across Europe were protesting the corruption and opulence that characterized much of the life of the Church in this age. Judged as decadent, the pre-Reformation Church was seen as inefficient and unable to meet the needs of either clergy or people.[3] As historian R. Po-chia Hsia writes, "The Protestants abhorred the Roman Babylon: there, ambition, not faith, reigned; laws not conscience, guided action; letters and arts, not the Word of God, were in fashion; and in this world of privilege and power, one advanced through patronage and family, with little regard, it seemed, for ecclesiastical laws or personal piety."[4] Many within the Church shared this view as well. Across Europe, conscientious theologians and churchmen called for a reform.

Although contemporary scholarship has adopted a more objective view of the issue than that embraced by past historians, noting that this was an age of unparalleled spiritual creativity, the need for reform was both real and perennial. Martin D.W. Jones notes that monastic leader and reformer Saint Bernard of Clairvaux (d. 1153) had condemned the Church of his day as having been "incurably degenerate".[5] While the specifics of past attempts at reform varied from time to time and from place to place, most reformers looked to a change in the individual, rather than a reform of the institutional

---

[1] R. Po-chia Hsia, *The World of Catholic Renewal, 1540–1770* (New York: Cambridge, 1998), 10. These represented only 5 percent of the prelates remaining in Catholic territories. See also Martin D.W. Jones, *The Counter Reformation: Religion and Society in Early Modern Europe* (New York: Cambridge, 1995), 68.

[2] The Smalkaldic League (*Schmalkaldischer Bund*) was a defensive alliance of Lutheran princes within the Holy Roman Empire that was formed on February 27, 1531, as a means of religious alliance. Members of the League pledged to defend one another's territories in the event of an attack by Emperor Charles V. In December 1535, the League began accepting any territory that subscribed to the Augsburg Confession.

[3] Jones, *Counter Reformation*, 28.

[4] Hsia, *Catholic Renewal*, 11.

[5] Jones, *Counter Reformation*, 28.

Church. "Until comprehensive, Church-wide reform was ordered by the papacy or a general council, reform of and by the individual was the target; everyone had to do what they could."[6]

More than a few reformers called for a transformation in the quality and commitment of the clergy. Many in the Church's hierarchy were all too aware of the abuses committed by bishops and clerics, and the corruption and immorality found within the ranks of the clergy were symptoms of an apparent lack of men who were truly dedicated to the spiritual and moral welfare of their congregations.[7] Indeed, the decrees of the Fifth Lateran Council (1512–1517) had been implemented to reform the lives of clerics, specifically in the areas of clerical celibacy and continence, "that nefarious pest simony", and the qualifications of candidates for holy orders.[8]

Catholic Europe looked to Rome for guidance and healing, believing that the only hope for reconciliation and unity lay in an ecumenical (general) Church council.[9] Pope Adrian VI (1522–1523), in a letter to the Diet of Nuremberg dated January 1523, allowed that "there have been great spiritual abominations and abuses in the Holy See for many years.... We will do everything in our power to reform first this See, from which the powerful evil advanced so that, even as corruption passed from Rome to every other part, so healing will spread from Rome."[10] However, for Pope Paul III (1534–1539) and the Roman Curia, the time for healing the schism had passed. Rather than work for reconciliation, this pope instructed the delegates at the Council of Trent to define the Church's doctrines, and both pope and emperor exerted great influence over the Council's proceedings[11] Over the course of the Council's twenty-five sessions,

---

[6] Ibid., 30.

[7] Ibid., 33.

[8] For text and commentary of the decrees of the Fifth Lateran Council, see H. J. Schroeder, *Disciplinary Decrees of the General Councils: Text, Translation, and Commentary* (St. Louis: B. Herder, 1937), 496–97, 505.

[9] Ecumenical councils are "assemblies of senior clergy, representing the whole church, at which key doctrinal or other matters are settled in decrees considered binding on all Christians. Instruments of church government, they have usually been summoned only in emergencies and have always been regarded as the best means of reform." Jones, *Counter Reformation*, 65.

[10] Adrian VI to the Diet of Nuremberg, January 1523, in *Documents Illustrative of the Continental Reformation*, ed. B.J. Kidd (Oxford: Clarendon Press, 1911), 109.

[11] Jones, *Counter Reformation*, 68.

an ever-increasing number of churchmen were in attendance. It was in the two final sessions that the Council dealt with the difficult subject of clerical reform (September to December 1563). These reforms touched on almost all aspects of clerical life: the strengthening of the authority of bishops over chapters and colleges; restrictions on appeals to Rome; regular episcopal visitations of dioceses; removal of unchaste priests from parishes; reform of all religious orders, including reestablishing the strict rules of enclosure for women religious.[12] Although there was a great deal of opposition, the Council Fathers were able to issue their reforming decrees, thanks in large part to the support of Pope Pius IV (1559–1565) and his nephew, the Cardinal-Archbishop of Milan, Saint Charles Borromeo (d. 1584). Saint John Leonardi (d. 1609), a contemporary of Aloysius and the founder of the congregation Clerks Regular of the Mother of God of Lucca, summarized this spirit of reform in a letter to Pope Paul V (1605–1621):

> Those who want to work for moral reform in the world must seek the glory of God before all else.... In this way they will gently entice the members of the Church to reform instead of forcing them, lest, in the words of the Council of Trent, they demand of the body what is not found in the head, and thus upset the whole of the Lord's household.... As far as remedies applicable to the whole Church are concerned, reform must begin with high and low alike, with superiors and inferiors. Yet reformers must look first to those who are set over the rest, so that reform can begin at the point from which it may spread to the others.
>
> Be especially concerned with cardinals, patriarchs, archbishops, bishops and priests, whose particular duty is the care of souls, and make them men to whom guidance of the Lord's flock can be safely entrusted.[13]

The decrees of the Council of Trent were promulgated by Pope Pius IV in June 1564. His successor, Pope Saint Pius V (1566–1572),

---

[12] C. C. Martindale, *The Vocation of Saint Aloysius* (New York: Sheed and Ward, 1946), 25–26.

[13] Saint John Leonardi to Pope Paul V, "Epistle concerning the Complete Reform of the Universal Church", from the archives of the Order of Clerks Regular of the Mother of God, excerpt in *The Liturgy of the Hours: According to the Roman Rite*, vol. 4, trans. International Commission on English in the Liturgy (New York: Catholic Book Publishing, 1975), 1478–79.

who was noted for his wisdom and indefatigable strength in the face of great opposition, worked to ensure that the reforms proposed by Trent would become a reality. Unfortunately, however, many of the expected reforms were implemented slowly and unevenly due to sustained opposition within local churches.[14] Thankfully, the spirit of reform prevailed in Rome. Four of the remaining seven popes of the sixteenth century had been participants at the Council: Gregory XIII (1572–1585), Urban VII (1590), Gregory XIV (1590–1591), and Innocent IX (1591).

In light of the reforms of the Council of Trent, the Church saw renewal within existing religious orders as well as a proliferation of new ones, particularly in Spain and Italy: the Capuchin Franciscans, the Theatines, the Barnabites, and the Somascan Fathers in Italy; the Congregation of the Mission (the Lazarists) in France; and among women, the Angelic Sisters of Saint Paul,[15] the Ursulines, the Visitation Nuns, and the "English Sisters"[16] won support among the male hierarchy and took their place alongside reformed convents of Carmelites, Benedictines, and Franciscans. While these communities worked to support and foster the new spirit of reform sweeping the Church through their preaching and ministry, it was the Society of Jesus (the Jesuits) that was to become the most significant religious community of early modern Catholicism.

Aloysius' station and his blood relationships and connections with the great political and religious leaders of Europe opened to him the doors of every vocation connected to the serious endeavors of his day. Whether he would leave his mark as a statesman, a soldier, a savant, or a priest was his choice to make. His father, the marquis, took it for granted that his son would become a soldier. Donna Marta, however, remembered her vow and maintained her hopes that her eldest son would one day dedicate his life to God in the service of the Church.

---

[14] Hsia, *Catholic Renewal*, 25.

[15] Saint Antony Zaccaria (d. 1539) founded the congregation of the Angelic Sisters of Saint Paul as the female branch of the Barnabites in Milan in 1535.

[16] The religious community of the Institute of the Blessed Virgin Mary, commonly known as the "Loreto Sisters" or "the English Sisters", was founded in England by Venerable Mary Ward (d. 1645) in 1609, following a way of life and spirituality based on that of the Society of Jesus.

Chapter 3

Aloysius' Childhood

Don Ferrante wanted to instill in his eldest son a taste for the soldier's life and commissioned a uniform and suitable weapons for the boy—little muskets and arquebuses that were small enough for him to use.[1]

The boy, now four years old, was delighted with the novelty of his new costume and toys. Aloysius' soldier-father also came to believe that if he left the boy in the care of his mother and nurses any longer, the child would never become the man-of-arms he believed he was destined to be. He decided that the time had come to introduce his son to the military camps, believing it would ensure the boy's interest in military life. As King Philip's commander of the Italian troops in the territory of Milan, the marquis was called upon to join an expedition to relieve the town and province of Tunis in North Africa, which had recently been taken by the Turks. (Tunis had originally been captured by the Christian forces of King Charles V in 1535.) Don Ferrante was ordered to bring a contingent of three thousand Italian infantrymen to join the forces of Don John of Austria and take command of the Italian fleet. With young Aloysius at his side, he chose the fortress of Casalmaggiore on the river Po to be his headquarters.

The sights and sounds of camp life, with its pageantry and the drilling of troops, made a favorable impression on the young boy. Father Meschler tells us: "Aloysius also wore a little plumed helmet, a light coat of mail short enough to let the Spanish breeches be seen, and a little rapier with a basket-hilt at his side. In his hand he carried the halberd, the distinguishing weapon of the captains and officers, and in this guise marched proudly by his father's side. Firearms had a special

---

[1] Virgil Cepari, S.J., *Life of Saint Aloysius Gonzaga*, ed. Francis Goldie, S.J. (New York: Benziger Brothers, 1891), 10.

attraction for him, and it was his great delight to let them off."[2] The "little captain" was well received by the other soldiers who readily allowed him to handle their muskets (which were becoming more commonly used during this period). However, on one of these occasions, the gunpowder flew out of the touchpan and burned his face. It seems that after this mishap he was no longer allowed to have powder.[3] Aloysius took this setback in stride and, as children are wont to do, looked for a more creative way to satisfy his desire to fire the artillery and guns, and this occasioned one of the most well-known events of the saint's early life. One afternoon, as the soldiers were taking their siesta, a shot suddenly sounded from one of the cannons on the outer perimeter of the camp. The alarmed marquis believed that mutiny had erupted and ordered his officers to investigate. It was soon discovered that Aloysius (who was only four or five years old) had wandered away, slipped into a soldier's tent, taken powder from a flask, and then loaded and fired a little piece of ordnance all by himself. The boy was nearly killed by the recoil of the gun carriage, which knocked him to the ground. More frightened than harmed, Aloysius always credited God's Providence for his safety when he recounted this story in later years.

A fascination with firearms was not the only thing Aloysius developed during this formative time. The conversation and behavior of the camp made quite an impression on the boy, and he began to repeat the vulgar jokes and bad language of the soldiers. His tutor, Pietro Francesco del Turco, who overheard Aloysius using such language, reproved him severely, explaining to him that such language was not only unbecoming but blasphemous. This was a lesson Aloysius never forgot.[4]

Early in the summer of 1573, the marquis sent Aloysius back to Castiglione, while he himself led the troops across the sea to Tunis. This marked the end of Aloysius' life as a soldier or, as he called it, his sinful life.[5] In reality, he had only committed the same sort of

---

[2] Maurice Meschler, S.J., *St. Aloysius Gonzaga: Patron of Christian Youth* (Rockford, Ill.: TAN Books, 1985), 15.

[3] Ibid., 16.

[4] Paul Burns and Kathleen Jones, eds., *Butler's Lives of the Saints: New Full Edition; June* (Collegeville, Minn.: Liturgical Press, 1997), 153.

[5] Meschler, *St. Aloysius*, 17.

trifling faults to which many children would be prone. By his own admission, he had justified to himself the taking of the powder with the thought that the soldiers would have given it to him, had he only asked.[6] As for the vulgar language he had used, he had not even understood the meaning of the words until they had been explained to him by his tutor. Aloysius later related that he was so ashamed of what he had said that he could not bring himself to repeat the words to his confessor. However insignificant these instances may seem, they reveal the beginnings of a spiritual sensitivity that the boy would conscientiously develop over the coming years. Father Meschler relates that Aloysius "afterwards said that he had not thought himself bound to confess them at this time, but he did not think he would have ventured to receive his First Communion, later on, with this fault upon his conscience".[7] Although we might be surprised that these minor faults would trouble him in his later years, we should understand that Aloysius, like Augustine confessing his stealing pears as a boy,[8] recognized that there was little in him that would prevent him from pursuing that which was easy and pleasant: "His temperament is indeed to reveal itself as passionate rather than sensual, but masterful in all conscience. Against this latter trend he had always to govern himself violently.... I think that neither this nor anything else that was good would have lasted in him, without that terrible self-discipline which after a while he was to begin to impose upon himself."[9] Indeed, the Gonzagas were known throughout Italy for their passionate nature and temper that could nurse a grudge in silent sulks for months, only to explode later in violent speech and actions. So well known was the Gonzaga temper that it was popularly known as *La Gonzaghina*.[10]

These occurrences ultimately benefited Aloysius in three ways. First, they provided the foundation for a deep and abiding spirit of humility that would mark his spiritual growth for the remainder of his life. Second, they constantly reminded him of the need to do

[6] Cepari, *Life of Saint Aloysius*, 10.

[7] Meschler, *St. Aloysius*, 17.

[8] Augustine of Hippo, *Confessions* II, 4, 9.

[9] C. C. Martindale, *The Vocation of Saint Aloysius* (New York: Sheed and Ward, 1946), 30.

[10] Margaret Monro, *A Book of Unlikely Saints* (Freeport, N.Y.: Books for Libraries, 1943), 15. See also ibid., 100.

penance and to cultivate a spirit of mindfulness. Finally, and perhaps most importantly, they made him cautious and reserved in his dealings with the world. It is in his response to these minor faults that we see the first steps of his gradual retirement from the world and his adoption of the asceticism and penance he was to embrace so eagerly. We can also glimpse the natural courage and strength of will that allowed him to recognize his faults and dedicate all his energy to conversion and wholehearted abandonment to God's Will.

Back in Castiglione, Aloysius, who was now five years old, began his studies and entered a particularly formative time in his spiritual development. He served Mass each day, and, alone or with his tutor, he daily recited the so-called Exercitium Quotidianum—a collection of vocal prayers that included the Little Office of the Blessed Virgin, the Gradual and Penitential Psalms, and a number of other prayers. It is recorded that the boy never used a prie-dieu or a cushion, but knelt on the floor—a penance he practiced throughout his life.[11]

Around this time, Aloysius was attacked by a disease known as "quartan ague", which troubled him for more than a year and a half and which left him so weak that he was confined to his bed.[12] Despite the pain and fatigue caused by the illness, he remained patient and continued, as much as possible, his devotions. When he was too weak to sit up in bed, he asked one of his mother's attendants to support him while he recited his prayers.

In later years, Aloysius would look upon this time of his life as having been one of grace and conversion. After his entrance into the Society of Jesus, he confidentially related to Father Mutius Vitelleschi (d. 1645), who later became the sixth general of the Society, that he had offered himself to God with his whole heart from the "very dawn of his reason".[13] Saint Robert Bellarmine, who served as Aloysius' spiritual director, considered this childhood abandonment and submission to God's Will to be one of the special graces bestowed upon the saint during his life.

---

[11] Meschler, *St. Aloysius*, 19.

[12] Quartan ague (also known as "Italian bad air") is an archaic English name for a tropical disease, similar to malaria, whose symptoms are fever, shivering, pain in the joints, vomiting, and convulsions, occurring at intervals of around seventy-two hours. If left untreated, the disease can lead to coma and even death.

[13] Meschler, *St. Aloysius*, 19.

The boy continued to have a close relationship with his mother. Because she had once shared with him that she would be glad to have one of her children enter a religious order, he told her that it might be very possible that God would grant her this favor. A little later, he returned to the subject, repeated his words, and then added that he hoped to be the one to give her this pleasure—words that Donna Marta never forgot. It is not known with any real certainty that he was already seriously thinking of becoming a religious. It seems more likely that his aim at this time was to serve God as best he could in his present state of life. This disposition was still more than enough to lead those around him to consider him to be a holy and angelic child.[14]

The early biographies of Aloysius recount a striking event that confirmed the general opinion many held of the boy. A Franciscan friar who was popularly thought to be a "living saint" came to the friary of Santa Maria, not far from Castiglione. The crowds circulated many wonderful stories about him, and he was believed to have the power to work miracles. People came in droves to hear him speak and to ask his prayers. Some possessed people were brought to him to be exorcised, and on one of these occasions, Aloysius and his brother Rudolfo were present with other members of the nobility. Suddenly, one of the possessed people turned to Aloysius, pointed his finger at him, and cried out: "Do you see him? He will be in Heaven one day, and be in great glory." The story spread quickly throughout Castiglione and was never forgotten.[15]

For Aloysius, the piety of his childhood reflected a spirit of real devotion that would only increase with the passage of time. The boy's pious habits formed and developed into a spirit of abandonment that he would come to understand only in his later years. No one can argue that this inclination was indeed a rare and precious gift, particularly in one so young.

[14] Ibid., 19–20.
[15] Ibid., 19.

Chapter 4

Florence

Don Ferrante's campaign against the Turks at Tunis came to a sad end for the Christian armies. After the defeat, Ferrante traveled to the Spanish court at Madrid, where he spent two years before returning to Castiglione toward the end of 1576. By then, Aloysius was eight years old. The marquis was surprised and pleased by the progress and maturity of his eldest son. Although his childish attraction to the military had faded, the boy exhibited a sincere piety, polished manners, and an intelligence beyond his years. Ferrante saw in his son a future prince who would bring honor to his family by ruling his subjects wisely and justly.

A short time after the marquis' return home, a terrible pestilence broke out, ravaging nearly all of Italy. Concerned for the welfare of his family, Ferrante chose to take them to the Marquisate of Monferrato, which lay outside the infected district. As he was making the arrangements for the trip, however, he suffered an attack of gout and was advised by his physicians to travel to Lucca so that he might benefit from that city's celebrated healing baths. Rudolfo was also ill at the time, so it was decided that both he and Aloysius would accompany their father. The marquis ultimately planned to take both boys to Florence so that he might introduce them to the Grand Duke of Tuscany and leave them in his care for the sake of their education. Florence was a center of the arts and sciences, and nowhere else was the Italian language spoken with such purity or the courtly manner so polished. These were advantages the marquis wished for his sons. While Donna Marta was hesitant to be parted from her two eldest children, the marquis prevailed, and the party started for Lucca in the early summer of 1577.

The baths of Lucca were a popular destination for those seeking cures for a variety of ailments. Expenses were low in the region, and the city of Lucca enjoyed all the privileges of the free towns of the Middle Ages. From Lucca, the marquis and his party, including the two boys, traveled to Tuscany. Florence was the seat of the powerful Medici family. Although the days of Cosimo and Lorenzo de Medici were but a memory, the younger princes of the family were known for their patronage of the arts, striving to uphold the dignity of the House of Medici. Since 1574, Francis I (d. 1587), the father of Marie de Medici, had been in power. It was to Francis and his wife, Joanna of Austria, daughter of Emperor Maximilian II, that Aloysius and Rudolfo were to be presented.

Because orders had been given by the city officials of Florence that no one could be admitted to the city without a certificate of health, the marquis' party was turned back when it reached the city's gates. Not even the powerful marquis and his sons were excused from this requirement, so the party traveled to the home of Aloysius' tutor, Pietro del Turco.

Del Turco's little country house, called Fontanella, still stands near the old Dominican friary of San Domenico, the religious house that had given the city of Florence its archbishop, Antonio Pierozzi (the future Saint Antoninus, d. 1459), and the immortal painter Blessed John of Fiesole (d. 1455), who is better known as "Fra Angelico". The small friary, with its well-kept gardens and peaceful setting, was a favorite spot for Aloysius, who often visited the friars, making San Domenico a sort of summer resort.[1] The room he used during his visit to del Turco's home has been turned into a chapel. An inscription placed there by the family states that Aloysius repeatedly sanctified the room by his presence and that the family erected its altar in 1726, the year of his canonization by Pope Benedict XIII (1724–1730).[2]

From Fiesole, the marquis sent word to the grand duke of his arrival and desire to visit with him. The duke invited him to come immediately, and Ferrante and his sons were received at court with all deference and honor. The grand duke was so pleased when the marquis introduced his sons and expressed his desire to leave them in Florence that he offered the boys apartments in the palace for their

[1] Maurice Meschler, S.J., *St. Aloysius Gonzaga: Patron of Christian Youth* (Rockford, Ill.: TAN Books, 1985), 24.
[2] Ibid.

use. Upon learning that Ferrante wanted his sons to study during their time in Florence, the grand duke arranged a residence for them and their attendants, at his own expense, on the Via degli Alfani.[3] The account book kept by Aloysius' tutor, del Turco, records that the two princes took up residence in the house on December 5, 1577, and left Florence on November 10, 1579.[4] Here, too, the room occupied by Aloysius has been converted into a chapel, and the house bears a picture of Aloysius on the exterior as well as a marble tablet with an inscription stating that the saint had once resided there.

After having ensured that his sons were well provided for and safely in the care of their tutor and servants, the marquis returned to Castiglione. The two princes stayed in Florence for more than two years, from Aloysius' ninth to his twelfth year. The boy devoted his energy to his education, which included both sacred and secular studies. He was very eager to learn and studied both Latin and Italian. At this time, Aloysius might also have begun to study French and German; before his death, at age twenty-three, he could speak Latin, Greek, Italian, Spanish, German, and French.

Two letters to his father, dating from his first year in Florence, have survived; they offer us a glimpse of the intelligence and interests of the ten-year-old prince.

Illustrious and honored Father,
    We were sorry to learn from your letter of the 6th day of April that you had again been suffering from gout in the foot and a slight fever; but we are glad, however, that both are abating. The other letter from our mother, of the 8th of April, consoled us, as we learned from it that you were recovered! Thanks be to God!
    Yesterday we went to see the funeral of the Grand Duchess [Joanna of Austria]; it was a beautiful sight, and lasted three hours. The following was the order of the procession: First came the standard of Saint Lawrence, and then the cross. These were accompanied by 150 poor persons dressed in mourning, and carrying lighted torches. They were

---

[3] The residence was actually three houses joined together and formed part of the housing used by members of Florence's weavers' guild. According to the surviving legal documents, the lease taken by the grand duke lasted from November 1, 1577, until the end of April 1580. See ibid., 25.
[4] Ibid.

followed by the friars, not only of the city, but also of the surrounding country within the radius of three miles—members of eighteen different religious orders in all, carrying white candles of a pound-weight. Then came the mourners with the usual trains,[5] and the priests with candles like those carried by the friars; these again were followed by the pages, knights, and courtiers, all in mourning, with torches in their hands. Next came the coffin under a canopy; the bearers of the body were gentlemen of the court, and the canopy was carried by noblemen of the city. Last came the Grand Duke in cap and mantle, with the rest of the court and the armed guard of honor. After accompanying the coffin to San Lorenzo, he retired to his palace.

We continue our devotions and studies, and are in good health. I have nothing else to say. In conclusion I kiss your hands and those of our honored mother, sister, and little brother.

April 1578.

> Your Lordship's dutiful son,
>
> Aluigi Gonzaga[6]

Four months later, he wrote this letter to his father:

On Sunday we were with Don Giovanni[7] on the Grand Duke's stand to the see the race for "Saint Anne's mantle," which was red in color. The Count di Bagno's race-horse won it. On Friday we paid Don Giovanni a visit, and as he did not want to go out, we spent the time together cooking all sorts of things. But he ate nothing at all himself, for he was fasting to gain the Jubilee indulgence proclaimed by the Pope, which absolves from sin and punishment. For the same reason, he also prayed for the ending of the disturbances in Flanders, for the exaltation of the Holy Church, the end of heresy, and the preservation of Christian princes. We wish to gain the indulgence next week, too, and we shall remember you in our prayers, as we always have done and always shall do.

Yesterday we were with Don Giovanni in the Pitti Palace, and while he was going with us to the fountain, the princesses came with a number of dogs and joined us, saying they wanted to let the dogs run

---

[5] "These trains were several yards in length, and attached to hoods." Ibid., 26n2.

[6] Aloysius Gonzaga to his father, n.d., [Letter I], in *Lettere di S. Luigi Gonzaga*, ed. Oliviero Iozzi (Pisa, 1889), 3ff., quoted in ibid., 27–28; translation adapted.

[7] "Don Giovanni" refers to Don Giovanni de Medici (1563–1621), the grand duke's youngest brother.

a race for a mantle.[8] While the race was going on, the Grand Duke
came through the garden gate, accompanied by only four gentlemen,
and watched the game. We all ran, the princesses, Don Giovanni, and
ourselves, and kept it up till evening. During these holidays we went
to Mass at the Nunziata, and prayed to Our Lady for all graces and
blessings, and a special increase in joy and comfort. We are well
and studying diligently. In conclusion we kiss your lordship's hand.
        Florence, Aug. 17, 1578.[9]

The account book kept by the princes' tutor provides us with a
glimpse of the lifestyle the two boys enjoyed during this time. The
successive entries offer a detailed account of Aloysius' wardrobe.
Father Meschler reports:

> There is mention of a long black mantle, a stiff short mantle with a
> hood, trimmings of silk and satin, and silk ribbons; the simple, every-
> day attire of coloured stuff,[10] and the gala doublets of white satin
> with gold and silver fastenings, fringes, and buttons, with button-
> holes stitched with red silk; blue and green stockings for the Spanish
> breeches; a velvet cap with trimmings of tulle and white or black
> feathers; embroidered gloves and white shoes with double soles; a
> dagger and a gold-hilted sword, the scabbard for which was of black
> velvet trimmed with gold lace and fringe.[11]

Although some of Aloysius' critics through the years have proposed
that the boy's preference for black clothing was an assertion of his
austerity or aversion to the rich, highly embroidered clothing of the
time, it should be noted that black (or at least dark-colored) clothing
was the custom for court.[12] What made Aloysius' clothing noteworthy was the simplicity of the design and decoration.

[8] The mantle mentioned here was most likely a piece of gold brocade, or another expen-
sive piece of scarlet, yellow, or green silk; these were often given as prizes in races and contests
during this period.

[9] Aloysius Gonzaga to his father, Aug. 15, 1578 [Letter II], in Iozzi, *Lettere*, 5f., quoted in
Meschler, *St. Aloysius*, 28.

[10] "Stuff", a word that first appears in the seventeenth century, became the common name
for fabrics made of wool or a blend of wool and linen. Clothing intended for the upper classes
was often made of this more coarse, base fabric, but would have been elaborately embroidered, giving them increased value and, of course, beauty.

[11] Meschler, *St. Aloysius*, 28–29.

[12] C. C. Martindale, *The Vocation of Saint Aloysius* (New York: Sheed and Ward, 1946),
47. See also Francis Corley and Robert Willmes, *Wings of Eagles* (Milwaukee, Wis.: Bruce
Publishing, 1941), 52.

Subsequent entries in the tutor's account book include records of payments for pomade, dancing lessons, a writing master, storybooks, letter paper and a seal, tops with string, clay marbles (for shooting birds), and a chain for Aloysius' small dog. The account book also shows that Aloysius gave several gifts during his time in Florence. Among these was a crystal vessel given to Don Giovanni and gratuities for Don Giovanni's dwarf and two of his servants, as well as the vergers of the cathedral on his visit to see the famous dome of the Cathedral of Santa Maria del Fiore.

The account book also reveals that Aloysius was often treated by a physician and surgeon, and that he used mustard oil for chilblains,[13] gum salve and oil as a poultice for his stomach, and dried roses and pomegranate peel as toothpaste.[14] There is also a record that between December 1578 and June 1579, Aloysius had to have two teeth pulled by a barber; a third was extracted in April 1580.

Although Aloysius was obliged to participate in the pageantry and diversions of the day, he tried to avoid activities that he deemed frivolous or unwholesome. Often required to appear at court, he was invited to join in the games of the princesses Eleanor, who in a decade would become Duchess of Mantua, and Mary, who later became queen of France. As duchess, Eleanor later related that Aloysius talked little, loved solitude, and often spoke of God, even during their games. He was often placed before the princesses as an example of holiness by their governess.[15]

Aloysius made great progress in holiness while in Florence. He would later look back on those years as the "cradle of his spiritual life". He began to celebrate the sacrament of reconciliation regularly and was always concerned for the state of his soul. He made a general confession and resolved to lose his life rather than sin, to watch constantly over all his actions, and to lead an austere life.[16]

It should be noted, however, that this discerning, pious boy was not without faults against which he truly struggled. His biographers record that he was prone to anger and impatience with himself and

---

[13] Chilblains (also known as *pernio* or *perniosis*) are acral ulcers (of the extremities) that occur when an individual is exposed to cold and humidity. The exposure to cold can damage capillary beds in the skin, which in turn causes redness, itching, blisters, and inflammation.

[14] Meschler, *St. Aloysius*, 29.

[15] Ibid., 30.

[16] Ibid., 31.

others.[17] He began to realize how often he made remarks that belittled others and determined to curb this habit. We also begin to see in Aloysius a greater tendency toward solitude and reflection. He ignored accusations that he was over-pious and scrupulous, because his one aim in life was to avoid offending God in any way. He always tried to obey those who were responsible for his care and education. He also exhibited a marked kindness to his servants, not only by requesting their help rather than giving orders, but also by reproving his brother Rudolfo for his behavior toward them.[18] One of the servants later testified: "I often disputed and quarreled with the Florentine Antonio del Turco [the cousin of Aloysius' tutor]. Then Aloysius used to come out of his room, take me gently by the arm and lead me in to reprove me for my conduct. He was really admirable in his humility, amiability, and gentleness; he despised no one but himself, honored everyone else, and shunned all honor shown him."[19] The piety exhibited by Aloysius was typical of the piety of the age. Although he had not yet been introduced to the practice of mental prayer, he recited vocal prayers morning and evening, attended Mass each day, and also attended Vespers on Sundays and feast days. On those days, he went to confession and attended Mass in the little Jesuit Church of San Giovanni, which was located behind the Medici palace. The future Carmelite saint Mary Magdalen (Catherine) de' Pazzi (d. 1607), who would later contribute greatly to the development of the cult of Saint Aloysius, also used to attend Mass at San Giovanni at this time. Aloysius' early biographers delight in observing that these two graced souls might often have prayed there at the same time.[20]

Aloysius' devotion to the Blessed Virgin also began to develop in a special way during this period. He frequently visited the popular Servite church Basilica della Santissima Annunziata. The Lady chapel of this basilica, which is decorated with painted scenes of the lives of

[17] See, for instance, Virgil Cepari, S.J., *Life of Saint Aloysius Gonzaga*, ed. Francis Goldie, S.J. (New York: Benziger Brothers, 1891), 20.

[18] Ibid., 21.

[19] Bollandists, *Acta Sanctorum Junii IV*, "Anno Apice 1707", quoted in Meschler, *St. Aloysius*, 31–32.

[20] See, for instance, Meschler, *St. Aloysius*, 32.

the Virgin and the Servite priest Saint Philip Benizi[21] by Andrea del
Sarto, houses a famous fresco of the Annunciation dating from the
thirteenth century. The Virgin is depicted sitting in a chamber—
radiant in her youthful beauty, her eyes raised to Heaven in contemplation. The archangel Gabriel kneels before her, while above,
descending through a small window, the Holy Spirit hovers, casting
upon her golden rays. While the image was ordinarily kept covered, Aloysius had the opportunity to see the image, for it had been
unveiled to honor the visit of Charles Borromeo, who celebrated
Mass in the chapel. This shrine was one of the young prince's favorite
places, and he often performed his devotions there.

The Counter-Reformation saw a renaissance of devotion to the
Virgin Mary and to the Eucharist; the piety that grew out of the reforms of the Council of Trent developed and gave new warmth to
many older devotions.[22] The laity were encouraged to receive Communion and go to confession more frequently. Theologians began
to embellish older Marian doctrines that celebrated the Virgin's
cooperation in the redemption of mankind, and, more practically,
members of the Society of Jesus gave witness to this renewal as they
carried rosaries in their hands or on their belts as they walked in the
streets.[23] Eucharistic devotions, including Benediction of the Blessed
Sacrament, took on new life, and these more formal devotions were
complemented by a newfound reverence for the humanity of Christ,
particularly as expressed in the infancy and Passion of Jesus. Another
devotion that flowed naturally from these reflections on the hidden
life of Jesus was a filial affection for Saint Joseph. The Carmelite
reformer and foundress, Saint Teresa of Avila (d. 1582), among others, promoted this devotion in her writings and reform, declaring,
"To other saints our Lord has given power to help in one sort of

---

[21] Saint Philip Benizi (1233–1285) was a native of Florence who, after earning doctorates
in medicine and philosophy, entered the Order of Servites, in 1254. After being ordained a
priest, he was appointed superior of several Servite houses before being elected prior general
in 1267. Known for unifying the Servites, he was highly regarded for his charity and efforts
to establish peace between the warring Guelphs and Ghibellines and was also celebrated as
a miracle-worker. Saint Philip Benizi was canonized in 1671, and his feast is celebrated on
August 22.

[22] Owen Chadwick, *The Reformation* (New York: Penguin, 1990), 293.

[23] Ibid., 294.

need, but this glorious saint, as I know by experience, helps us in every need. I cannot remember ever having asked him for anything which he did not obtain for me."[24] Ultimately these symbols, themes, and ceremonies contributed to a tendency for spirituality to become an increasingly interior, emotional experience, and they significantly nurtured Aloysius in his own spiritual development. His commitment to the Blessed Virgin was representative of the evolving devotional life of the Church after Trent.[25]

It was at this time that Aloysius acquired an introduction and commentary on how to meditate upon mysteries of the Rosary written by Father Gaspar de Loarte, S.J., which served to heighten his devotion to the Mother of God and to introduce him to meditative prayer.[26] Through his reading, Aloysius began to understand the value of thinking about what he was reciting. From this point onward, he would continually draw benefit from his meditations upon the mysteries of the lives of Jesus and Mary honored in the Rosary.[27] "With his little book in hand, he went to the altar of the *Annunziata* and before the altar of *La Santissima Annunziata* in that church he pondered on the vision of holiness that had taken hold of his mind, with a hunger for God that was the root of it, and there determined that this would be his life's goal."[28] Aloysius would always acknowledge the special graces he received during his prayer in this chapel.

One day, as he was kneeling before the image of the Annunciation in the Basilica della Santissima Annunziata chapel, Aloysius was inspired to dedicate himself to the Blessed Virgin by offering her the most precious gift that he possessed: the gift of his purity. Acting on this inspiration, he consecrated himself to her service through a vow of perpetual chastity. Years later, he would tell his confessor

[24] Quoted in Paul Burns and Teresa Rodrigues, eds., *Butler's Lives of the Saints: New Full Edition; March* (Collegeville, Minn.: Liturgical Press, 1999), 188. See also Keith P. Luria, "The Counter-Reformation and Popular Spirituality", in *Christian Spirituality: Post-Modern and Modern*, ed. Louis Dupré and Don E. Saliers (New York: Crossroad Publishing, 1989), 113.

[25] Luria, "Counter-Reformation", 104, 107–8.

[26] Gaspar de Loarte, S.J., *Istruttione e avvertimenti per meditar i misterii del Rosario della santissima Vergine Madre* (*Instructions and Advertisements on How to Meditate upon the Mysteries of the Rosary of the Most Holy Virgin Mother*).

[27] Meschler, *St. Aloysius*, 34.

[28] Clifford Stevens, "Four Centuries of Aloysius", in *Aloysius*, ed. Clifford Stevens and William Hart McNichols (Huntington, Ind.: Our Sunday Visitor, 1993), 19.

that he had always been aware of Mary's patronage and protection of his purity.[29]

While Aloysius' biographers are quick to assert that he went through his life without experiencing any temptations against chastity, it is highly unlikely that Aloysius was ignorant of sexuality or its expressions. Gonzaga family historian Kate Simon notes that in the cultural transition from the Middle Ages to the Renaissance, the "delicacy of courtly love and the softness of its verbiage disappeared into broad sensuality and heated words of dance songs."[30] During this period, both pages and young nobles were often used as sexual objects by noble women and men.[31] Although there is no proof that Aloysius was ever abused himself, he was certainly aware of the practice, and his well-known "custody of the eyes", his aversion to being alone in the presence of women, his refusal to participate in the often highly eroticized dances and games of the day, and ultimately his vow of virginity were all an attempt to safeguard the gift of innocence. We cannot doubt that Aloysius was aware of the implications of this vow, even though he was only nine years old. As the novelist and painter A'Dora Phillips notes, to be "virgin" is to be free.[32] To be "virgin" is to be able to assert one's own identity against the claims of culture and custom. Although Aloysius' purity would later be ridiculed for being "not of flesh and blood", his insistence on modesty and discretion offer a valuable lesson to those of us who live in a culture of relativism and permissiveness. His primary objective was not simply to avoid sin, but to do what he believed was necessary to become holy.

Life in Florence's court was filled with violent contradictions. We can learn from contemporary literature such as *Libro del Cortegiano* (*The Book of the Courtier*), published in 1528 by Baldassare Castiglione (d. 1529), or the writings of Pietro Fortini (d. 1562) about how

[29] Meschler, *St. Aloysius*, 34.

[30] Kate Simon, *A Renaissance Tapestry: The Gonzaga of Mantua* (New York: Harper and Row, 1998), 16.

[31] Ibid., 149. Father Martindale notes that "boys were married off at ages that to us seem incredibly immature, and girls even younger. Bridegrooms of fourteen and girls of twelve were no rarities. Women began to throw themselves at the heads of boys, when a brilliant match could be hoped for: Aloysius must have been simply suffocated with feminine advances." Martindale, *Vocation of Saint Aloysius*, 36.

[32] A'Dora Phillips, *Mortal Saints and Immortal Callings: Vocation in the Lives of the Saints* (Brewster, Mass.: Paraclete Press, 2006), 62.

the ideal of courtly love was celebrated and how the external signs of religion pervaded almost every aspect of the culture. But these books also allow a glimpse of a life that was coarse, sophisticated, and worldly.[33] In the midst of Florentine grandeur and excess, Aloysius began to stand out as an austere figure, guided by the Mother of God; her blessing accompanied him henceforth, and "[a]ll good things came to [him] along with her, and in her hands uncounted wealth" (Wis 7:11).

[33] Martindale, *Vocation of Saint Aloysius*, 44–46; Richard Hermes, "On Understanding the Saints", in Stevens and McNichols, *Aloysius*, 70; and Simon, *Renaissance Tapestry*, 176–80.

Chapter 5

Discernment and Prayer

In November 1579, the marquis called his sons to Mantua, while he himself assumed control of the Marquisate of Monferrato. Aloysius and Rudolfo traveled to Mantua, where they befriended Vincenzo[1] who, as the son of William (Guglielmo),[2] the Duke of Mantua, was the future head of the House of Gonzaga. Mantua was a flourishing center of the arts, under the patronage of the Gonzagas. The city was also famous for the Basilica of Sant'Andrea, the mother church of the Order of the Knights of the Most Holy Redeemer.[3] Every year, pilgrims flocked to this church, whose treasury boasted reliquaries containing drops of the Blood of Christ.[4]

Aloysius, who was now eleven years old and living in the palace of Abbot Gonzaga, resumed his classical studies. At this time, he also began reading a book of saints' lives, from which he drew great benefit and of which he often spoke. Aloysius continued to develop his habits of prayer, and he frequently visited various religious communities and monasteries on his trips outside of the palace. His servants related that the prince did much good for members of

---

[1] Vincenzo Gonzaga (1562–1612) was twenty-five when he was crowned 4th Duke of Mantua. He was, by all accounts, the antithesis of Aloysius, although he was genuinely fond of his younger cousin.

[2] William (Guglielmo) Gonzaga (1538–1587) was the 3rd Duke of Mantua.

[3] The Basilica of Sant'Andrea had been commissioned by Aloysius' ancestor Ludovico II, who ruled the city of Mantua from 1444 until his death in 1478. Built on the site of a former Benedictine abbey, the church was begun in 1462 and took more than three hundred years to complete.

[4] Ancient tradition maintained that Saint Longinus, the Roman soldier who pierced Christ's side with a lance as he hung on the Cross, carried a vial of Christ's Blood to Mantua, where the relic was preserved at the Basilica of Sant'Andrea and became the most sacred possession of the city. Today, these relics are exposed only on Good Friday, when they are carried in solemn procession through the streets of the city.

the household, instructing them in the Christian life by his words and example: "When we called him 'my lord' or 'your highness', he answered: 'To serve God is better than all the glory of the world.' I have often heard him say this, and even while he was a child, I regarded him as a Saint."[5] Although Aloysius continued to absent himself from certain activities (as he had in Florence), it seems that he did attend the masques of the court, as masks and costumes for these events are included in del Turco's account book.[6]

While in Mantua, Aloysius began to show signs of "strangury", for which the physicians prescribed a strict diet.[7] His biographers record that he took their advice seriously, but, while the disease was checked by that treatment, his general health was weakened. Although he had been a healthy, active boy until this time, he now began to grow thin and developed a weak stomach, a condition that plagued him for the rest of his life. Nonetheless, he decided to stick to his meager diet, believing that the extreme fast was good for his soul as well as for his body. Here we may think of the early Abbas and Ammas of the Egyptian desert, and numerous other ascetics, who insisted on denying their bodily needs.

> Abba John the Short said: "If a king wanted to take possession of his enemy's city, he would begin by cutting off the water and the food and so his enemies, dying of hunger, would submit to him. It is the same with the passions of the flesh: if a man goes about fasting and hungry the enemies of his soul grow weak." ...
>
> ... Amma Syncletica said: "Just as the most bitter medicine drives out poisonous creatures so prayer joined to fasting drives evil thoughts away."[8]

It was during his stay in Mantua that Aloysius first conceived the idea of renouncing his inheritance and dedicating his life to the

[5] Quoted in Maurice Meschler, S.J., *St. Aloysius Gonzaga: Patron of Christian Youth* (Rockford, Ill.: TAN Books, 1985), 38.

[6] Ibid., 38.

[7] Stangury, urethral pain occurring at the end of voiding, is a symptom of a urinary tract infection caused by a decreased washing-out ability of the urinary mechanism and the presence of stagnant urine remaining in the bladder.

[8] Quoted in Benedicta Ward, *The Sayings of the Desert Fathers: The Alphabetical Collection*, rev. ed. (Kalamazoo, Mich.: Cistercian Publications, 1984), 86, 231.

service of God in the Church. Having already given up the possibility of marriage by his vow of chastity, he now began to form a plan to resign his legacy in favor of his brother Rudolfo. After careful reflection, he resolved to become a priest, hoping to enjoy greater peace of soul and complete freedom to do good. In the meantime, he requested that he be dispensed from the obligations of court so that he might devote himself more completely to his studies. Aloysius' brief stay in Mantua was a time of remarkable spiritual growth. Although he was surrounded by the glories of the Gonzaga dynasty, he came to recognize his true vocation lay in the service of God.

In the summer of 1580, the marquis, having heard of Aloysius' illness, wrote to his sons, telling them to return to Castiglione. Don Ferrante and Donna Marta were greatly alarmed to see the change in their eldest son. Seeing how thin and weak Aloysius was, his mother reproached the boys' tutor, who replied that his pupil would not be interfered with.[9] While his mother tried to restore him to health, he resisted her solicitude and care, continuing his austerities, believing that he drew spiritual benefit from his practices of abstinence and fasting.

Not surprisingly, Aloysius remained physically weak for a long time, a fact that caused him to be cut off from the world more than he already was. Spending his time in spiritual reading and in reciting devotional prayers, he began to experience the grace of contemplation. As Father Meschler says, "A glorious and hitherto unsuspected interior life was opened out to Aloysius in meditation upon the mysteries of the Redemption and contemplation of the Divine Attributes."[10] He began to lengthen the time he spent in meditation each day, and his biographers record that he was so overwhelmed by the experience of God's grace and mercy that he would often weep. His attendants began to watch him secretly, and they reported seeing the prince prostrate himself before his crucifix, kneeling with his arms outstretched while tears rolled down his cheeks. These biographers are also quick to assert that the prince was always, as Meschler puts it, "rapt in prayer".[11] Although he had been accustomed primarily to reciting only vocal prayers before, his return to Castiglione witnessed

[9] Meschler, St. Aloysius, 41.
[10] Ibid., 42.
[11] Ibid., 43.

a marked advance in his piety and spirituality. While he maintained many of his pious habits (although idiosyncrasies might be a more fitting word in some instances—one of these was his reported habit of greeting the Blessed Virgin at every step when mounting the stairs[12]), he was introduced to the practice of formal meditation by an essay composed by Saint Peter Canisius, a priest and missionary of the Society of Jesus. This work contained practical instructions on mental prayer and became an important tool for Aloysius.[13] The book was instructive rather than devotional; Aloysius said he liked it because he considered it especially suited to his character.[14]

Saint Peter Canisius

Saint Peter Canisius, one of the many outstanding and influential early Jesuits, was born in Nijmegen, Holland, in 1521. After entering the Society of Jesus in 1543, he distinguished himself for his learning and spiritual perfection. He dedicated himself to the reevangelization of Germany through preaching, teaching, and leading the Counter-Reformation there with charity and zeal.

Peter recognized that in order to combat the Protestant Reformers, the Church must reform herself in her own pastors and prepare new generations of laymen capable of defending their Faith. A prolific writer, he is especially remembered for his catechism *Summa Doctrinae Christianae* (*Summary of Christian Doctrine*), which was a popular catechetical tool throughout Europe with more than two hundred editions appearing before the end of the seventeenth century. First published in 1555, this work was intended for use in colleges and universities. It presented Catholic doctrine in 211 questions and answers and became one of the most significant books of the Counter-Reformation.[15] (The essay that instructed Aloysius in the practice of mental prayer was appended to Canisius' catechism.) In addition to his *Summa*, Canisius composed catechisms for children and adolescents; a complete list of all his writings

---

[12] Virgil Cepari, S.J., *Life of Saint Aloysius Gonzaga*, ed. Francis Goldie, S.J. (New York: Benziger Brothers, 1891), 26.

[13] Ibid., 43.

[14] C.C. Martindale, *The Vocation of Saint Aloysius* (New York: Sheed and Ward, 1946), 63.

[15] John F. Fink, *The Doctors of the Church: An Introduction to the Church's Great Teachers*, vol. 2, *Doctors of the Second Millennium* (Staten Island, N.Y.: St. Paul's, 2000), 153.

fills more than thirty pages of the bibliography of Jesuit authors.[16] Peter, known as the Second Apostle of Germany, died at Fribourg, Switzerland, in 1597. He was canonized and proclaimed a Doctor of the Church in 1925.[17]

* * * * *

It was around this time that Aloysius first began to think of entering the Jesuits. Partly influenced by the writings of Canisius, he was also inspired by reading copies of the letters written by Jesuit missionaries serving in the Society's Indian missions.[18] His heart was enflamed with the apostolic zeal that filled the heart of Saint Francis Xavier (d. 1552) and his missionary companions. Aloysius began to instruct the poor children of the city in the catechism on Sundays and feast days, and many were edified by his charity and skill as a teacher. He would allow no dissension, oaths, or immoral conduct among his servants, and he dedicated himself to "spiritual conversation"— he would speak of practically nothing other than spiritual matters.

In 1580, when Aloysius was twelve years old, Saint Charles Borromeo made a pastoral visitation of Brescia, the diocese in which Castiglione was located. Because the cardinal's sister, Camilla, had married Don Cesar Gonzaga-Guastalla, Borromeo was well known within the Gonzaga family.

Saint Charles Borromeo

Charles ("Carlo") Borromeo was born in Arona, Italy, on October 2, 1538. His father was Count Gilberto Borromeo, and his mother was a Medici from Milan and the sister of the man who would become

---

[16] Ibid. Interestingly, one of Peter's works appeared on the Church's *Index of Forbidden Books* for a time because it was considered to have too much of a conciliatory tone toward Protestants. Ibid., 155.

[17] For a fuller treatment of the life of Saint Peter Canisius, see Paul Burns and Kathleen Jones, eds., *Butler's Lives of the Saints: New Full Edition; December* (Collegeville, Minn.: Liturgical Press, 2000), 163–66.

[18] These "Lettere delle Indie" were written by Jesuit priests, recounting their experiences in the missions of India. Aloysius would have probably possessed Italian editions that appeared in parts in 1565 (under the title *Diversi avisi particolari delle Indie di Portogallo ricevuti dall'anno 1551 fino al 1558 dalli Padri della Compangia di Gesù*), 1568, and 1572.

Pope Pius IV (1559–1565). Remembered as having been a devout and serious young man, Charles also suffered from a speech impediment that caused some to dismiss him as being dull or unintelligent.[19] In fact, he was a very intelligent boy who displayed numerous gifts and who was not afraid of hard work.

Charles received the clerical tonsure at the age of twelve and inherited the Benedictine Abbey of SS. Gratinian and Felinus at Arona Arras, which had long been held by his family *in commendam*. In 1559, he was awarded a doctorate in theology by the University of Pavia. Returning to Milan, he learned that his uncle had been elected pope, taking the name Pius IV. The following year, his uncle named the twenty-two-year-old Charles, who was only in minor orders, a cardinal. Then, on February 8, 1561, he was appointed administrator of the vacant see of Milan. This was a prestigious appointment but one that Charles was unable to fill because of his many responsibilities in Rome. In addition to his post as administrator of Milan, Charles was appointed head of the *Consulta* (making him the pope's secretary of state); papal legate to Bologna, Romagna, and the March of Ancona; and cardinal-protector of Portugal, the Low Countries, the Catholic cantons of Switzerland, as well as of the Knights of Malta and the orders of Friars Minor and the Carmelites.

The young cardinal dedicated himself to his new duties with an intentionality and goodwill that illustrated his considerable administrative gifts. A supporter of the arts and letters, he believed that it was important for him to live according to the standards of the papal court, and yet, despite the luxury surrounding him, he managed to remain detached from that way of life. Throughout this period, his absence from his duties in Milan and his many responsibilities in Rome caused Charles to feel a certain anxiety. Even with his misgivings about the luxuries of the papal court, however, Cardinal Borromeo supported his uncle's intention to reconvene the Council of Trent. Once that occurred, Charles took an active role in drafting the new catechism (*Catechism of the Council of Trent*) and in the reform of the liturgical books and church music.[20]

[19] Paul Burns and Sarah Fawcett Thomas, eds., *Butler's Lives of the Saints: New Full Edition; November* (Collegeville, Minn.: Liturgical Press, 1997), 30.
[20] A staunch supporter of church music, Charles commissioned Giovanni Pierluigi da Palestrina (d. 1594) to compose his famous *Missa Papae Marcelli* (Pope Marcellus Mass, 1562).

While the Council was still in session, Charles' brother Federigo died. Profoundly affected by his brother's passing, he resolved to live an even holier life. Because he was now head of the Borromeo family, it was assumed that he, not having been ordained, would abandon his ecclesiastical duties and marry. But Charles was a man who knew his own mind, so he decided to resign his position in the family in favor of one of his uncles, seeking ordination to the priesthood. Ordained in 1563, he was consecrated bishop two months later, although his duties still prevented him from assuming his responsibilities in Milan. Pope Pius IV did give Charles permission to visit Milan, and he used this visit as an occasion to hold a provincial council. He succeeded in implementing the reforms of Trent, giving particular attention to those related to the education and discipline of the clergy and the celebration of the liturgy.

While returning to Rome, he received word that his uncle the pope was dying. Although he remained in Rome for a time at the urging of the new pope, Pius V, Charles decided to return to his see. Finally, in April 1566, he returned to Milan and implemented a full program of reform that included the convocation of a number of synods and councils, regular visitations of the parishes, and the establishment of seminaries for training the secular clergy. For his part, Charles lived a simple life of prayer and penance that effectively bespoke his dedication to the ideals he was seeking to impart to his flock. Although he faced some opposition from the civil authorities and disgruntled clerics, he enjoyed the support of his people, who appreciated their bishop's benevolence and humility. When the city was struck by plague in 1576, Charles arranged for the care and support of more than seventy thousand poor people, a task that exhausted all of his resources.

Charles Borromeo died in Milan during the night of November 3, 1584, at the age of forty-six. Devotion to this holy bishop spread quickly, and he was canonized by Pope Paul V in 1610.

* * * * *

During his visit to Castiglione, Cardinal Borromeo stayed with the archpriest of the parish of Saints Celsus and Nazarius. Within a few hours of the cardinal's arrival, Aloysius came to pay his respects, representing his father, who was absent at the time. The cardinal took Aloysius to his private sitting room, where the two had a long conversation. Borromeo was astonished by the grace and wisdom of the boy who sat before him. For his part, Aloysius opened his heart to the cardinal, begging him for instruction and guidance in the spiritual life. Borromeo recommended that Aloysius study the *Catechism of the Council of Trent* and asked if the young prince had made his First Communion. Aloysius replied that he had not. The cardinal, who would not allow the event to be postponed any longer, took it upon himself to prepare him to receive the Blessed Sacrament. Consequently, on July 22, 1580, the Feast of Saint Mary Magdalen, Aloysius received the Eucharist for the first time, from Saint Charles during a public Mass in the parish church.[21]

The young prince received Communion frequently, always preparing himself by celebrating the sacrament of reconciliation and by looking for ways to increase his devotion. He prepared the day before by prayer, spiritual reading, and meditation upon the mystery of Christ's Presence in the Blessed Sacrament. His demeanor as he received the Eucharist edified many who saw him, and he made a long act of thanksgiving afterward. The Eucharist became the center of his spiritual life. Aloysius was often seen to weep, especially while he attended Mass on feast days and on the days he received Holy Communion. This special grace, the gift of tears, was to remain with him throughout his life. As Father Meschler notes, the gifts of tears and consolations "were a reward to Aloysius for the purity of his youth, and at the same time a source of strength for the hard and thorny path he had still to tread".[22] Aloysius' spirit of prayer, particularly his newly acquired habit of mental prayer, combined with his remarkable devotion to the Blessed Sacrament and the Mother of God, was to be a hallmark of this young man throughout his short life.

---

[21] It seems that Father Cepari was not aware of this event when he published the first edition of his *Life of Saint Aloysius*. It is recounted in the second edition. Despite this omission, Clement Ghisoni, who knew Aloysius from age seven until his entrance into the Society of Jesus, attested to Aloysius' reception of Holy Communion from the hand of Saint Charles. Ghisoni offered the following deposition as part of the investigation for Aloysius' process of canonization on July 15, 1608: "Afterwards Aloysius returned from Mantua to Castiglione. At this place the blessed Cardinal Charles Borromeo, when making a visitation there, instructed him in the manner of receiving the Holy Sacrament of the Altar, and with his own hand gave him his first communion." Quoted in Cepari, *Life of Saint Aloysius*, 352n23.

[22] Meschler, *St. Aloysius*, 46.

During this time, the marquis had been residing in Monferrato, where he was acting as governor.[23] Greatly disturbed by the reports he had received about his son's failing health, he sent word to Donna Marta at the end of the summer of 1580, telling her to bring Aloysius and Rudolfo to him in Monferrato. The family traveled by coach, a primitive form of which had just come into fashion. (Prior to this time, people had journeyed on horseback or by foot.) Between Milan and Casale the group had to cross the Ticino River, which had overflowed its banks because of recent rains. The marchioness and her attendants crossed safely and were driving on, when, suddenly, the coach carrying Aloysius, Rudolfo, and their tutor broke in two in the middle of the river. The front part of the carriage, carrying Rudolfo, was pulled safely to shore. The back part, carrying Aloysius and the tutor, was carried downstream. The two might have been lost had not the piece of carriage struck against the trunk of a large tree that was floating in the middle of the river. A man quickly rode to where Aloysius and del Turco were stranded and, placing Aloysius behind him on his horse, brought him safely to shore. He then returned and saved the tutor. There was a small chapel dedicated to the Virgin Mary nearby, and the party stopped there to offer thanks to God for the rescue. Following a brief rest in Vigevano, where the boys and their tutor changed into dry clothing and prepared for the rest of their journey, the group eventually reached Casale di Monferrato, where they were greeted by an anxious Don Ferrante.

While in Monferrato, Aloysius dedicated his time to his classical studies, making good progress in ancient languages. His favorite writers were Seneca, Plutarch, and Valerius Maximus. "He was in the habit of copying out extracts from their works which he thought he could make use of in conversation, to encourage others to practice virtue and strive after perfection. But in spite of his liking for these pagan authors, he still preferred to read spiritual works, such as those of Louis of Granada."[24]

---

[23] The Marquisate of Monferrato lay between Genoa, Milan, and Piedmont and had been claimed by the Duke of Mantua in 1536.

[24] Meschler, *St. Aloysius*, 49. Louis of Granada (1504–1588)—born Luis de Sarriá in Granada, Spain—became a Dominican at the Priory of the Holy Cross. While pursuing studies at the College of Saint Gregory at Valladolid, he was influenced by Thomistic Scholasticism, Christian humanism, and zeal for the apostolate of preaching as exemplified by

The marquis did all he could to convince Aloysius to abandon his austere lifestyle, and went to great pains to distract him by hosting parties and other amusements. There were tournaments, foot and horse racing, pageants, and fireworks, in addition to a regular round of plays and masques. Although there were no theaters, plays were performed in great halls with actors dressed in elaborate and costly costumes. The longer dramas were broken up by skits, pantomimes, music, and singing.[25] Relics of Greek plays were translated by scholars, Roman plays were delivered in the Italian vernacular, and sacred plays were all performed to the delight of the wealthy and elite.[26] And yet, as much as the wealthy enjoyed theater, it was actually dancing that was the most celebrated and favored form of entertainment.

Beyond theater and dancing, high feasting was as theatrical as life in the court. Meals included dishes and utensils of gold and silver plate, tablecloths of damask and brocade (which were changed frequently because their edges were used to wipe hands and faces), and endless hours of dining through meals of two-dozen courses.

> Not only the fervid eating and drinking and the leisured pace imitated Rome, but the utensils themselves: ewers of crystal shaped like mythical birds, bowls painted in grotesque designs surmounted by harpies' heads and studded with breasts. Pottery from Faenza and Urbino told the cherished old stories: Diana turning Actaeon into a stag; Apollo in his sun chariot; Daphne becoming a laurel tree— characters who often came to actual life in the pageantry of the banquet itself. A fanfare of trumpets and the flare of torches introduced

---

the Dominican Savonarola. Renowned as a preacher, he served as confessor and chaplain to Queen Catherine of Portugal. Between 1554 and 1559, he published twelve books, which were granted ecclesiastical approval in 1562. Louis was one of the first ascetical writers to formulate methods of prayer specifically for the laity. Inspired by Sacred Scripture, the Fathers of the Church, Thomistic theology, Saint Catherine of Siena, and the spiritual writers of the Rhineland, among others, his teachings were Christocentric. He emphasized the practice of prayer, the cultivation of virtue, contempt for the world, contemplation of God in nature, the practice of mortification, obedience to the Commandments, celebration of the sacraments, and imitation of the saints. His writings strongly influenced Saints Charles Borromeo, John of Avila, Francis de Sales, Alphonsus Liguori, Rose of Lima, Teresa of Avila, Louise de Marillac, and Vincent de Paul.

[25] Kate Simon, *A Renaissance Tapestry: The Gonzaga of Mantua* (New York: Harper and Row, 1998), 216.

[26] Ibid., 71.

a live Diana leading off platters of venison and hare. Juno ushered in the display of peacocks, deplumed, stuffed, and reassembled. Ceres appeared with the highly prized Mantuan cheese and sausage; Mercury flew before trays that carried the dessert, hundreds of figurines of dough, sugar, and gold dust.[27]

It was from all these diversions that Aloysius began to withdraw. The young prince had no mystical notions—he saw only that he must avoid offending God at all costs. He began to excuse himself from playing games, especially with girls, and once, during a game of "forfeits", he was ordered to kiss the shadow of a girl who was also playing. He abruptly broke off the game and left the room. In this action we get a glimpse of Aloysius' temper and disposition. His tutor later reported that Aloysius did not care how much he upset the others who were playing. He was keenly aware of his station and the expectations placed upon a young nobleman. Father Martindale notes that he exhibited a strong masculine sense, dismissing those things which to him seemed "soft". When Aloysius was jokingly accused of being a "woman-hater", he flatly replied that he could not stand the smell of the perfumes that were so liberally used during this period.[28] In his responses we can see a boyish reaction to those things of which he disapproved or thought to be ridiculous. Fashion reigned supreme and extravagance was the norm. Aloysius responded to this type of life and its accompanying values by simply loathing what seemed to him to be nothing more than "shameless effrontery". This was expressed in a certain modesty and shyness that, combined with a spirit of independence, moved Aloysius to distance himself from the theatrics of court life where ladies hoped to see and be seen by him.[29] He did not want to be coddled and hated having footmen dress and undress him. Contrary to popular misconceptions, timidity, nervousness, or prudery were never characteristics of the young prince.[30]

Aloysius began visiting the small chapel of Our Lady of Crea, or he would visit the Capuchin monastery. Most often he visited

[27] Ibid., 213.
[28] Father Martindale notes that even mules and paper money were perfumed. Martindale, *Vocation of Saint Aloysius*, 53.
[29] Meschler, *St. Aloysius*, 51.
[30] Martindale, *Vocation of Saint Aloysius*, 54; translation adapted.

the house of the Barnabite Fathers, with whom he would converse about spiritual subjects and his studies. In fact, the young man visited them so frequently, going to confession and receiving Communion in their church, that the Barnabites began to think he intended to join their order. Although Aloysius was certainly considering religious life, it does not appear that he seriously considered a vocation to the Barnabites. He was, however, greatly edified by their detachment from material goods, their fraternal charity, the joyful atmosphere of their community, and their regular and quiet manner of life. One day, as Aloysius was visiting their community, he wrote the following reflection in his notes:

> See Aloysius, how happy is the life of a religious! These Fathers are free from all the snares of the world, and far removed from the occasions of sin. The times that others spend in acquiring perishing riches and vain pleasures is employed by them in storing up imperishable treasures, and thus they gain great merit in God's eye and are secure in His favor forever. They have no need to fear that the labor they undergo for their sanctification will be lost. Religious are guided by reason in the ordering of their lives; they are not swayed by the concupiscence of the senses. They are not ambitious, they strive after no honors; they have no esteem for earthly, perishable things; they are not jealous of others, nor do they envy any man's goods. They are happy in serving God alone, whom to serve is to reign. No wonder, then, that they are always happy and at peace, and fear neither death, nor judgment, nor the torments of hell; for they have no mortal sin upon their souls, but are busy night and day amassing heavenly treasures, since they are always occupied in doing some good work for God or with God. From the testimony of their good conscience springs peace and tranquility reflected even in the joyousness of their faces, and a firm hope of eternal life. What joy do they not feel at the thought of Him whom they serve and in whose court they dwell?
>
> What are you doing, and of what are you thinking? Why can you not choose this state of life? Think of the great rewards God has promised to it! Think how much time and opportunity you would have to attend to the care of your soul! If you carry out your resolution and yield the Marquisate to Rudolfo, and yet remain with him, you may have to see many things done of which you cannot approve. Will you shut your eyes to them? If you do, your conscience will continually reproach you with neglecting your duty. If you blame him, he will

pay no heed to you, or else grow impatient. Do you think you will attain your end by becoming a priest and living like any other secular cleric? On the contrary, you will have taken upon yourself graver obligations than a layman, and yet be exposed to the same and in a certain sense greater dangers than those in holy matrimony. You will find it impossible to avoid hearing the views of worldly-minded men, conforming to their manners and yielding to their wishes; for if you allow yourself to be persuaded to remain in the world, your social position will oblige you to visit first one prince and then another. If you shun the society of your female relatives and other ladies, you will excite remarks; if you mix with them, you will break your resolution. If you accept high offices in the Church you will have far more cares to perplex you than at present; if you refuse them, your relatives will be displeased, they will say you are a disgrace to the family, and do all they can to overcome your reluctance.

But if you join a religious order, you will cut off all those fetters with one stroke; you will put aside all obstacles, free yourself from all considerations of human respect, and be able to enjoy perfect peace and serve God perfectly.[31]

These reflections often occupied Aloysius' thoughts, and it was only after many prayers that he came to understand, at last, that this religious vocation came from God. He also realized that because of his age—he was only thirteen—he would not receive his father's permission. He understood that he should keep his resolve to himself, speaking of it to no one and deciding on no particular order. He did, however, decide that he would live like a religious as much as possible. Aloysius made constant efforts to divide his time between study and prayer. If he were disturbed, he would seek out quiet, secluded places for his meditation and devotions. He refused to have a fire in his room, and his hands became so tender that they were often swollen and chapped from the cold.

The marquis became increasingly annoyed by his eldest son's absences, and he constantly tried to persuade him to pursue princely amusements and pleasures. But Aloysius was no longer the four-year-old child who would be charmed by the sight of cavalry reviews and military drills. He felt at home in his study or in a church or

[31] Quoted in Meschler, *St. Aloysius*, 51–53.

religious house, engaging in spiritual conversations, spiritual reading, and prayer.[32]

* * * * *

In 1581, the marquis' term as governor of Monferrato expired, and he, along with his family, returned to Castiglione. After the family arrived home, Aloysius increased his austerities and prayers to an immoderate degree. One of the possible reasons for this excess was the dismissal of his tutor—it had been decided that Aloysius was old enough to be his own master.

On May 21, 1581, Aloysius wrote to his "dearest friend", Pietro del Turco, who was then in Florence. "I have received your most welcome letter. The only thing I did not like in it was that you should think me so foolish as to be annoyed or angered by words which could only increase my love for you. That was not the case, and it never will be; but I shall always remember you, wherever I may be.... In conclusion I greet you and beg to be remembered to James, Bastiano, the Lady Mary, little John, and Angelino."[33] With no one to temper Aloysius' penances, he added to his ascetical practices. He would allow nothing costly to be purchased for him or his room, which was rather small and contained only a simple bed and minimal furnishings.[34] In addition to his already severe diet, Aloysius began to fast three days each week, taking nothing but bread and water on Wednesdays, Fridays, and Saturdays.[35] It is impossible for us truly to judge the extent of his fasting and abstinence. Oral tradition related that his servants often weighed his food, finding it did not exceed an ounce, morning and evening. In the time immediately preceding his entrance into religious life, he is said to have had it weighed, and he could never be prevailed upon to take more than

---

[32] Cepari, *Life of Saint Aloysius*, 34.

[33] Quoted in Meschler, *St. Aloysius*, 55; translation adapted.

[34] Ibid., 58.

[35] It should be noted that this practice reflected the popular piety of the time. Numerous monastic and mendicant communities fasted or abstained on these days, and they are still considered days of penance in many religious communities today. Father Cepari tells us that these fasts were kept every Saturday, in honor of the Blessed Virgin; on Fridays, as a means of honoring the Passion of Christ; and on Wednesdays. Cepari, *Life of Saint Aloysius*, 36.

a fixed amount.[36] While these details may only be pious exaggerations, Aloysius would certainly have heard the stories from the lives of the saints of prolonged fasts and instances where saints were said to have abstained from all food for many years. Among those saints whose stories Aloysius would have most likely known was the mystic Catherine Benincasa (d. 1380). Canonized in 1461, the woman who is most commonly known as Saint Catherine of Siena was a wildly popular saint, and her vita, composed by her spiritual director, Blessed Raymond of Capua (d. 1399), was one of the most widely read books of that time. In it, Raymond dedicates a substantial chapter to Catherine's eating habits, writing that "not only did she not need food, but she could not even have eaten without pain. If she forced herself to eat, her body suffered greatly, she could not digest and she had to vomit."[37] Other saints, almost all women who would have been known to the young prince, were celebrated for their extreme fasts. These included Saint Clare of Assisi (d. 1253), Blessed Angela of Foligno (1309), and Saint Margaret of Cortona (d. 1297). Aloysius' contemporary Saint Mary Magdalen de' Pazzi would herself be remembered for the extremity of her fasts and penances. Whatever the inspiration for his own penances and the form his fasting would have actually taken, we can be certain that because of Aloysius' disposition, he would have eaten only what he believed was necessary—anything more he would have considered superfluous.[38]

In addition to his fasts and protracted times of prayer, the prince began to take the discipline (i.e., flagellate himself) three times each week. Later, this became a daily practice.[39] The custom of scourging one's own flesh (or being scourged by another) has a rich and varied history. Originally a penal practice imposed on delinquent clerics, it eventually became a feature of monastic discipline. Voluntary flagellation was a development of the earlier punitive form. It was intended to be an expiation for one's sins and the sins of others, a means of conquering temptation, and a way to imitate (literally) Christ's

[36] Meschler, *St. Aloysius*, 58. See also Cepari, *Life of Saint Aloysius*, 36–37.

[37] Raymond of Capua, *Legenda Major*, quoted in Rudolph M. Bell, *Holy Anorexia* (Chicago: University of Chicago Press, 1985), 25.

[38] Meschler, *St. Aloysius*, 58.

[39] Father Cepari asserts that Aloysius sometimes disciplined himself several times a day. See Cepari, *Life of Saint Aloysius*, 37–38.

Passion.[40] Monks were the first to adopt scourging as an ascetic exercise, but the practice soon spread to the secular clergy and even the laity. Saint Peter Damian (d. 1072), monastic reformer and Doctor of the Church, advocated the practice. In monasteries and religious houses, the practice eventually became more systematized. Provisions for the "discipline" were made in nearly all religious rules composed from the sixteenth to the eighteenth centuries. In the sixteenth century, self-flagellation was a common practice, and there were groups of *Disciplinati* who were supervised by the Church and under the supervision of bishops, including Saint Charles Borromeo. Inspired by the often fantastic penances contained in the lives of the saints and by the writings of Louis of Granada (among others), Aloysius also began to fasten spurs together, wearing them around his body like a girdle.[41]

While Aloysius' penances certainly seem spectacular to us today, they were an important component of his spiritual life and growth.[42] However, it is Aloysius' habits of prayer that provide us with the most meaningful insight into his spirituality. He began each day with meditation, after which he recited certain vocal prayers and attended Mass. During the day, he often attended the Divine Office with the various religious of Castiglione, read spiritual books, and revisited the subject of his morning meditation. Before retiring to bed, he again spent an hour in meditation. He often passed a good part of the night in prayer, kneeling on the stone floor and wearing only his nightshirt.

Needless to say, the continued fasting and penance had a serious effect on his already delicate health. He began having severe headaches, which caused him much suffering, and from which he was never again completely free. When he reflected on these headaches, he thought of the crown of thorns worn by Christ, accepting them as an opportunity for grace.

[40] Martin D. W. Jones, *The Counter Reformation: Religion and Society in Early Modern Europe* (New York: Cambridge University Press, 1995), 21.

[41] Cepari, *Life of Saint Aloysius*, 38.

[42] Father James Martin notes that "the prevailing Catholic piety at the time, which warmly commended such practices, obviously exerted a strong influence on Aloysius. The young nobleman was, like all of us, a person of his times." James Martin, *My Life with the Saints* (Chicago: Loyola Press, 2006), 333.

One evening, Aloysius had been suffering from a particularly severe headache. Retiring earlier than usual, he suddenly remembered that he had not yet recited the Penitential Psalms (as was his custom), and he asked his servant to place a light by his bed. Falling asleep, he forgot to extinguish the candle, which either burned down or fell over. The bed, mattress, two coverlets, and bed curtain caught fire. Aloysius awoke, running to the door to call for help. No sooner had he opened the door than the whole bed burst into flames. The servants and soldiers hurried to his room and threw the burning bed out of the window, preventing further damage. Aloysius later recalled that he experienced divine protection in this instance and "a thousand others, and however hopeless the matters might seem about which he prayed, whether his own concerns or his father's, never were his prayers unanswered".[43]

As Aloysius began to mature spiritually, he began to see the things of the world as base and of little worth. Growing in his faith and union with God, he became all the more attached to the priests and religious of Castiglione. He especially enjoyed visiting the Benedictines and Dominicans, with whom he conversed on various spiritual topics, and he was always pleased when the monks and friars presented him with little devotional objects, such as rosaries, medals, or Agnus Dei.[44]

The virtues of Aloysius stand out in sharp contrast with the frivolity and excesses of his age. He had learned how to live poorly amid riches and luxury, and unnoticed among honors and respect. He presents a picture of renunciation, austerity, and self-denial that, while sometimes extreme and overzealous, offers a valuable witness, even today.[45]

With time, the prince came to believe that it was his special vocation to offer penance for the sins of the world. Surprisingly, no steps

---

[43] Meschler, *St. Aloysius*, 61.

[44] Ibid. "Agnus Dei" here refers to oval disks of wax blessed by the pope on which the figure of a lamb is stamped. The wax comes from the remains of paschal candles and is solemnly blessed on the Thursday after Easter in the first and seventh years of the pope's pontificate. They are sacramentals and are typically carried or worn as medals around the neck. An Agnus Dei is traditionally regarded as protection against the attacks of the devil, sickness, or sudden death, or as a source of divine help for expectant mothers.

[45] Quoted in Cepari, *Life of Saint Aloysius*, 42–44; translation adapted.

were taken by his family to curb his zeal. As Father Meschler says, "God had chosen this child as a sacrificial lamb."[46] In his later years, Aloysius himself wrote these words:

> The pillars of heaven have fallen; who can promise me that I shall per-severe? The world is now full of iniquity; who shall appease the wrath of the Almighty? Very many priests and religious think but little of their vocation. How can God suffer longer such a devastation of His Kingdom? The faithful rob Him of honor through their carelessness; who is to make reparation? Woe to the worldly who put off their penance until the hour of their death; and woe to the clergy who slumber on! Such thoughts ought to rouse us from our lethargy and renew our resolution to do penance and to serve God with constancy and sincerity.[47]

It was this spirit of reparation that motivated Aloysius to adopt his dramatic behaviors. But if we look deeper into his reasons for these actions, we can see the intensity with which Aloysius loved God, the Church, and those around him. His penance was not only self-serving. He offered it in reparation to God for the faults and failures of the Church and the sins of his family and world.

[46] Meschler, *St. Aloysius*, 63.

[47] Aloysius Gonzaga, "For the Exercises of the First Week" (n.d. from personal papers), quoted in Cepari, *Life of Saint Aloysius*, 44.

Chapter 6

Spain and the Jesuits

The court of King Philip II of Spain (d. 1598) was a center of political and spiritual power whose influence spread throughout Europe and the New World. It was to Philip (who had assumed the throne in 1556 upon the death of his father, King Charles I) that the Italian princes and nobles offered their allegiance. Philip acted as ruler of Milan, Sardinia, Naples, and Sicily, and he eagerly took advantage of every opportunity to draw the Italian princes to his court and retain their allegiance.

In 1581, the empress Maria (d. 1603), daughter of Emperor Charles V (d. 1558) and widow of the emperor Maximilian II (d. 1576), had returned to Madrid and to her brother, Philip. The king intended to entrust to her the government of Portugal, which he had claimed after the death of the cardinal-king Henry in 1580. It was his hope that, since Maria was the granddaughter of the Portuguese king Manuel, this appointment would make him more popular in Portugal. The Italian princes through whose provinces she passed on her way from Bohemia to Spain were instructed to escort her to Madrid, and it was the empress' special wish that Donna Marta of Castiglione accompany her personally. The marquis, who had many ties to King Philip, readily obeyed. Ferrante, however, was motivated by more than his obedience to his lord, King Philip. It is likely that he also recognized the benefit of presenting his sons at court, believing that this would persuade Aloysius to give up his thoughts of renouncing the world. The boys' former tutor, Pietro del Turco, was commissioned to act as traveling companion to the princes. Aloysius wrote to del Turco on June 1, 1581:

Dearest Friend,
I have already written you two letters, one from Mantua and the other from Venice. But as I am in doubt whether you received them,

and desire your presence so much, I am sending this one by our Peter
(who made 50 leaps into the air at the news), to beg you to come
without fail and to start as soon as possible. I assure you that my father,
the Marquis, greatly wishes you to come, and we all, especially Julius
and myself, desire it very much.[1]

However, as the days passed, del Turco did not come. Aloysius wrote
to him again on June 23, with another letter following on June 25.
We do not know if del Turco ever joined the group.

The marquis, his wife, and their five children joined the empress,
and we know that they were with her when she arrived in Verona.
In Brescia and Lodi, she was met by Saint Charles Borromeo, who
celebrated Mass in her presence and gave her Holy Communion.
Everywhere the empress stopped, she was received with highest honors. She continued her journey by way of Genoa, where she was
joined by an escort of ships of the Spanish fleet on November 8. The
group went ashore at Marseilles, Collioure, Barcelona, and Saragossa,
where an attack of gout obliged the marquis to remain behind while
Aloysius and the others continued on to Madrid.

Throughout the trip, Aloysius was affirmed in his piety and devotions by the empress, who visited all the famous shrines and sanctuar-
ies along the route. She venerated the relics of Saint Mary Magdalen
in the Church of Saint Maximinus at Marseilles and visited her cave at
Sainte-Baume in Provence.[2] The party also visited the famous shrines
of Our Lady of the Pillar in Saragossa, the famous "Black Madonna"
in the Benedictine abbey Santa Maria de Montserrat, and the relics of
Saint Didacus of San Nicolás at Alcalá. Although he was surrounded

[1] Aloysius Gonzaga to Pietro Francis del Turco, June 1, 1581, in *Lettere di S. Luigi Gonzaga*, ed. Oliviero Iozzi (Pisa, 1889), 8f., quoted in Maurice Meschler, S.J., *St. Aloysius
Gonzaga: Patron of Christian Youth* (Rockford, Ill.: TAN Books, 1985), 66. Internal evidence
suggests that this letter, though dated June 1, 1581, was, in fact, composed after the letters
dated June 23 and June 25. The date "June 1" was most likely a clerical error and should have
been "July 1".

[2] Ancient tradition states that Mary Magdalen died in France near the village of Villa Lata
and was buried by Saint Maximinus. Her relics were discovered in 1279 and enshrined in a
reliquary above the main altar of the Church of Saint Maximinus in May 1280. The Dominicans have served as the custodians of this shrine since 1295. The cave at Sainte-Baume was,
according to tradition, the grotto where Mary Magdalen lived for the last thirty years of her
life. For a more complete treatment of the history of this shrine and the relics of Saint Mary
Magdalen, see Joan Carroll Cruz, *Relics* (Huntington, Ind.: Our Sunday Visitor, 1984), 156–58.

by wealth and grandeur, Aloysius remained quiet and reflected, and the empress came to regard him as a little saint.[3] Finally on March 7, 1582, they entered Madrid, the city that Philip had transformed from a small Moorish village into his splendid capital.

Philip II was a serious, earnest man who loved simplicity but who also appreciated the prestige and majesty that were part of his status as king of Spain. Although he was a faithful son of the Church, he was also fully aware of his own importance and power. Philip regarded himself as the "sword of faith against heresy, but as God's representative in matters temporal, and became thus the occasion of much unpleasantness for the Church".[4]

Sixteenth-century Spain was a profoundly Catholic nation, whose identity was forged in the "Reconquest" against Islam and the Moors in the early part of the century.[5] Spain's Catholicism was intimately connected with the monarchy, even as it was tightly controlled by the Inquisition. In 1564, Philip II had ordered that the decrees of the Council of Trent were to be obeyed in his dominions. Spanish bishops returned from the Council eager to begin the work of reform, and in 1565 Philip called upon the bishops to organize provincial and diocesan councils to see to the implementation of the reforms.[6] Although King Philip's relationship with the papacy was often tense and even coercive, he was staunchly dedicated to the defense of the Church.[7] This tension can be evinced in a letter from Philip to Pope Sixtus V (1585–1590) dated June 1589.

> While the enemies of God are thus advancing you are content to look and let things be. I, on the other hand, who look upon all these interests as my own, and who have recourse to Your Holiness as a beloved and venerated Father, and who as a good son call your attention to the duties of the Holy See, receive in return nothing but insults! Heaven and earth are witnesses of my veneration for the Holy See.... By this

[3] Meschler, St. Aloysius, 67.

[4] Ibid., 68.

[5] R. Po-chia Hsia, The World of Catholic Renewal, 1540–1770 (New York: Cambridge, 1998), 46.

[6] Ibid., 47.

[7] Martin Jones, The Counter Reformation: Religion and Society in Early Modern Europe (New York: Cambridge University Press, 1995), 154.

present letter I wish to defend the Church. I shall believe in the affection which Your Holiness says that you feel for me, when I see from
your actions that Your Holiness is following my advice, paying heed
to my prayer.... If Your Holiness, in correspondence with your duty,
and the assurances which you have so often made, will act in this way,
I will lend my aid as your devoted son.[8]

Despite Philip's often tenuous relations with the papacy, his contributions to the Church's efforts of reform were as considerable as
his efforts to defend the rights of the Church. He freely offered Spanish money and arms to defend the Catholic cause. Although attempts
to suppress Dutch Protestant rebels and his plan to invade England
failed, he successfully checked the advance of the Ottoman Empire at
the famed Battle of Lepanto (1571), and he financially supported the
work of the Catholic League as it tried to bring peace and stability to
a France that was being torn apart by civil war.

Within the Spanish Church, there was a deep commitment to nur-
turing the Faith within Spain and in its colonies in the New World
and in Asia. Printed sermons, devotional prints, and catechisms were
published in large numbers, and charitable works (often undertaken
at the initiative of the new religious orders) were well endowed.
This was the Spain of Ignatius of Loyola (d. 1556); the founder of the
"Observant" Franciscans, Peter of Alcántara (d. 1562); Francis Borgia, the third general of the Society of Jesus (d. 1572); and the great
Carmelite reformers, Teresa of Avila (d. 1582) and John of the Cross
(1591)—all of whom worked and died during Philip's reign.

Ironically perhaps, despite the king's religious sensibilities, the
decadence of Spanish culture and fashion influenced all of Europe.
The members of the court loved fine music and good art, but also
pomp and grandeur, costly clothing, and gambling for high stakes.
The Spanish court was regarded as the school of good breeding, and
yet there were pride and flattery along with gallantry and splendor.

Upon arrival in Madrid, the marquis' daughter, Isabella, became
the maid of honor to the princesses Clara Eugenie (d. 1633) and
Catherine (d. 1597). (They were the daughters of Queen Elizabeth
[Isabella] of Valois, whose maid of honor Donna Marta had been).

[8] Quoted in ibid., 156.

The marquis assumed duties as chamberlain to the king. King Philip and his current wife, Anna Maria of Austria (d. 1580), had two living children—the princes Diego (d. 1582), who was the heir apparent, and Philip (d. 1621). It was to Prince Diego that Aloysius and Rudolfo were to serve as pages of the first rank.

As royal pages, Aloysius and Rudolfo would not only accompany the crown prince and wait upon him, but they would be educated with him. Aloysius continued to devote his energy to his studies. In a short time, he had completely mastered the Spanish language and passed on to higher studies. He learned logic and attended lectures on astronomy and mathematics, a subject for which he showed a natural proficiency. He also began to study philosophy, particularly the field of natural theology.

Aloysius' biographers record two events that illustrate the progress Aloysius was making in his studies. In March 1582, Aloysius was in Alcalá, where he was invited to take part in a theological debate. Although he was only fourteen years old, he argued with great skill against the thesis being defended, trying to prove (for the sake of argument) that the mystery of the Trinity could be understood by human reason alone. An interesting footnote to this incident is that Jesuit Father Gabriel Vasquez, who presided at the debate, later served as Aloysius' teacher of theology at the Roman College.[9]

The second event recounted by the young prince's biographers occurred in March 1583. In 1581, following the death of King Henry of Portugal, Philip of Spain laid claim to the throne of Portugal and subdued the people by force of arms. On the king's return to Madrid on March 29, 1583, Aloysius was chosen to welcome him with an oration. Composed in Latin, the speech praised Philip's illustrious ancestry, his virtues as a ruler, and his military triumphs in the wars with the Turks, the French, the Portuguese, and the English.[10] It is obvious from the fact that Aloysius was chosen for this honor that he was held in high regard by the other members of the court.

The particular esteem with which the court and king regarded Aloysius comes to light in the recounting of an exchange that Aloysius had

[9] Virgil Cepari, S.J., *Life of Saint Aloysius Gonzaga*, ed. Francis Goldie, S.J. (New York: Benziger Brothers, 1891), 46.
[10] See, for instance, Meschler, *St. Aloysius*, 70.

with the young Prince Diego. On one occasion, Aloysius was standing at a window with the prince, who, being annoyed at the wind,
shouted, "Stupid wind, be still, I command you!" Aloysius replied with
a smile, "Your Royal Highness can give commands to men, and they
obey you; but you have no power over the elements, for they are
subject to God alone, Whom you are also bound to obey." Courtiers
reported Aloysius' words to the king, who dismissed the criticism of his
son, recognizing the good sense and appropriateness of the response.[11]
Aloysius' obvious maturity and composure made a profound impact
on all whom he encountered, and it was a common saying of the court
that the young marquis was not made of flesh and blood.[12]

Historical evidence seems to indicate that Aloysius received the
habit of the Knights of the Order of Saint James of Compostela while
he was residing in Spain.[13] The marquis was a member of the Knights
of Saint James, as were others among Aloysius' family. This noble fel-
lowship had the dual distinction of caring for pilgrims on their way to
the shrine of Saint James at Compostela (for whom they are named)
and of being of great aid to the Spanish crown in its efforts to expel
the Moors from Spain. Having received its first rule of life in 1171
from the man who would later become Pope Celestine III (1191–
1198), the Order of Santiago (as they were also known) adopted the
Rule of the Canons Regular of Saint Augustine. Officially recognized by Pope Alexander III (1159–1181) in 1175, the order was
comprised of several affiliate classes: canons (who were charged with
the celebration of the sacraments), canonesses (who served the pilgrims), knights bound by religious vows who lived in community,
and married knights. The Knights of the Order of Saint James were
very influential and held numerous possessions throughout Spain
and in Portugal, France, Italy, Hungary, and the Holy Land. These

[11] Cepari, Life of Saint Aloysius, 49.

[12] Meschler, St. Aloysius, 72.

[13] See Cepari, Life of Saint Aloysius, 360n32; Margaret Monro, A Book of Unlikely Saints
(Freeport, N.Y.: Books for Libraries, 1943), 34. According to note 32 in the Goldie edition of
Cepari's Life of Saint Aloysius (p. 360), there exists an oil painting in a church in Uclés, Spain,
representing Saint Aloysius in the habit of the Knights of Saint James. On a side altar in the
same church is a full-length statue of Aloysius, clothed in the habit on which is emblazoned
the symbols of the order: a red cross terminating in a sword (which recalls their title de la
Espada) and a shell in honor of their patron, the apostle James.

possessions included parishes, hospitals, schools, convents, and a college in Salamanca. In 1499, King Ferdinand was awarded administration of the order by the pope, and this was confirmed by Pope Alexander VI (1492–1503), who united the three great military orders of Spain under one government, that of the king of Spain.

Despite the esteem he enjoyed at court, Aloysius continued the penitential and ascetical practices he had adopted in Italy. Although Aloysius would conform to the expectations of court etiquette when required, he had no great love for the fine apparel that was such a prominent feature in the Spanish court. While his father initially opposed Aloysius' habit of wearing worn or patched clothes, the marquis soon realized that it would be futile to try to impose his own will in the matter.[14] It was in Spain that we see for the first time the ascetical practice for which Aloysius has been perhaps most highly criticized: his practice of never looking a woman in the face.

As has already been noted, Aloysius struggled to conquer his fiery and passionate Gonzaga blood. Although he had made his vow of chastity at the age of seven, he nonetheless remained a highly desirable match for ladies of the court. Temptations would have also included the possibility of casual sexual liaisons with both women and men seeking to benefit from forming a connection with the heir of the Marquis of Castiglione.[15] There is one aspect of this habit of Aloysius in which it seems that his early biographers were mistaken: the belief that he extended this habit of never looking a woman in the face even to his own mother.[16] This report by his biographers may have been little more than an attempt to identify Aloysius all the more closely with his patron, Saint Louis of Anjou, whose own life resembled that of Aloysius in so many ways.[17] While he was certainly capable of applying ascetical principles and ideals in extreme ways, he himself gives no evidence that he extended this practice to his mother, nor is there any contemporary evidence for it. Father

[14] Cepari, Life of Saint Aloysius, 48.

[15] C. C. Martindale, The Vocation of Saint Aloysius (New York: Sheed and Ward, 1946), 88.

[16] James Joyce, possibly acting here as a spokesman for many others, dismisses Aloysius as being "a pig" when alluding to this practice in The Portrait of the Artist as a Young Man (New York: Bantam, 1992), 236.

[17] Jodi Bilinkoff, Related Lives: Confessors and Their Female Penitents, 1450–1750 (Ithaca, N.Y.: Cornell University Press, 2005), 40. See also chap. 1, n. 9, above in this book.

Martindale asserts that one aspect of this strict custody of the eyes was an extension of Aloysius' habit of extreme concentration and of keeping in his mind and imagination thoughts and images that he believed to be of value for his spiritual advancement.[18] It is obvious that he was capable of great mental discipline, as we can see both in his extended periods of meditation and in his academic achievements.

It would be a great disservice to the young prince to suggest that he did not love his mother. Donna Marta was the predominant influence in his life, and it was to her that he spoke and wrote with an unparalleled freedom.[19] It would also be incorrect to try to assert that Aloysius was a prude. Prudery or a puritanical spirit was virtually impossible in the permissive society of royal courts of that age. As Father Martindale succinctly states, "Not a soul in that society had the least chance of being a prude, even if he or she wanted to."[20]

Years before, Aloysius had discovered an "interior chamber" where he could commune freely with God. Surrounded as he was by the pageantry of court and a flurry of servants and other courtiers, the call to enter that "chamber" was insistent. In practicing a custody of the eyes that seems nearly heroic if not excessive, Aloysius did not necessarily intend to shut the world out. Rather, he sought to shut himself in.[21] In point of fact, Aloysius did not look at anything very much. All his biographers note that when he entered the Jesuit novitiate, his superiors ordered that his collars be stiffened to prevent his head from bending forward. This particular ascetical practice had, by then, become second nature.[22]

In spite of the many challenges and distractions provided by the court, Madrid proved to be a place of growth and continuing discernment for the young prince. More than ever, Aloysius was convinced that the life of a prince was not for him.[23] Besides his continued spiritual growth, we can also see how Aloysius' studies served to enlarge his horizons: with new knowledge of distant lands and foreign cultures

[18] Martindale, *Vocation of Saint Aloysius*, 89.

[19] Cepari, *Life of Saint Aloysius*, 41, 54.

[20] Martindale, *Vocation of Saint Aloysius*, 90.

[21] Monro, *Unlikely Saints*, 25–26.

[22] See, for instance, Meschler, *St. Aloysius*, 141.

[23] Ibid. See also Francis Corley and Robert Willmes, *Wings of Eagles* (Milwaukee, Wis.: Bruce Publishing, 1941), 51.

came the realization that these were new lands where one should desire to spread the Christian faith.[24] A great deal of his energy was devoted to the study of mathematics, chronography,[25] astronomy, and "the use of globes". He also exhibited a great proficiency in philosophy, the study of which allowed him to further his understanding of the nature and attributes of God.

We see in the prince in this period the emergence of a new disposition and temperament. Gone was the childish obstinacy—Aloysius had learned right judgment. Although he never budged when his principles or convictions were at stake, he began, at this time, to show that he was willing to take risks. This ability to yield served to make him a more powerful adversary and ultimately a more popular character.[26] Yes, God remained everything to him, but he was beginning to learn how to lead more effectively by example and to be less severe. It is now that we begin to recognize a vibrancy and an inner dynamism that shows that he had begun to understand how to harness *La Gonzaghina*, his fiery Gonzaga temperament. Aloysius was, by all accounts, an amazing young man, and his family and the officials of the court recognized the qualities of a great statesman in the making. Although he would always struggle with the tendency to belittle others, his charm and manners were highly refined and endeared him to nearly all who knew him.

During his time in Madrid, Aloysius took Father Ferdinand Paterno, S.J., as his confessor. This priest, who was rector of the Jesuit college of Madrid, was a great ally and aid to him. Father Paterno later related three things about his direction that he believed were particularly noteworthy. The first of these was Aloysius' maturity of judgment; second was his dislike of idleness—one of his favorite occupations was the study of Scripture; and third was his constant vigilance to say nothing unkind to or about another person.[27]

Aloysius' father also recognized the strengths of his son's character, and it is because of Don Ferrante's desire to make use of these gifts that we have an interesting sort of footnote to this period of Aloysius'

[24] Corley and Willmes, *Wings of Eagles*, 92.
[25] Chronography is the science of the study of historical time and the placing of events within their historical context.
[26] Monro, *Unlikely Saints*, 36.
[27] Meschler, *St. Aloysius*, 76.

life. Although the marquis was, at heart, a good man who sought to
live a Christian life (as much as anyone of his time and station did),
he had a severe gambling addiction. As has already been noted, gambling was a favorite pastime among courtiers and nobles. The stakes
were often very high, and Don Ferrante's gambling was a source of
pain and embarrassment to his family. Recognizing Aloysius' prudence and levelheadedness, Ferrante came to rely on his teenage son
to manage certain aspects of the family's finances. This was undoubtedly a source of discouragement and annoyance for the young prince,
but, as we see in two letters he wrote to his uncle Horace Gonzaga,
the Marquis of Solferino, he complied with his father's wishes.[28]

Very Illustrious Sir,
    The favor and aid you have ever deigned to show to our father
and to all of us has been far beyond any service we have been able to
render you, although our will and trust have been so great. I thank
you accordingly for everything in the name of my father, who is today
suffering from his usual malady of gout, and is not able to write and
acknowledge the kindness you have done him by sending the sum
which he received today. He will hardly have returned before it will
be his duty to repay it.
    With this, I respectfully kiss your hands and, in my Father's name,
I conclude.
    Madrid, May 18, 1582.
                              Nephew and servant,
                                          Aluigi Gonzaga.[29]

A second letter followed a short time later:

Very Illustrious Uncle,
    I should often have written to you, if I had not doubted whether
these letters would have reached you, as I did not know where to

[28] Ferrante apparently used Aloysius to write letters that he did not want his secretary to see.
A fragment of a third letter to Horace Gonzaga (Letter X), dated June 25, 1582, is included in
the Goldie edition of Father Cepari's *Life of Saint Aloysius*, 407; translation adapted.
    [29] Aloysius Gonzaga to Horace Gonzaga, May 18, 1582 (Letter VIII), in Cepari, *Life of
Saint Aloysius*, 406. Many of Aloysius' letters, translated from Prof. Oliviero Iozzi's collection,
Lettere di S. Luigi Gonzaga (Pisa, 1889), were added as "Letters of Saint Aloysius Gonzaga" to
the end of the Goldie edition of Cepari's work.

address them, nor where you were, and if our duties with our serene master [Don Diego, the young Spanish prince], in whose service our father wishes us to be always engaged, had not hindered me. But at length, as I feared my great and unmeasured delay would make you somewhat suspect me of neglect, I resolved to put everything aside, and take the pleasure, which is over and above my other occupations, to pay you by this letter my humble respects, and to tell you that our father went nine days ago to Lisbon, and that we are here in Madrid with our mother, who, as you must have heard, was obliged by our father's illness to remain at Saragossa and give up attendance on the King, who is now in Lisbon, and he has sent his brother with the King.

So kissing your hands I conclude.

Madrid, May 28, 1582.

Your nephew and servant,

Luigi Gonzaga.[30]

In the midst of this family drama, Aloysius remained single-minded in his resolve to seek and serve God alone.

Aloysius was greatly influenced by a compendium of meditations by Louis of Granada, whose writings had had such a profound influence on him years earlier. This book encouraged him to work ever harder for discipline in prayer and to strive to make his one-hour daily meditation without any mental distraction.

The most important event of this time in the young prince's life was his decision to enter the Society of Jesus. Aloysius, who was now fifteen years old, entered into a period of discernment with that same intensity that characterized so much of his life. As Father Meschler says, "It is no wonder that the great responsibility of this choice, a matter of such momentous consequences for time and eternity, occupied his thoughts [this] early.... He was led on step by step to the clear recognition of God's Will, and guided by His gentle, Fatherly Hand."[31]

In looking back over the past several years of Aloysius' life, we recognize a marked transition from one spiritual stage to another. In Florence, he surpassed many ordinary Christians by his vow of chastity, an

[30] Aloysius Gonzaga to Horace Gonzaga, May 28, 1582 (Letter IX), in Cepari, *Life of Saint Aloysius*, 407. Some historians assert that this letter was, in fact, written by Rudolfo in the name of Aloysius.

[31] Meschler, *St. Aloysius*, 77.

act which clearly reveals his desire for the freedom to serve God with all his heart. In Mantua, he came to understand that he was being led to renounce the marquisate and dedicate himself to the service of God and the Church. Recognizing the dangers and challenges faced by the secular clergy, he came to appreciate the value of the religious life. And his time in Castiglione was marked by a resolve to follow God by dedicating himself to life as a vowed religious. Having decided to enter religious life, he dedicated much time and energy to discerning which community God was calling him to enter.[32]

Aloysius considered this question from a number of angles, but in all things his aim was to glorify God.[33] He was initially attracted to the austerity of the Capuchin Franciscans.[34] Founded by an Italian Franciscan, Matteo da Bascio (d. 1552), the Capuchins sought to live the primitive simplicity of the early Franciscans and to observe as closely as possible the teachings of Saint Francis of Assisi. The Capuchins were officially recognized by the Church in 1528, and they dedicated themselves to works of pastoral charity in ministry to lepers, service in hospitals, and evangelization. Initially limited to Italy, they were granted permission to establish houses outside of that country in 1572. They are remembered as being second only to the Jesuits in the influence they had on the life of the Church during the period of the Counter-Reformation.[35]

Although he was strongly attracted to the Capuchin way of life, Aloysius soon recognized that it would be nearly impossible for him to live the harsh life of the Capuchins. Knowing how delicate his health often was, he feared that he would not be able to endure the demands of such a life. Father Cepari also notes that, although Aloysius recognized that he had already dedicated himself to a life of penance and self-denial, it was actually his mother who convinced him to abandon this plan. Cepari writes, "He had broached it to her, and she assured him that he would not live much longer if he either continued his austerities in the world, or entered an order with a very severe and penitential rule."[36]

---

[32] Ibid.

[33] Cepari, *Life of Saint Aloysius*, 50.

[34] Ibid.

[35] Owen Chadwick, *The Reformation* (New York: Penguin, 1990), 254.

[36] Cepari, *Life of Saint Aloysius*, 51.

Aloysius next, rather zealously, wondered whether it was God's Will for him to join a religious order that had fallen into a poor observance of its rule. It seemed to him that he could not only be of service to any monastery or community he might enter, but he might also reform the community. However, he recognized that he himself lacked the necessary virtues to undertake such a task and he might, in time, lose himself.[37] Following this realization, Aloysius next considered the contemplative life. He recalled the positive influence the Benedictines had been for him in Castiglione. The splendor of monastic liturgies and commitment to contemplation was very attractive to him.[38] On the other hand, he also understood that he possessed certain gifts and talents that would allow him to serve God's people more broadly very well.

Aloysius remembered that in his *Summa theologica*, Saint Thomas Aquinas had written that "the first rank among the religious orders is held by those which combine with the contemplative also the active life, and utilize for the spiritual welfare of their neighbor what they have gained by contemplation."[39] Although this passage from Aquinas reveals a certain preference for the Angelic Doctor's own Dominican Order, with its emphasis on a balance of contemplation and service, Aloysius heard in these words a call to imitate, as perfectly as possible, the life of Christ. He knew that he must begin to leave behind the pleasure that he drew from solitude and meditation and to seek out a religious order that combined aspects of the contemplative and apostolic lives, seeking the good of others.[40]

Aloysius ultimately decided upon the Society of Jesus. At this time, the Society was still young; having been founded by Saint Ignatius in 1534, it was still in the vigor of its early years. The Jesuits were especially devoted to the education of the young, and Aloysius believed that he had the gifts needed to be a good teacher.[41] Of special importance for him was the fact that Jesuits were forbidden by their Rule to accept any ecclesiastical honors. This not only ensured that Jesuits

---

[37] Ibid.

[38] Ibid., 51–52.

[39] Meschler, *St. Aloysius*, 79. Here, Father Meschler is paraphrasing *Summa theologica* II, 2, 188, 6.

[40] Cepari, *Life of Saint Aloysius*, 52.

[41] Martindale, *Vocation of Saint Aloysius*, 95.

were to keep their individual vows of poverty, but that they would always remain poor. Aloysius was also drawn to the Society's missionary activities in Asia and the New World. It was, in fact, his hope that he would someday be able to join these missions.[42] Finally, having come to believe that this was God's Will for him, he prayed for certitude.

Aloysius dedicated himself to prayer and the reception of the sacraments. Entrusting his intention to the Blessed Virgin, he prepared with great devotion to honor Mary on the Feast of her Assumption, and he planned to receive Holy Communion in the Lady chapel of the Jesuit church in Madrid. He made his act of thanksgiving kneeling before the miraculous image of Our Lady of Good Counsel that was enshrined in this chapel.[43] As he was praying, he heard in his heart a voice, giving him the instruction he desired: he was to join the Society of Jesus.

Aloysius returned to the palace filled with joy. That same day, he went to see Father Paterno to tell him of what had happened and to ask his spiritual director to do what he could to assist him in his endeavor. After listening to what the young man had to say, the priest judged that Aloysius' call was indeed from God. Despite his belief that the call was genuine, he told Aloysius that he would need his father's consent, because without it, the Society would never accept him. The first thing he must do was inform the marquis of his resolve to enter the Jesuits and receive his permission to carry it out. For once, Aloysius flinched.[44]

Returning home, the prince went straight to his mother. Donna Marta rejoiced to learn of Aloysius' decision, and she agreed to be the one to tell Don Ferrante of his intention. True to form, the marquis erupted in anger. Although Donna Marta did everything she could to soothe Ferrante's wrath, nothing could assuage him. The marquis, suspicious of his wife's intentions, went so far as to accuse her of

[42] Cepari, *Life of Saint Aloysius*, 53.

[43] This ancient image came to Spain from Italy and was originally housed in the church of the Imperial College in Madrid. It is because of the singular experience that Aloysius had while praying before this image that it has come to be known as Our Lady of Good Counsel. Sadly, the statue before which Aloysius received his inspiration was destroyed in the 1930s during the religious persecutions of the Spanish Civil War.

[44] Martindale, *Vocation of Saint Aloysius*, 96.

favoring Rudolfo, hoping to secure the marquisate for him instead of Aloysius.[45]

After this initial outburst had subsided, Aloysius went to see his father. With all his characteristic humility and deference, he laid open the desires of his heart to Don Ferrante. The marquis, however, would hear none of it and sent Aloysius away, threatening to have him stripped and beaten.[46] Aloysius, for his part, replied simply that he hoped that God would allow him to suffer something for love of him, and left the room.[47]

Don Ferrante remained angry and anxious for several days. He sent for Father Paterno and blamed the priest for the family's disturbance. The outraged marquis accused the Jesuit of wishing to kidnap his son for the Society. Father Paterno quickly replied that it had only been a few days before that Aloysius had come to tell him of his resolution and that Aloysius would himself witness to this. He added that, because of the life the young man had led up to this point, he was not at all surprised that Aloysius had made a decision to enter religious life.[48]

Paterno's reply seems to have surprised Don Ferrante. Almost immediately he softened. He asked his son why he did not choose some other order in which he would be free to accept high dignities within the Church. Aloysius replied that it was precisely because Jesuits were forbidden to accept ecclesiastical honors that he had chosen that community. If he had any desire for honors and dignities, he could very easily stay in his current state, since God had seen fit to give him the rights of the firstborn son.[49] The marquis could find no response to his son's words, and so the storm passed for a time without having led to any definite result.

As Ferrante began to reflect on these events, he came to believe that Aloysius was simply using this threat as a ploy to induce him to give up gambling. The marquis had recently lost a large amount of money, and he had lost six thousand more gold pieces the very evening his son told him of his intentions.[50] The day after Aloysius

[45] Cepari, *Life of Saint Aloysius*, 54; Martindale, *Vocation of Saint Aloysius*, 96.
[46] Cepari, *Life of Saint Aloysius*, 55.
[47] Ibid.
[48] Meschler, *St. Aloysius*, 82.
[49] Ibid.
[50] Cepari, *Life of Saint Aloysius*, 56–57.

made his resolution, his father forced him to write to a relative, Fabio
Gonzaga, about Don Ferrante's creditors.

> To My Most Excellent and Honored Lord,
> My Lord Father being gravely ill with gout in the hands, to such an
> extent that it hinders him from writing, at his order and by his charge
> I write myself to recommend to you the affair you know of with
> the gentlemen responsible for the "Mount" [i.e., the official money-
> lenders] of Mantua who continually molest my Lord Father and desire
> at all costs to be paid, threatening him even with the confiscation of
> his goods which would be a grave loss and ruin of our house and a
> scandal: seeing that the heavy expenses that have hold on him here at
> Court do not make it convenient for him to be able to satisfy at once
> and *quamprimum* his creditors: I beg that Your Lordship would inter-
> vene, kissing whose hands I finish.
> Madrid, August 16, 1583.
> Your Lordship's most humble and devoted servant,
> Aluigi Gonzaga[51]

The boy was greatly troubled by his father's gambling habits and
would often go to his room in tears when his father was at the card
table, but he used to say to his servants that it was not the monetary
losses that upset him; rather, it was the offenses his father was com-
mitting against God.[52] The court also knew how severe Don Ferrante's addiction was and how much money he lost in gambling; the
courtiers shared the marquis' view that Aloysius was simply making a
threat to make his father change his ways.[53]

Aloysius remained steadfast in his request to be allowed to renounce
his inheritance and enter the Society of Jesus. His direct and earnest
requests eventually convinced his father that he was sincere. As Ferrante looked back on his son's life, he remembered the constant piety
and devotion, and he too recognized that this call to religious life
came to him from God.[54] However, that Aloysius had a call to religious life did not necessarily mean that he was called to the Jesuits.

---

[51] Martindale, *Vocation of Saint Aloysius*, 86, which is the first printed appearance of this
letter, which is preserved at Saint Aloysius Church at Oxford.

[52] Cepari, *Life of Saint Aloysius*, 57; Meschler, *St. Aloysius*, 83.

[53] Monro, *Unlikely Saints*, 34; Cepari, *Life of Saint Aloysius*, 57. See also Martindale, *Vocation
of Saint Aloysius*, 97.

[54] Cepari, *Life of Saint Aloysius*, 58.

Ferrante appealed to a relative, Francesco (Hannibal) Gonzaga. The son of Charles Gonzaga, Ferrante's cousin, Francis had entered the Franciscan Order in 1562 after holding a high position in the Spanish court. When he met with Aloysius in 1583, he was serving as the superior general of the Franciscan Order. At Don Ferrante's request, he met with Aloysius, and for more than two hours he carefully examined the youth, who satisfied all his doubts. He told the marquis that there could be no doubting the divine origins of his son's vocation.[55]

It seems that King Philip also questioned Aloysius about his intention to enter the Society; we have no record of his views, but Father Martindale speculates: "Perhaps the tired and disheartened king, destined so soon to grow sadder still, more morose, more self-isolated, saw in the young man something that he took to resemble his own disgust with things, and half-envied him the possibility of abdicating."[56]

Prince Diego, for whom Aloysius and Rudolfo served as pages, died suddenly of smallpox on November 21 of that year. Perceiving that he had no further duties at court, Aloysius resolved that the time had come for him to enter the Society. Walking one day with Rudolfo and some attendants, he made his way to the Jesuit college in Madrid. Stopping, he informed his companions that he would remain there, and that they were to go home and tell his father the news. The servants were shocked and afraid to return to Don Ferrante. The Jesuits were no less surprised.[57] Upon hearing the news, the marquis flew into a rage and, because he was confined to bed by gout, ordered his physician, Dr. Sallust Petrocini, to go to the college and retrieve his son. Upon hearing his father's demand, the prince replied by saying that what had to be done tomorrow might as well take place today. He asked his father to allow him to stay where he was.[58] The marquis was unwilling to accept this reply and ordered

---

[55] Ibid. Venerable Francesco Gonzaga, who in 1593 became Bishop of Mantua, died in Mantua on March 11, 1620. See http://www.catholic-hierarchy.org/bishop/bgonzfra.html. The cause for his beatification was introduced in 1627; although his writings were declared to be free from any doctrinal errors in 1924, its seems that his cause has become (practically speaking) inactive.

[56] Martindale, *Vocation of Saint Aloysius*, 97. Neither Cepari nor Meschler make any mention of a meeting between Aloysius and Philip II.

[57] Ibid., 98.

[58] Meschler, *St. Aloysius*, 84; Cepari, *Life of Saint Aloysius*, 58.

the physician to return to the college and tell the prince that he must absolutely come back. Aloysius obeyed and returned home.

Don Ferrante again summoned Francis Gonzaga and asked him to be his ally in dissuading Aloysius. He begged him to persuade his son to remain in the world and lead a pious and holy life as a secular ruler. Father Francis objected to being part of the game being played, observing that his duty as a Christian and as a religious forbade him to oppose such an obvious vocation.[59] The marquis then asked the Franciscan at least to persuade Aloysius not to enter religious life until the family had returned to Italy. However, Father Francis refused to do even this. It seems that years before, the same suggestion had been made to him when, in the same court, he had decided to join the Franciscans.[60] The only thing he would agree to do for the marquis was neutrally to relay to Aloysius Don Ferrante's wishes without attempting to influence him. Aloysius was willing to concede to his father's request to wait until the family returned to Castiglione. He also told Francis that he understood the opposition he would have to overcome in Italy, but he believed that, with God's grace, he would not falter in his resolution.

In the end, Aloysius had gained something in his struggle. The marquis was now convinced of the sincerity of his son's desire and that his call came from God. Aloysius trusted that his father would give his permission as soon as they reached Italy.

[59] Meschler, *St. Aloysius*, 84.
[60] Martindale, *Vocation of Saint Aloysius*, 99.

Chapter 7

Saint Ignatius and His Society

The end of the fifteenth century was a time like no other in history. The world grew with the discovery of the limitless prospects of America. Medieval tradition was beginning to fade. As historian Jean Lacouture notes, "with almost everything either in exuberant flux or coming hesitantly into bloom", this was a threshold between two ages.[1]

Iñigo López de Oñaz y Loyola was born sometime around the year 1491, about two miles from the town of Azpeitia in the Basque province of Guipúzcoa.[2] At the time of his birth, the great humanist Erasmus was twenty-five, Machiavelli was twenty-two, Copernicus was eighteen, Michelangelo sixteen, Thomas More was eleven, and Martin Luther had just turned seven.[3] The Protestant Reformation was still years off, and the earth was still the center of the universe.

Born into a noble family still embracing the vestiges of medieval feudalism, Iñigo entered the household of Juan Velázquez de Cuéllar, the treasurer of the king of Castile, as a page. He received the chivalric and academically sparse education for men of his rank, and he accompanied his patron on his travels with the court, no doubt doing all he could to win the notice of the king and his courtiers.[4] In his autobiography (which was written toward the end of his life), the man who would come to be known as Ignatius describes himself as "a

[1] Jean Lacouture, *Jesuits: A Multibiography*, trans. Jeremy Leggatt (Washington, D.C.: Counterpoint, 1995), 4.

[2] He assumed the name "Ignatius" during his years as a student in Paris, probably out of devotion to Saint Ignatius of Antioch.

[3] Lacouture, *Jesuits*, 4.

[4] Paul Burns and Peter Doyle, eds., *Butler's Lives of the Saints: New Full Edition; July* (Collegeville, Minn.: Liturgical Press, 2000), 248; and John W. O'Malley, S.J., *The First Jesuits* (Cambridge, Mass.: Harvard University Press, 1993), 23.

man given over to vanities of the world; with a great and vain desire
to win fame he delighted especially in the exercise of arms".[5] Vain,
handsome, and hot-blooded, Iñigo enjoyed tales of chivalry and
knightly conquest.[6] A ladies' man, the young Ignatius was described
by one of his later followers as "satis liber in mulierum amore" (freely
sated in the love of women). It was even rumored that he fathered
an illegitimate child.[7] In 1515, Iñigo was arrested with his brother
Pedro López (himself a priest), for assaulting a priest during a visit to
Loyola. The court records reveal that the attack was a premeditated
ambush, with Iñigo in armor, carrying a sword, dagger, and pistol.[8]
It seems that sometime before this, he had received clerical tonsure,
and, because of this, he asked to be tried by an ecclesiastical court.
The judge dismissed the appeal based on his clerical state (which
seems to have meant little to nothing to Iñigo) and ordered that the
brothers be tried by a secular court. There is, however, no existing
record of how this incident ended.

Sometime after 1517, Iñigo joined the forces of the Duke of
Nájera, who, as viceroy, was responsible for the defense of Navarre.
In the spring of 1521, France invaded the region and, in the course of
the invasion, occupied the city of Pamplona. In spite of the French
occupation of the town, the Spanish garrison in the city's citadel
stubbornly refused to surrender. Ignatius was among the defenders,
and on May 20, 1521, he was severely wounded during the French
bombardment of the citadel. It is at this point that he begins his autobiography, writing,

> Until the age of twenty-six he was a man given over to the vanities of
> the world; with a great and vain desire to win fame he delighted espe-
> cially in the exercise of arms. Once when he was in a fortress that the

[5] Ignatius of Loyola, *The Autobiography of Saint Ignatius Loyola with Related Documents*, trans.
Joseph F. O'Callaghan, ed. John C. Olin (New York: Fordham University Press, 1992), 21.
Ignatius of Loyola dictated his autobiography to secretaries in 1553 and 1555. This work, in
which Ignatius refers to himself in the third person, covers the years 1521 (after the siege of
Pamplona) to his arrival in Rome in 1538. The primary focus of the work is to offer his follow-
ers an account of his "years of pilgrimage", and it offers a unique perspective on his conversion.

[6] Ibid., 33; Burns and Doyle, *Butler's; July*, 248.

[7] O'Malley, *First Jesuits*, 23; James Martin, *My Life with the Saints* (Chicago: Loyola Press,
2006), 75.

[8] Burns and Doyle, *Butler's; July*, 248.

French were attacking, although all the others clearly saw that they could not defend themselves and were of the opinion that they should surrender provided their lives were spared, he gave so many reasons to the commander that he persuaded him at last to defend it.... When the day arrived on which the bombardment was expected, he confessed to one of his companions in arms. After the bombardment had lasted a good while, a shot hit him in the leg, breaking it completely; since the ball passed through both legs, the other one was also badly damaged.[9]

Following the battle, the French returned Iñigo to his family's castle, where he had a long and painful convalescence. The broken leg was set, but had to be broken again and reset. Iñigo's condition grew worse, and it seemed he was near death.[10] "He was advised to confess; he received the sacraments on the vigil of Sts. Peter and Paul.... As the sick man had devotion to St. Peter, Our Lord willed that he should begin to improve that very midnight. His improvement proceeded so quickly that some days later it was decided that he was out of danger of death."[11]

During his long period of recuperation, he asked for some books to read. However, rather than receiving the tales of chivalry that had captured his imagination so often before, he was given a copy of the *Life of Christ* by the Carthusian monk Ludolph of Saxony (d. 1377) and a copy of the well-known collection of saints' lives by Jacopo de Voragine (d. 1298), *The Golden Legend*.

The *Life of Christ*, which Iñigo read in a Castilian translation, is a series of meditations on the Lord's life in which Ludolph made liberal use of both the Old and the New Testaments with frequent quotations from Church Fathers and other theologians. The goal of the work, which was also peppered with Ludolph's own commentaries and reflections, was intended to help the reader learn to meditate more "effectively".[12] Jesuit scholar Joseph Tylenda notes: "It was Ludolph who first taught him how to meditate, and it was

---

[9] Ignatius, *Autobiography*, 21.

[10] Ibid., 22.

[11] Ibid.

[12] Joseph Tylenda, "The Books That Led Ignatius to God", in *Sharing the Spiritual Exercises of St. Ignatius*, ed. David L. Fleming (Saint Louis: Review for Religious, 2007), 14.

Ludolph who told him of the need to have a composition of place in which to situate himself so that he could be a witness to the mystery, be near enough to see the characters, hear their words, and note their reactions."[13] These insights and practices found their way into the *Spiritual Exercises*.

The other book that the future Ignatius read during his convalescence was the *Legenda aurea*. As Iñigo learned the stories of the Christ and his mother, he also began to appreciate the lessons contained in the lives of the saints. The 182 chapters of this amazingly popular book (written around the year 1265) were arranged according to the Church's liturgical calendar, and Iñigo himself relates the influence this seminal work of hagiography had on his own life. The insights Iñigo drew from this book remained with him all his life.

Despite their influence, Iñigo was initially put off by these spiritual books, with their tales of self-denial and bodily penance.[14] Slowly, however, a change began to take place in the mind and heart of Iñigo:

> Putting his reading aside, he sometimes stopped to think about the things he had read and at other times about the things of the world that he used to think of before.... While reading the life of Our Lord and of the saints, he stopped to think, reasoning within himself, "What if I should do what Saint Francis did, what Saint Dominic did?" So he pondered many things that he found to be good, always proposing to himself what was difficult and serious, and as he proposed them, they seemed to him easy to accomplish.[15]

In the record Ignatius provides of his conversion, there are three saints who stand out. Two of these, as we have seen, are Saint Francis of Assisi and Saint Dominic, both of whom are founders of great religious orders, whose members would have been well known to him. The other is the Desert Father Saint Onuphrius.[16] The influence of

[13] Ibid.

[14] Burns and Doyle, *Butler's; July*, 249.

[15] Ignatius, *Autobiography*, 23.

[16] Ibid., 33. See also Burns and Doyle, *Butler's; July*, 249. According to the legend, Onuphrius (Humphrey) was a hermit in the Egyptian desert whose story was retold by Paphnutius, an abbot of Lower Egypt. He relates that he came upon Onuphrius, whose hair and beard reached to the ground and were so matted and thick that they seemed to be fur, and he wore only a loincloth of leaves. For a more complete presentation on the life of Saint Onuphrius, see Paul Burns and Kathleen Jones, eds., *Butler's Lives of the Saints: New Full Edition; June* (Collegeville, Minn.: Liturgical Press, 1997), 94–96. See also, Tylenda, "Books", 65.

these three particular saints is noteworthy because each, in his own way, embodied a spirit of complete self-surrender that Iñigo was beginning to embrace as he sought to harness his energies and passionate nature. Although his conversion was not sudden, these new religious sentiments did take root. He writes, "From this reading he obtained not a little insight, and he began to think more earnestly about his past life and about the great need he had to do penance for it. At this point the great desire to imitate the saints came to him, though he gave no thought to the circumstances, but only promised with God's grace to do as they had done."[17]

Inspired by these new ideals and empowered by a profound experience of the Virgin and Child, Iñigo made a resolution to travel to Jersusalem.[18] He had become a man on fire with God: "When he thought of going to Jerusalem, barefoot and eating nothing but herbs and undergoing all the other rigors that he saw the saints had endured, not only was he consoled when he had these thoughts, but even after putting them aside, he remained content and happy."[19] He records that he imagined what his life might be like after he returned from his pilgrimage, and he resolved to enter the charterhouse in Seville where he could live as a penitent. This resolution was short-lived. While he longed to leave for Jerusalem, Iñigo was still too weak and his leg had not yet sufficiently healed. To pass the time, he spent his days copying out quotations from his reading. He himself tells us that he covered three hundred pages, with Jesus' words copied in red and Mary's in blue. At night, he drew great consolation from contemplating the stars and the sky.[20]

In the spring of 1522, Iñigo traveled from Loyola to the great shrine of our Lady at the Benedictine Abbey of Montserrat before continuing on to Manresa. This was a decisive time for Iñigo, who had exchanged his knightly regalia for the dress of a poor pilgrim. He spent several months in Manresa living as a hermit, begging in the streets, and studying how to advance in the spiritual life he had chosen.[21] The caballero had become a soldier of Christ.[22] Manresa

---

[17] Ignatius, *Autobiography*, 24.
[18] Ibid.
[19] Ibid.
[20] Ibid., 25; Lacouture, *Jesuits*, 14.
[21] Ignatius, *Autobiography*, 37–40.
[22] Burns and Doyle, *Butler's; July*, 250.

has since been described as "a psychological upheaval for him, a journey through the flames, the womb of 'Ignatianism.' He himself called Manresa his 'Early Church'."[23] Jesuit historian John O'Malley describes Iñigo's time in Manresa in this way:

> Iñigo meditated on the life of Christ and discovered *The Imitation of Christ*, a book to which he remained devoted all his life. At the same time he gave himself up to a regimen of prayer, fasting, self-flagellation, and other austerities that were extreme even for the sixteenth century. He surrendered all care for his appearance and, in defiance of convention, let his hair and fingernails grow. Shortly after his arrival at Manresa, moreover, he began to experience an excruciating aridity of soul, obsessive doubts about the integrity of his sacramental confessions, and even temptations of suicide.[24]

Iñigo faced these trials with a spirit of resignation and abandonment, and, slowly, he was able to find the guidance he sought. By the time Iñigo left Manresa, he had matured spiritually and emotionally. Out of his experience of suffering emerged the essential elements of what would become his *Spiritual Exercises*. The book was a simplified presentation of his own experiences of conversion presented in a way that would be helpful to others in attaining perfection in the spiritual life. Although he would continue to revise the book for the next twenty years of his life, he had the majority of the text in hand when he left Manresa to complete his pilgrimage to Jerusalem.[25]

The *Exercises* contain two central elements. The first of these is a systematized examination of conscience that focuses on overcoming sin. The second element is a planned approach to meditation as a prayer intended to fix the imagination on a particular biblical event or point of doctrine. Iñigo presents two options or "standards" to those making the *Exercises*: Christ or the world. Personal conversion and individual sanctification had become, and would remain, the focus of Iñigo's mission.[26]

---

[23] Lacouture, *Jesuits*, 17. Here we can assume that Ignatius was referring to a spirit of simplicity and evangelical authenticity. See O'Malley, *First Jesuits*, 25.

[24] O'Malley, *First Jesuits*, 25.

[25] Ibid.

[26] Burns and Doyle, *Butler's; July*, 251.

In September 1523, after experiencing many frustrating delays, he finally reached the destination of his pilgrimage—Jerusalem. Although he desired to stay in Jerusalem and to be of use to the Franciscan custodians of the shrines there, he was ultimately advised to return to Spain for fear that he would be captured or possibly killed by the Muslim authorities.[27]

After his return to Spain, he came to the realization that if he was to be of benefit to souls, he must receive some formal training in theology.[28] By the autumn of 1524, he found himself in classes in Barcelona, learning Latin with children who were less than half his age. Iñigo drew great benefit from this time of study, and he fulfilled his desire to help souls by sharing his spiritual insights with others and by taking them through the early form of the *Exercises*.

After two years in Barcelona, he began attending lectures at the University of Alcalá. Although he lacked guidance, he dedicated himself to his studies and began to teach catechism to people in the streets.[29] He was joined by other men who began to dress in the same pilgrim's garb worn by Iñigo, and rumors soon spread that these "sack wearers" were *Alumbrados* (Enlightened Ones), followers of a religious sect that taught that its adherents could attain spiritual perfection through internal illumination.[30] Iñigo was questioned by the Inquisition but was released on the condition that his followers did not dress as though they were members of a religious order.[31] He would be questioned by the Inquisition again the following year. Ordered to dress as other students and told not to hold any more meetings, he flatly refused to accept the Inquisition's conditions for his ministry and fled to Salamanca. After a short time, he was again arrested and imprisoned for three weeks while his *Exercises* were examined. Following his release, he decided to leave Spain. In 1528, Iñigo traveled to France, where he enrolled at the University of Paris.

It would be impossible to overestimate the value of his time in Paris. Iñigo entered into an intellectual and theological world

---

[27] Ignatius, *Autobiography*, 49–51.
[28] Ibid., 54.
[29] Ignatius, *Autobiography*, 61; O'Malley, *First Jesuits*, 27.
[30] O'Malley, *First Jesuits*, 27.
[31] Burns and Doyle, *Butler's; July*, 252.

markedly different from anything he had encountered in Spain, and the educational system he experienced there significantly influenced his vision for the educational apostolate of the Society of Jesus.

In Paris, Ignatius (as he was now calling himself) was joined by followers who formed the core of a new society: (Saint) Francis Xavier, Alfonso Salmarón, Diego Laínez, Simon Rodriguez, Nicolas Bobadilla, and (Saint) Peter Favre.[32] Following Peter Favre's ordination in 1534, this group of friends decided to make a vow to travel to Jerusalem, where they would work for the conversion of the Muslims. Should that plan fail, they would offer themselves to the pope's service.[33] On the morning of August 15 of that same year, the companions gathered in the crypt of the church of the historic Benedictine Abbey of Saint-Denis, where Peter Favre celebrated Mass. At Communion, Father Peter turned to the kneeling group and holding the Host before them, each, in his turn, in a clear voice, pronounced his religious vows. Peter himself then turned to the altar, pronounced his vows, and received the Blessed Sacrament. It was in this simple ceremony, without pomp or ritual, that the first members of the Society of Jesus were bound together as religious.[34] The companions were eager to enter into their ministry, but Ignatius recognized the need for more organization if this work was to be effective, and he set about revising the *Exercises*. So essential were the *Exercises* to the work of the Society that, years later, Francis Xavier would remark that the *Exercises* "converted more souls than it contains letters".[35]

Ignatius was forced to return to Spain in 1535 because of ill health, but before his departure, he and his companions agreed that they would meet in Rome in two years' time and set out for Jerusalem. During this time, he traveled to Venice, where he continued his theological studies and met with others interested in reform. He continued to make use of the *Exercises*. In 1537, the original group (plus Claude Le Jay, Paschase Broët, and Jean Codure) reassembled

---

[32] Francis Corley and Robert Willmes, *Wings of Eagles* (Milwaukee, Wis.: Bruce Publishing, 1941), 17. For an account of Ignatius' meeting with Francis Xavier and Peter Favre, see William V. Bangert, *To the Other Towns: A Life of Blessed Peter Favre, First Companion of St. Ignatius* (San Francisco: Ignatius Press, 2002), 40–41.

[33] Bangert, *To the Other Towns*, 51.

[34] Ibid., 51–52.

[35] Corley and Willmes, *Wings of Eagles*, 16.

in Venice, and together they worked at a hospice for the incurable, nursing those suffering from typhus and syphilis. Later that year, the group traveled to Rome, where they hoped to obtain the blessing of Pope Paul III. Receiving the hoped-for support, they returned to Venice, where six of them, including Ignatius, were ordained priests.

The friends now called themselves the "Company of Jesus". Shortly after the ordinations, the group disbanded, with Ignatius, Favre, and Laínez returning to Rome to offer their services to the pope. They dedicated themselves to teaching catechism to children, hearing confessions, and preaching. They were joined by the rest of the group in the winter of 1538, and together the Company worked to alleviate the suffering brought on by a famine that ravaged the city in 1539. Pope Paul III proved to be a faithful supporter of the work of the Company, and with his encouragement, Ignatius wrote out a formalized plan of life for the group. This early rule specifies that the work of the community was to teach catechism, preach, hear confessions, lecture, and care for the sick and prisoners.[36] It is important to note that in this early document many references to traditional practices common to religious communities are missing.

For Ignatius, the key to the Company's efficacy was flexibility in lifestyle and ministry. Ignatius would struggle throughout his time as the general of the Society against movements to make the Jesuits into a conventional, more contemplative order.[37] Unlike traditional religious orders, the Jesuits did not share a common liturgical life. Rather than gathering for the Hours of the Divine Office, their clerics were expected to pray privately, with their priority being their ministries on the streets, in hospitals, prisons, and in foreign lands.[38] Although it took more than a year for the pope to decide on the question of canonical recognition, the new foundation (now known as the Society of Jesus) was approved by Paul III on September 27, 1540, in his bull *Regimini Militantis Ecclesiae*.[39] Ignatius was elected the first general of the Society in 1541, and on April 22 of that year,

---

[36] Burns and Doyle, *Butler's; July*, 254.

[37] Owen Chadwick, *The Reformation* (New York: Penguin, 1990), 260.

[38] R. Po-chia Hsia, *The World of Catholic Renewal, 1540–1770* (New York: Cambridge, 1998), 31.

[39] Chadwick, *Reformation*, 259.

the six members of the Society still present in Rome made vows together. Ignatius Loyola spent the rest of his life in Rome, leading and guiding the Society and serving the poor, prostitutes, Jews, the sick, and orphans.[40]

The Society's commitment to educate and to evangelize took the early Jesuits to Asia and the Americas, where they were among the first to make contact with and document non-Western cultures.[41] It was in 1541, only one year after the Society's approval, that Francis Xavier, bound for the Indies, left Lisbon with three Jesuit companions. Before Ignatius' death in 1556, members of his Society would be ministering in England, Ireland, India, Japan, Brazil, Abyssinia, and China.[42] During its first century, the Society of Jesus would also play a decisive role in the Counter-Reformation in almost every part of Europe.

The mission of the early Jesuits was characterized by a triad of ministries of Word, sacrament, and works of mercy.[43] These early Jesuits recognized their ministry of the Word to include both preaching and education, which was to become a hallmark of the Jesuit mission and identity in the middle of the sixteenth century.[44] As the Society grew, their work became more diverse, but a commitment to serve among heathens and heretics, as preachers and educators, remained the primary focus of the missionaries.[45] In fact, one of the Society's principal means of bringing new vigor into the Roman Catholic Church was through their mission of education. In 1579, the Jesuits administered 144 colleges; by 1749, this number would grow to include 669 colleges and 24 universities. Their chosen curriculum included rhetoric and oratory, in addition to philosophy and theology.[46] Throughout

[40] Burns and Doyle, *Butler's; July*, 255. Saint Ignatius died in Rome on July 31, 1556. His remains were interred in the Church of Santa Maria della Strada, which had been entrusted to the Jesuits by Pope Paul III. This church was later torn down and replaced by the Gesù. Ignatius was canonized in 1622, along with Francis Xavier, Teresa of Avila, Philip Neri, and the humble farmer Isidore.

[41] Christopher Chapple, ed., introduction to *The Jesuit Tradition in Education and Missions: A 450-Year Perspective* (Scranton, Penn.: University of Scranton Press, 1993), 7.

[42] James Brodrick, *The Origin of the Jesuits* (Chicago: Loyola Press, 1997), 103.

[43] O'Malley, *First Jesuits*, 85.

[44] Corley and Willmes, *Wings of Eagles*, 18.

[45] Chadwick, *Reformation*, 261.

[46] Chapple, *Jesuit Tradition*, 7.

this period, individual Jesuits would make significant contributions to a wide range of subjects, including moral and ascetical theology, historical studies, and the sciences of mathematics, astronomy, and geography. In addition to their work in these fields, the Jesuits also promoted the arts, architecture, drama, and dance.[47]

The Jesuit schools of the sixteenth century were fairly typical of their times. The curriculum was the so-called Latin curriculum, based on the same texts and exercises used by the humanist educators of the Latin schools. The first Jesuit colleges and universities were, in fact, modeled on the University of Paris, where Ignatius and his first companions were students.[48] However, the members of the Society added more structure to this curriculum by introducing a more systematic chronological progression of classes based on ability and age.[49]

Recall that, during the period of his conversion, Ignatius dedicated himself to learning so that he might more effectively help souls—he did not pursue learning for its own sake; as Jesuit historian Francesco Cesareo notes, with the Jesuit model, "Education was to serve a greater end as it assisted humanity in its quest for God."[50] In understanding his own vocation more clearly, Ignatius recognized that education would be an important work of his new Society. While he never intended to found a teaching order, he did recognize the value of providing a sound education that would lead the student upward academically and in the life of virtue.[51] This point was later brought home by Pope Paul III in his bull approving the Society of Jesus. Concerning the work of the Society, he declares:

> Whoever shall desire to bear the arms of God under the banner of the Cross, and to serve the one God and the Roman Pontiff, His Vicar upon earth, in our Society, which we wish to be called by the name of Jesus, having made a solemn vow of perpetual chastity, must

---

[47] Ibid.

[48] Paul G. Crowley, "Theology in the Jesuit University: Reassessing the Ignatius Vision", in ibid., 156.

[49] Francesco Cesareo, "Quest for Identity: The Ideals of Jesuit Education in the Sixteenth Century", in Chapple, *Jesuit Tradition*, 17.

[50] O'Malley, *First Jesuits*, 208; Cesareo, "Quest for Identity", 18.

[51] Chadwick, *Reformation*, 262.

purpose to become a member of a society principally instituted to
work for the advancement of souls in Christian life and doctrine, and
for the propagation of the faith by public preaching and the ministry
of God's Word, by spiritual exercises and works of charity, more
particularly by grounding in Christianity boys and unlettered persons,
and by hearing the confessions of the faithful, aiming in all things for
their spiritual consolation.[52]

The *Autobiography of Saint Ignatius* makes clear the relationship
between education and the progress of the soul. This idea became the
nucleus around which Ignatius developed his vision for education.[53]

The Jesuit college at Goa, India, established by Saint Francis Xavier
in 1543, became the model for future Jesuit colleges. Beginning in
1546, the Jesuit college at Gandía, Spain, began to accept extern students, giving rise to mixed colleges, designed to serve both Jesuit and
secular students. As early as 1548, the Society began to open colleges
intended for lay students who had no intention of becoming priests.
As the Jesuits established themselves in the largely Protestant lands
of northern Europe, a number of high-ranking Protestants began
attending their colleges. Some of these men would eventually con-
vert to Catholicism.[54]

The involvement of Jesuits in the educational apostolate led them
to develop a particular outlook and understanding of what they
hoped to attain for their students. "Foremost in Ignatius' mind in
accepting education of the laity was his belief that this would promote the salvation and perfection of the students, as they penetrated
their world with Christian doctrine and spirit."[55] To accomplish this
end, he brought together diverse educational methods that he transformed into a uniquely Jesuit system. Whether they were religious
or lay students, Ignatius' aim was clear—he was preparing leaders for
society and the Church.

The *Constitutions of the Society of Jesus* clearly state that the Jesuits undertake the educational apostolate because of their apostolic

[52] Pope Paul III, *Regimini Militantis Ecclesiae* (1540), quoted in Cesareo, "Quest for Identity", 18–19.
[53] Quoted in Cesareo, "Quest for Identity", 19.
[54] Hsia, *Catholic Renewal*, 32.
[55] Cesareo, "Quest for Identity", 19.

motives to help guide men to salvation, emphasizing that the task of education was not literary but the "inculcation of Christian doctrine and good customs".[56]

> To accomplish this, Ignatius added to the humanist educational program the study of philosophy and theology, to serve as the foundation of a "theistic philosophy of life—a philosophy which gives true significance and worthwhile meaning to the life of man both in this world and the next. There is constant encouragement of the student not only to moral and sacramental living but also to the exercise of all the supernatural virtues which lead to the highest union with God."[57]

Ignatius' mission was to form good Christian leaders who could exert a positive influence on the social, political, and cultural environment, and, by means of this, to allow for the progress of the soul on the pilgrimage of salvation. The vision of Pope Paul III was reiterated by Pope Julius III in his bull *Exposcit Debitum* of July 21, 1550.[58]

One of the principal tasks of the Jesuit educator was to illumine the relationship between studies and man's end: knowledge and love of God should come first as these lead to salvation. In Chapter 16 of the Society's *Constitutions*, Ignatius wrote: "The masters should make it their special aim, both in their lectures when occasion is offered and outside of them too, to inspire the students to the love and service of God our Lord, and to a love of the virtues by which they will please Him. They should urge the students to direct all their studies to this end."[59] In light of this aim, the curriculum in Jesuit schools came to emphasize subjects such as human letters, logical, natural and moral philosophy, metaphysics, scholastic theology, and Sacred Scripture.[60] Obviously, Ignatius urged that special emphasis be given to theology.

Students in Jesuit schools were prepared to reenter the world with an education that compared favorably with that of their secular

---

[56] Ibid.
[57] Ibid., quoting Ignatius of Loyola, *The Constitutions of the Society of Jesus*.
[58] Cesareo, "Quest for Identity", 21.
[59] Ignatius of Loyola, *Constitutions*; quoted in ibid., 23.
[60] Cesareo, "Quest for Identity", 23.

counterparts. However, they drew added benefit from the Jesuit system that combined the needs of the spiritual life with more practical and mundane concerns. It was Ignatius' goal to "mold the nature and actions of his students in the image of Christ".[61] His concern was for a practical theology that would allow for the cultivation of piety, assisting people to know and love God more deeply and to save their souls. Within Jesuit institutions, "future prelates, princes, and professors hobnobbed, learning the 'Jesuit way of proceeding'—memorizing their Latin, striving to excel, and undergoing the *Spiritual Exercises*."[62] Their high-ranking alumni and the influence they exerted on the secular clergy and the nobility allowed the Jesuits to provide an unparalleled service and influence across the Continent.

The formation of character was another essential part of the Society's plan for the education of the young. For the princes of Europe, the Jesuits formed loyal and pious servants of the Catholic states, and the service the Society provided for diocesan bishops offered a much-needed leaven for poor dioceses unable to support their own seminaries.[63] Students were exhorted to make progress in those virtues that would enable them to become good Christian leaders. Ignatius' hope that his educational model would have a pronounced influence on society as a whole can be recognized in his vision for the Roman College, which he founded in 1551:

> If he is zealous for the common good and the help of souls and the spread and increase of the Catholic faith, this is a work which is especially destined to such an end. For not only will the youth of Rome be taught and trained in learning and good morals, but in time students can come from all parts of Italy and beyond for the same purpose.... Likewise, a large number of apostolic workers of our own Society will be educated there, with their studies directed solely to the same end of the common good.... Thus this college will be a never failing nursery of ministers of the Apostolic See for the service of the holy Church and the good of souls.[64]

[61] Ibid.
[62] Hsia, *Catholic Renewal*, 33.
[63] Ibid.
[64] Ignatius of Loyola to N.N., Letter 41, n.d., quoted in Cesareo, "Quest for Identity", 27.

Ignatius had the same hopes that his beloved German College could provide for the people of Germany what his Roman College would do for the Italian people.[65]

Among the religious communities founded during the Catholic Counter-Reformation, the Jesuits experienced the most dramatic growth and influence. The Theatines, who were founded by Saint Cajetan (1480–1547) in 1524, and who resembled the Jesuits in some ways, had only thirty members by the middle of the sixteenth century. The Barnabites of Saint Anthony Mary Zaccaria (1502–1539) and the Clerics Regular of Somasca, founded by Saint Jerome Emiliani (1486–1537), two other congregations founded around the same time, also had comparatively small membership. The Society of Jesus, however, could boast more than three thousand members by 1565. The Society recruited new members at a rapid pace, and wherever Jesuit schools flourished, large Jesuit communities soon developed.[66] The well-known *Exercises* of Saint Ignatius proved to be a great asset in attracting new members, as was the recruitment of high-profile members such as Saint Francis Borgia (1510–1572), who would serve as the third general of the Society; Saint Stanislaus Kostka (1550–1568); and Saint Peter Canisius (1521–1597), whose catechism *Summa Doctrinae Christianae* would have such a profound influence on the spiritual life of Aloysius. The Jesuits did not wait passively for young men to come to them. By 1562, it was expected that every local Jesuit community would have a *promotor*, who would be responsible for seeking out likely candidates and offering guidance to those discerning their call.[67]

The Society maintained high standards for admission. Although they sought out candidates who were academically gifted, they also showed special concern for the character and emotional maturity of new recruits.[68] Typically, new members came from the merchant or professional classes, although a few like Borgia, Kostka, and Aloysius came from the ranks of the nobility. The idealized profile of what

[65] Brodrick, *Origin of the Jesuits*, 213. Rome's Pontifical German College (Pontificium Collegium Germanicum et Hungaricum de Urbe) was founded on August 31, 1552, and formally opened by Saint Ignatius on October 28.

[66] O'Malley, *First Jesuits*, 54.

[67] Ibid., 55.

[68] Ibid., 56, 81.

Ignatius hoped every Jesuit would be calls for the man to be "prayer-ful, virtuous, compassionate but firm, magnanimous and courageous, not without learning, unswervingly committed to the Society and its goals, a person of sound judgment".[69]

[69] Ignatius, quoted in ibid., 88.

Chapter 8

The Battle Continues

In an essay written to commemorate the fourth centenary of the death of Saint Aloysius in 1991, Jesuit activist and writer Daniel Berrigan offered this reflection:

> All too easy to make of this youngster, fighting for his soul's ransom against enormous odds, an icon just short of bizarre, carefully and studiously remote, nose in air, rapt gaze, crucifix, lilies delicately in hand, cleaving his way to heaven with scant interest or attention to mere earthlings.
>
> He was tougher than his would-be admirers would have him, both tougher and more tender, enormously more complex, his heaven won by way of many a detour—through hell ...
>
> The heartbreaking effort called for, if he was to break free, to cut the noose so delicately woven, of money and prestige and lust and altitudinous pride of life. The tyranny of bloodline (the world's offertory), the family's ambiguous tie.
>
> And then the fraying of these bonds, by prayer and tears and bloodletting. His own blood. More than fraying, a clean cut of the lifeline.
>
> The scandal, plainly put, offered by one so young, so singularly summoned, so eager to risk everything, so paying up. Cut the lifeline!
>
> It was strangling him.[1]

Aloysius trusted that when his family returned to Castiglione, Don Ferrante would give him permission to enter the Society of Jesus. The young prince could not have foreseen the struggles and temptations that would still have to be endured before he would be free to follow his call to leave all to and for God.

[1] Daniel Berrigan, "Short and Sweet; and Against All Odds: A Life of Some Moment", in *Aloysius*, ed. Clifford Stevens and William Hart McNichols (Huntington, Ind.: Our Sunday Visitor, 1993), 127–28.

In the spring of 1584, the marquis entrusted his family to the care of Admiral Giovanni Andrea Doria, whose fleet was preparing to leave Madrid for Genoa.[2] Only Aloysius' sister, Isabella, was to remain in Spain to serve as a maid of honor to Princess Clara Eugenie. To Aloysius' delight, Father Francis Gonzaga, the general of the Order of Friars Minor Conventual, who was returning to Rome, would accompany the family on their voyage. Aloysius took advantage of the priest's presence during the trip, asking him to resolve certain difficulties he encountered in his reading of Sacred Scripture and talking to him of other spiritual topics to his heart's content. The young prince considered Francis to be a model of virtue and holiness: "Every time he looked at him, he appeared to see a real and living image of religious life and of regular observance."[3]

As the Gonzaga family traveled through Saragossa, they were invited to stay for a time with the marquis Espez y Mendoza. While they were staying in the marquis' home, his wife gave birth to a child. The delivery was difficult, and there seemed to be little hope of saving the life of the mother or the infant. Tradition credits the intercession of Aloysius, who was moved by the tears of the frightened husband, with saving the lives of both mother and child.[4] After his death, a memorial was placed in the palace chapel to commemorate the miraculous intervention.[5]

The voyage to Genoa was largely uneventful, and the fine weather of early summer made for a pleasant trip. The passengers' peace was interrupted near Genoa when the fleet was in danger of being attacked by Algerian cruisers under the command of Asan Agar, the bey of Algiers. The pirates followed Admiral Doria nearly all the way to Genoa. All that is recorded of Aloysius' response was that he remarked that it would be a great joy if they were all martyred for the Faith.[6]

[2] Maurice Meschler, S.J., St. Aloysius Gonzaga: Patron of Christian Youth (Rockford, Ill.: TAN Books, 1985), 86. The great-nephew of the famed Genoese admiral Andrea Doria (d. 1560), Giovanni Andrea Doria (d. 1606) was named admiral of the fleet of Genoa in 1556. He commanded the fleet of the Christian "Holy League" at the Battle of Djerba (1560) and was a participant in the famed Battle of Lepanto (1571).

[3] Virgil Cepari, S.J., Life of Saint Aloysius Gonzaga, ed. Francis Goldie, S.J. (New York: Benziger Brothers, 1891), 60; Meschler, St. Aloysius, 87.

[4] Virgilio Cepari, The Life of St. Aloysius Gonzaga, of the Society of Jesus, vol. 1 of Library of Religious Biography, ed. Edward Healy Thompson (London: Burns and Oates, 1867), 86.

[5] Meschler, St. Aloysius, 86.

[6] Ibid.

During the trip, Aloysius found a small stone marked with red spots among the rocks on the seashore. The markings on the stone reminded him of the Lord's Passion, and this sign encouraged him to persevere in his resolve to enter the Jesuits. With great delight he showed the stone to his mother, exclaiming, "See, Signora, what God has let me find, and yet my father will not allow me to become a religious!"[7] Although he held on to few worldly possessions, he kept the stone for a long time.[8]

The party reached Genoa on July 28 and immediately headed for Castiglione. Aloysius was now sixteen years old. Expecting his father to give him the necessary consent, he was surprised when the marquis announced that he wished for Aloysius and Rudolfo to pay their respects, in their father's name, to all the princes and dukes of Italy.[9] It was Ferrante's hope that the luxuries and attentions of the courts of their relatives would turn Aloysius away from his desire to become a religious.[10] The prince saw through the plan immediately, but again submitted to his father's wishes and set out with his brother and a large suite of attendants. Father Cepari records that Rudolfo was magnificently dressed, as suited his station, but Aloysius wore only a plain suit of black serge, and would have nothing elegant about him.[11]

The brothers visited the courts of Mantua, Ferrara, Parma, and Turin. In Pavia, Aloysius became acquainted with Federico Borromeo (d. 1631), the cousin of Charles Borromeo. Federico would succeed his uncle as Archbishop of Milan in 1595 and do a great deal to advance devotion to Aloysius after the young man's death by promoting the cause for his beatification.[12] It could be imagined that a tour such as this would be a great temptation to many young men in Aloysius' position.[13] Not only was he greeted with all the marks of

---

[7] Bollandists, 950, *Acta Sanctorum Junii IV*, "Anno Apice 1707", quoted in ibid., 87.

[8] Ibid. See also C. C. Martindale, *The Vocation of Saint Aloysius* (New York: Sheed and Ward, 1946), 102.

[9] Cepari, *Life of Saint Aloysius*, 60. This and all subsequent references, unless specified otherwise, are to the Goldie edition.

[10] Ibid., 61, 87; see also Martindale, *Vocation of Saint Aloysius*, 103.

[11] Cepari, *Life of Saint Aloysius*, 61.

[12] Meschler, *St. Aloysius*, 88.

[13] Walter Burghardt, "Aloysius Gonzaga: Role Model for Today's Youth?" in Stevens and McNichols, *Aloysius*, 28.

respect due to him because of his rank; he was also able to broaden his understanding of what might be possible for him should he remain in the world. But rather than give in and embrace the splendor that was paraded before him, the sixteen-year-old prince "flung his glove" in the face of the life he had by now come to despise. Aloysius Gonzaga had pledged himself to a different kind of kingdom. He was making it clear where his allegiance lay.[14]

It would be naïve to assume that Aloysius was unaware of the good he could do for his subjects as a secular prince. Certainly there were the examples of those royal saints who used their power to benefit their subjects: Saints Henry the Emperor (d. 1024) and Cunegund (d. 1033) of the Holy Roman Empire, Saint Edward the Confessor of England (d. 1066), Saint Louis of France (d. 1270), Saint Elizabeth of Hungary (d. 1231)—all of whom would have been known to Aloysius. It would also be unfair to assume that he was blind to the good that he could have done as a member of the secular clergy or another religious order in which he could have accepted ecclesiastical honors and influence. As Walter Burghardt notes, "Above all these considerations was a single overriding fact: God was calling him elsewhere, to vowed life in the Society of Jesus. It was as simple as that. *God* was calling. Not human reasoning; not objective argument. Simply, God."[15] It was probably at this time, more than any other in his life, when the "Standards" meditation of the *Exercises* came to have special meaning in Aloysius' life.[16] His father's command brought him face-to-face with a choice that could only be his: Would he choose to carry the standard of the earthly kingdom or that of Heaven? Aloysius knew what it was like to be both subject and master in the secular world.[17] But as he grew in the love and knowledge of Christ, discerning the total demands of true discipleship, he came to recognize that "once one has heeded the call of Christ the King, any other allure, any other fundamental attachment, falls under the banner of Satan."[18] Aloysius would not compromise his commitment or his vision.

[14] Clifford Stevens, "Four Centuries of Aloysius", in Stevens and McNichols, *Aloysius*, 18; see also Meschler, *St. Aloysius*, 90.
[15] Burghardt, "Aloysius Gonzaga", 32.
[16] James Martin, *My Life with the Saints* (Chicago: Loyola Press, 2006), 336.
[17] Richard Hermes, "On Understanding the Saints", in Stevens and McNichols, *Aloysius*, 79.
[18] Cepari, *Life of Saint Aloysius*, 62.

Throughout the eighteen-month journey, Aloysius never omitted his regular devotions.[19] Praying and meditating as he had at home, he made it his practice to seek out the local Jesuit community in the city where he happened to be staying. Once there, he immediately went to the chapel to honor the Blessed Sacrament, and afterward he would converse with his future confreres.[20]

During Aloysius' visit to the Jesuit novitiate in Novellara, he was introduced to a novice who recorded his impressions of the prince:

I was a novice in the Novellara house of the Society of Jesus when Aloysius and his brother [Rudolfo] and their suite arrived in the town. He was received with high honors by the princes of the palace, who also belonged to the Gonzaga family. I noticed that [Rudolfo], who was taller and much more richly dressed than Aloysius, always gave place to his brother and walked after him. A great crowd of people had assembled to see Aloysius, not only because he was the eldest son and heir of the Marquis, but because his sanctity had been spoken of everywhere, and it was rumored that he intended to become a religious. We novices stood in rows in the courtyard as Aloysius and his suite entered. The modesty and holiness of his bearing filled me with such a feeling of reverence that I scarcely dared to look at him. It was a great consolation to us all, and helped to strengthen us in our vocation to know that the young Marquis wished to enter our Order, though he could find no way to do so.[21]

After all the visits had been paid, Aloysius and company returned to Castiglione at the end of September 1584. Now seventeen years old, he expected that his father would soon let him go.[22] The marquis would hear none of it. Ferrante still doubted that his son was serious about his decision to enter the Society of Jesus, believing it to be only a youthful impulse or imprudent fervor.[23] The marquis enlisted the help of Duke William of Mantua, who sent a bishop to see Aloysius at Castiglione. This prelate tried to convince Aloysius to become a secular priest. Father Cepari summarized the bishop's argument: "There were plenty of examples of holy men, in bygone

[19] Cepari, *Life of Saint Aloysius*, 62.
[20] Ibid.; Meschler, *St. Aloysius*, 89.
[21] Quoted in Meschler, *St. Aloysius*, 89.
[22] Ibid., 91.
[23] Meschler, *St. Aloysius*, 91; Cepari, *Life of Saint Aloysius*, 63.

days as in our own times, like Saint Charles Borromeo and others, who in positions of high dignity were more useful to the Church than many religious. And he [the bishop] promised *in fine*, to make use of his best endeavors and influence to gain him Church promotion."[24] Aloysius asked the bishop to thank the duke for his kindness, but "assured him that he must decline the offer of such favors, for he wished to have no treasure but God alone, and had chosen the Society of Jesus precisely because it forbade the acceptance of Church dignities".[25]

Some of Aloysius' other relatives weighed in as well. Don Alfonso Gonzaga of Castel Goffredo, his uncle, approached the young man, but received the same reply as that given to the duke's bishop. Giovanni Vincenzo Cardinal Gonzaga (of the Guastalla-Molfetta Gonzaga) tried to induce Aloysius to give up the idea of entering the Jesuits, proposing that he should join the Carthusians or Capuchins instead.[26] Father Cepari proposes that the real reason for this suggestion might have been to induce Aloysius to abandon the idea of a religious vocation altogether by convincing him to consider religious orders whose austerities were beyond the prince's weak health.[27] Aloysius replied that the Society was far enough from the world for him, since riches and honor would be impossible there.[28]

The third attempt to discourage Aloysius came from two priests recruited by the marquis. The first of these, the Archpriest of Castiglione, John Baptist Pastorio (who had baptized the prince), was so impressed by Aloysius' sincerity and determination that he became his most enthusiastic supporter.[29] The other priest, a Franciscan, Francis Panigarola, who was a popular preacher and who would later become Bishop of Asti, was also unsuccessful.[30] Aloysius remained unmoved.

Ferrante was blind to the truth and was by now convinced that his son could not have withstood the arguments of such learned and

---

[24] Cepari, *Life of Saint Aloysius*, 63–64. See also Meschler, *St. Aloysius*, 91; Martindale, *Vocation of Saint Aloysius*, 108.

[25] Meschler, *St. Aloysius*, 91.

[26] Ibid. Although these orders are quite distinct in their spiritualities and charisms, both made allowances for their members to be promoted within the Church.

[27] Cepari, *Life of Saint Aloysius*, 64.

[28] Ibid. See also Meschler, *St. Aloysius*, 92.

[29] Cepari, *Life of Saint Aloysius*, 65; Meschler, *St. Aloysius*, 92; Margaret Monro, *A Book of Unlikely Saints* (Freeport, N.Y.: Books for Libraries, 1943), 39.

[30] Cepari, *Life of Saint Aloysius*, 65. See also Martindale, *Vocation of Saint Aloysius*, 108–9.

influential churchmen.[31] Calling Aloysius to his chamber, where he was again confined to bed because of gout, the marquis asked his son what he now intended to do. The young prince responded with his characteristic simplicity and directness that he had not changed his mind and still intended to enter the Society of Jesus.[32] The *Gonzaghina* erupted and a ranting Ferrante, unable to control his anger, ordered his son out of his sight. Aloysius took this to mean that he had been commanded to leave the castle altogether and requested that his valet collect his books, bedding, and a few other personal items, and bring them to the Franciscan friary of Santa Maria, which stood near the lake not far from Castiglione.[33]

Near the Franciscans' house was a small villa, a sort of summer retreat built by the marquis for family. The villa stood on the banks of the lake, which had been made by damming up the streams that flow down the hills. Water from the lake entered into subterranean vaults richly ornamented with mosaic tiles and then rose in a great fountain in front of the villa.[34] It was in this idyllic setting that Aloysius took up residence, passing his time in prayer in the Franciscans' church or in his room.

Ferrante refused to talk about his son, and the other members of the family and the servants were too anxious and upset to tell him that Aloysius had left the castle. After a few days, however, the marquis finally asked where Aloysius was. Being told that he was at the villa, Don Ferrante angrily ordered that he be sent for at once. When Aloysius appeared before him, Ferrante berated him for causing him more grief and vexation by leaving the house.[35] With calmness and simplicity, Aloysius responded that he thought he was obeying his father's orders by leaving. The marquis again lost his temper, and after another angry outburst, he ordered Aloysius to his room.[36] The prince bowed and went out.

Father Cepari records, "As soon as he had reached his apartment, he closed the door, and kneeling before a crucifix he began to weep

[31] Cepari, *Life of Saint Aloysius*, 66.

[32] Ibid.; see also Meschler, *St. Aloysius*, 92.

[33] Cepari, *Life of Saint Aloysius*, 66.

[34] Ibid.; Meschler, *St. Aloysius*, 93; Martindale, *Vocation of Saint Aloysius*, 109. The room in which Aloysius stayed was converted to a chapel by Pope Saint Pius X during his time as Bishop of Mantua.

[35] Cepari, *Life of Saint Aloysius*, 66.

[36] Ibid., 66–67; Meschler, *St. Aloysius*, 93.

bitterly, calling on God for constancy and courage in his many trials;
he then stripped off his shirt and disciplined himself for a long time."[37]
As this was happening, the marquis was experiencing his own interior
struggle, a battle between his conscience and his affection for his son.[38]
Although Ferrante was given to frightening fits of rage, he did truly
love and admire his son. The marquis understood that should Aloysius
abdicate, none of his other children would be able to bear the burden
of the marquisate.[39] Moreover, while he did not wish to offend God,
he could not bear the thought of being parted from Aloysius.[40]

Fearing that Aloysius might have been made ill by his outburst, Ferrante sent one of his attendants, the governor of the town, to check on
the prince. When he went to Aloysius' room, the governor found the
door locked and the young man's footman sitting outside. The governor explained that he had orders from the marquis to see what the boy
was doing. "Accordingly he came to the door, and as he could not get
in, he made a little hole in the crevices and looking through it he saw
Aloysius half undressed, on his bare knees upon the floor, in front of a
crucifix, weeping and scourging himself."[41] The governor was deeply
moved by what he saw and returned to the marquis in tears, telling
him that if he knew what Aloysius was doing, he would no longer
prevent him from carrying out his resolve.[42] The astonished father
asked what he had seen. The governor told him everything, assuring
him that no one could look upon such a scene without weeping.[43]

The following day Ferrante was told that Aloysius was again dis-
ciplining himself. Because of his gout, he had himself carried to his
son's room. "There through the hole already made, he could see
his son again in tears and scourging himself. So moved was he by
the spectacle, that for a time he remained quite amazed and as if lost
to all around."[44] Regaining control of himself, Ferrante ordered the
servants to knock on the door, then he and Donna Marta entered

[37] Cepari, *Life of Saint Aloysius*, 67.
[38] Ibid.
[39] William Hart McNichols, "Saint Aloysius: Patron of Youth", in Stevens and McNichols,
Aloysius, 40.
[40] Cepari, *Life of Saint Aloysius*, 67.
[41] Ibid.
[42] Ibid.; Meschler, *St. Aloysius*, 94.
[43] Meschler, *St. Aloysius*, 94.
[44] Cepari, *Life of Saint Aloysius*, 67.

the room. Father Cepari tells us, "He found the floor marked with drops of blood from the discipline and the place where the saint had been kneeling all wet with his tears, as if water had been spilt there."[45]

This sight was too much for the marquis. Commenting on this, writer Margaret Monro observes, "The sight produced an extraordinary impression. At last he realized what he was up against. There was no more *Gonzaghina*—things were too serious for that."[46] After this, Aloysius continued, each day, to ask for permission to go and join the Society. Finally, after all the years of struggle, the marquis gave in to his son and to God—Aloysius was free to go.

Reflecting on all these events, William Hart McNichols writes:

> It seems amazing now that Ferrante did not see what everyone saw so clearly in his son: a full-grown sage and saint in a child's body, much the same way the little Mozart held a full-grown genius and composer of symphonies in a child's body. Finally, Ferrante could no longer fight the concentrated single-mindedness of a boy visited, like the young King David, with the power of God. Aloysius won the contest for his own life through a flood of prayer and penances, which included taking upon himself the resistance and anger of his father, scourging these in his own body with a dog whip until he drew blood.[47]

* * * * *

Ferrante wrote to Scipione Gonzaga (the brother of Father Francis and the Patriarch of Jerusalem), in Rome, asking him to offer in the marquis' name his eldest son to the Father General of the Society of Jesus.[48] He also asked him to learn from the general where he would like Aloysius to make his novitiate.

The general of the Society of Jesus at that time was Father Claudio Aquaviva.[49] The son of the Duke of Atri and a distant relative of the

[45] Ibid., 68.
[46] Monro, *Unlikely Saints*, 40.
[47] McNichols, "Saint Aloysius", 40.
[48] Cepari, *Life of Saint Aloysius*, 68.
[49] Claudio Aquaviva (1543–1615) was the fourth general of the Society of Jesus, governing from 1581 to 1615. His rule was marked by a period of rapid expansion for the Jesuits from about five thousand serving in twenty-one provinces to thirteen thousand members in thirty-two provinces. His work strengthened the order internally, and he is credited with systematizing the Jesuits' educational system by drawing up a practical code for their schools, *Ratio atque Institutio Studiorum*, in 1586.

Gonzagas, Aquaviva accepted Aloysius for the Society and responded that it would be best that his novitiate be at Rome.[50]

Aloysius himself wrote to the general, thanking him for his acceptance, placing himself entirely at Aquaviva's disposal.

> Most Reverend Father in Christ,
>
> Your Reverence can scarcely believe what great consolation God has vouchsafed to grant me during these last few days. I have always put my trust in the infinite mercy of His Divine Majesty, and hoped that He would let this hard and painful struggle turn out for the best, and for the salvation of my soul. And as I do not doubt that Your Reverence will accord me the final comfort, I can say with assurance: *Facta est tranquillitas magna* [There is a great calm]; and, when I take leave of my father's house: *Domus mea hodie salva facta est* [Today is salvation come to my house]. I beg Your Reverence to let me soon have directions about my journey *ad sanctam civitatem*, where the Vicar of Our Lord Jesus Christ is enthroned, in order that I may there enjoy the intercourse of so many holy persons, derive profit from their holy admonitions, amend my life and, with the help of God and in imitation of their holy example, put on the *novum hominem* (new man). My father will give you all necessary information. In token of my obedience to you henceforth, I kiss Your Paternity's hand, and remain
>
> Castiglione, August 15, 1585.[51]
>
>   Your obedient son in Christ,
>
>   Aloysius Gonzaga

Aquaviva responded kindly to Aloysius' letter, calling him his son and expressing his willingness to receive him at Rome.[52] Two years had passed between the day when Aloysius had clearly understood his vocation and the date of his letter to Aquaviva.

Needless to say, Aloysius was overjoyed by these developments, and he readily agreed to whatever course of action his father might think advisable. The marquis felt that Aloysius should renounce all

[50] Martindale, *Vocation of Saint Aloysius*, 110.

[51] Aloysius Gonzaga to Father Claudio Aquaviva, Aug. 15, 1585, in *Lettere di S. Luigi Gonzaga*, ed. Oliviero Iozzi (Pisa, 1889), 17f., quoted in Meschler, *St. Aloysius*, 95. Father Martindale notes that there has been some question as to the legitimacy of this letter, although he does not offer any other explanation or argument. Martindale, *Vocation of Saint Aloysius*, 110.

[52] Meschler, *St. Aloysius*, 95; Martindale, *Vocation of Saint Aloysius*, 110.

his rights to the Marquisate of Castiglione and any other fiefs he might inherit in favor of his brother, Rudolfo. Ferrante also decided that Aloysius should receive four thousand ducats on account and an annuity of four hundred ducats. Because Aloysius was willing to accept any conditions, a document was soon drawn up, examined by lawyers and the Senate of Milan, and finally sent to the emperor for his approval. Aloysius went so far as to ask the Duchess of Mantua (the emperor's aunt) to use her influence to aid his cause. She promised to do what she could.[53]

Aloysius endured a hard battle, but, by the grace of God, he had obtained victory. His struggle for freedom had cost him tears and blood, but he faced all adversity with courage and with hope that God's Will would be done. Aloysius sought to live out the potential of his baptism, and he abandoned himself to Providence. He was not driven by logic in his quest. He was guided and driven by God's grace and with that deliberateness and zeal that were uniquely his.

Having received the permission he had so long desired, Aloysius was now forced to wait. The young prince, who was growing more impatient by the day, continued to fill his role as his father's arbiter, tending to the marquis' business. Don Ferrante was still confined to bed with gout and sent Aloysius to manage affairs in Milan. Most likely the business concerned the marquis' many loans, consequences of his gambling addiction.[54] Aloysius focused his energies on his father's business and was able, during his seven or eight months there, to arrange everything as the marquis wished, in spite of the complicated and involved nature of the business.[55] As we have seen, and as Father Meschler reiterates, "He had an extraordinary talent for managing people and business, and this was precisely what made his father feel his departure so much."[56]

These months of waiting were not wasted. Always seeking to improve himself, the young prince took advantage of his time in Milan to attend lectures regularly, continuing his courses in philosophy and natural science at the Brera, the city's Jesuit college. It

[53] Cepari, *Life of Saint Aloysius*, 69.
[54] Martindale, *Vocation of Saint Aloysius*, 112; Monro, *Unlikely Saints*, 41.
[55] Cepari, *Life of Saint Aloysius*, 70.
[56] Meschler, *St. Aloysius*, 98.

was his practice to attend both morning and evening lectures, and if he was prevented from attending in person, he had notes taken for him. His biographers record that he readily joined in the debates, and his skill and amiability endeared him to many of his peers. He also attended mathematical lectures, showing a remarkable intelligence and proficiency.[57] Father Cepari relates that because the lecturer did not dictate his course, "Aloysius, for fear of forgetting what he had heard, on his return home, used at once to dictate to his servant [Clement Ghisoni] what he had heard. . . . Never had he forgotten a proof or misplaced the figures, the measures, the calculations, the points, lines, or corrections with which those pages are filled."[58] While attending the lectures, he was always dressed simply and was very conscientious and courteous in his dealings with others.[59]

During this time Aloysius grew very close to the Jesuit lay brothers who worked at the college. He often spent time in conversation with the brother-porter, and he was even entrusted with the keys from time to time while the porter delivered a message in the house. This simple act of trust gave the young man the sense that he was already a Jesuit.[60]

On Thursdays, which were always free days, the Fathers of the college had the custom of walking to a villa known as La Chisolfa. Located about a mile and a half from the Porta Comasina, this house and its grounds provided a quiet escape for the Jesuits and their students. Aloysius would start out early on these days, leaving his servants behind, and, book in hand, he would walk along the road in the hopes of meeting some of the Fathers. He envied those who possessed what he was seeking, and he longed to share in their life and mission.[61] To his young, idealistic mind, these men were but one step from Heaven because they were free to follow their vocation of service to God and the Church.

---

[57] See, for instance, ibid.

[58] Cepari, *Life of Saint Aloysius*, 71. Cepari notes in the text that he has seen the copies of the lectures dictated by Aloysius, which were being kept by one of his former servants as a relic.

[59] Ibid.; Meschler, *St. Aloysius*, 99.

[60] Cepari, *Life of Saint Aloysius*, 71.

[61] Martindale, *Vocation of Saint Aloysius*, 113.

During Carnival, Aloysius decided to take up residence in the college, refusing to participate in the riotous celebrations that overtook Milan. Only once during the pre-Lenten festival did he emerge from the college, and this was to be present at a tournament and an exhibition of horsemanship. Riding schools were quite popular throughout Italy, and the Gonzagas were known for their love of horses. Aloysius himself had a number of horses in his father's stables, and one of these, magnificently draped in velvet embroidered with the family's coat of arms, was led behind him wherever he went.[62] However, on this day, Aloysius chose to appear on a mule and to be attended by only two servants. The response to his behavior was mixed. Some laughed at the prince, while others were edified by the behavior of one who had become known throughout Milan because of his intention to renounce his title and enter the Society of Jesus.[63] We can only guess at Aloysius' motivation for this display. Had he been pressured to attend? And, if so, had he decided that he would go, but only on his own terms? This would certainly be in keeping with his disposition and his contempt for the wealth and grandeur that were always being displayed by his peers, both in secular society and in the Church.[64]

These months in Milan saw no change in Aloysius' religious devotions, and he often made visits to the shrine of the Madonna di San Celso. He frequently received Communion in the Jesuit Church of San Fidele, which had been built for the Society by Saint Charles Borromeo in 1569. Father Cepari tells of one Jesuit preacher who recalled that "whenever he wished to rouse himself to earnestness and devotion in his sermons, he turned to look at Saint Aloysius who was always present at his discourses, and who took up his position in front of the pulpit."[65]

Finally, during the months Aloysius was in Milan, the ratification of his abdication arrived from the emperor. Don Ferrante appeared, unannounced and in person, in Milan. Although he had given his son permission to go to the Jesuits, he still hoped that his son's vocation might simply have been only a phase. Questioning the prince,

[62] Cepari, *Life of Saint Aloysius*, 72.
[63] Martindale, *Vocation of Saint Aloysius*, 114.
[64] Ibid.
[65] Cepari, *Life of Saint Aloysius*, 72.

he found him as firm in his resolve as ever before.[66] Speaking first in angry tones, Ferrante soon softened as he sought to convince his son that he was not a bad Christian and that he had no desire to resist God's Will. However, in his view, Aloysius' plan was not God's Will, but a youthful impulse.[67] Father Cepari records:

> The Marquis began to argue, with every motive that affection could dictate, that his entry into religion would be the complete ruin of the family. He set before him the excellent dispositions God had given him, wherein there was no danger of his being turned from a good life, so that there was no occasion to fear remaining in the world. For even in the world he could lead the life of a religious, and he would maintain the subjects whom God had given him in the observance of His laws, and, by his example, lead them to Christian piety.... He laid before him the ardent character of his younger brother [Rudolfo], to whom he was about to resign his States; his youth, his inexperience, which made him less fit for the exercise of authority; the danger there was of his committing follies, if he were to be left his own master when so young. "See," he said, "how ill I am, scarcely able to move on account of being tortured and enfeebled by continual attacks of gout, I require to be relieved of the burden of government, which you could this very moment undertake. Whereas if you enter a religious order and abandon me, affairs will arise to which I shall not be able to give my attention, and I shall be crushed by troubles and misfortune, and you will be the cause of my death." And at this point the Marquis burst into a flood of tears and went on to say words full of sorrow and deep emotion.[68]

The pressure placed on Aloysius by his father's attack was very great.[69] The prince listened to what his father had to say, humbly thanking him for his love and affection, then explained to Don Ferrante that he had considered all (or at least most) of what he had said. He was aware of his duty, and, had not God called him to another state of life, he would have been contented to accept the duties and obligations of his birth. As it was, he wished to enter religious life

[66] Ibid., 74.
[67] Ibid.; Meschler, *St. Aloysius*, 101.
[68] Cepari, *Life of Saint Aloysius*, 74–75.
[69] Monro, *Unlikely Saints*, 42.

because he believed it was God's Will.[70] Aloysius could not have foreseen that his father would, in fact, die very soon. But the marquis would die a peaceful death, convinced at last that his son was where he belonged—in the Society of Jesus.[71]

Don Ferrante again tried to have influential men dissuade Aloysius from pursuing his true vocation. Many in Milan tried to "reason" with the young prince, even going so far as to try to frighten him by speaking of the trials and sacrifices of religious life.[72] Each of these learned men was in turn persuaded of the truth of Aloysius' vocation, and many even began to admire the prince for his resolution and fortitude. They explained to the marquis that they believed this vocation was from God.[73]

After this unanimous verdict by Aloysius' inquisitors, Don Ferrante made one last effort. He had himself carried to the Jesuit house at San Fidele, to see Father Achille Gagliardi, who was highly regarded throughout Milan for his learning and piety. He asked the priest to examine his son in his presence about his vocation, begging him to present to the youth strong reasons against it. On his own, the marquis promised that, after that, he would be at peace with the decision, as far as was possible.[74] After Father Gagliardi had given his consent, Aloysius was summoned, and the Jesuit examined him very carefully for more than an hour. He presented to him the difficulties of religious life and questioned him about his choice of the Society in particular. Father Cepari records that Aloysius himself later related to him that the priest was so severe in his questions and objections, he began to believe that Gagliardi was serious in his objections.[75] The respect Aloysius had for the priest made him hesitate for a moment in his resolve. Cepari writes, "For as the Saint often said, no one had ever before so thoroughly felt his pulse, or used arguments against him exactly as if they were his own convictions."[76] Unexpectedly, Gagliardi declared defeat. Aloysius had replied to the priest with such

[70] Cepari, *Life of Saint Aloysius*, 75; Meschler, *St. Aloysius*, 102.

[71] Martindale, *Vocation of Saint Aloysius*, 115.

[72] Meschler, *St. Aloysius*, 102.

[73] Cepari, *Life of Saint Aloysius*, 76.

[74] Ibid.

[75] Ibid.

[76] Ibid., 77.

openness to his questions, responded to his objections with such humility and learning (drawing on both Scripture and other spiritual writers), that the Jesuit was not only edified, but he was amazed to see how well grounded Aloysius was in his vocation. The priest's declaration was a great comfort to Aloysius, who now understood that it had been his duty to test him. The marquis himself, having witnessed the exchange, dismissed Aloysius from the room and admitted to Father Gagliardi that he recognized the divine origin of his vocation. He began to recount the events of his son's life, ending by stating that he was willing to allow him to enter into religious life.

A few days later, the marquis returned to Castiglione while Aloysius remained in Milan to conclude business there. Upon his return to his family, he would sign the document of renunciation.

Chapter 9

Surrender

Aloysius had now obtained yet another promise from his father, but, as the time for his return to Castiglione drew near, he came to believe the struggle was still not yet ended.[1] Before he left Milan, he sent a letter to the Father General, Claudio Aquaviva, in which he told him his troubles and asked for his advice. Although the general felt sorry for Aloysius, he explained that he felt the prince should have his father's permission. He encouraged Aloysius to do all in his power to obtain that consent.[2]

Before returning to Castiglione, Aloysius traveled to Mantua, arriving there sometime in July 1585. The young prince used his stay in Mantua as an opportunity to make the *Spiritual Exercises* at the city's newly founded Jesuit college and to seek the support of the duchess, who had been so helpful in obtaining the needed approval of the emperor. As it turned out, this was not a propitious time to seek the duchess' support.[3] Mantua at the time was preparing to receive ambassadors from Japan, who were expected to arrive any day.[4] These Japanese Christians had come from Japan to Rome with their Jesuit guides to visit Popes Gregory XIII (1572–1585) and Sixtus V (1585–1590). After traveling through Portugal and Spain, the group was fêted throughout Italy. This visit to Rome came to serve as something of a climax to the reign of Gregory XIII, whose pontificate saw the establishment of a number of national groups (including

[1] Virgil Cepari, S.J., *Life of Saint Aloysius Gonzaga*, ed. Francis Goldie, S.J. (New York: Benziger Brothers, 1891), 78.

[2] Ibid.; Maurice Meschler, S.J., *St. Aloysius Gonzaga: Patron of Christian Youth* (Rockford, Ill.: TAN Books, 1985), 104.

[3] Margaret Monro, *A Book of Unlikely Saints* (Freeport, N.Y.: Books for Libraries, 1943), 43

[4] C. C. Martindale, *The Vocation of Saint Aloysius* (New York: Sheed and Ward, 1946), 117.

students from England, Germany, and Greece, all studying in their respective colleges) in the city of Rome. Arriving only a month before the pontiff's death, the three Japanese princes—"slim and modest in their white silk coats embroidered with birds and flowers in different colors, wide-sleeved and open at the front, with rich scarves crossed over the breast and round the waist again as girdles"— and their accompanying courtiers were honored with a tumultuous reception in Rome. "Gregory wept as they knelt to kiss his feet, and said, 'Master, now you are dismissing your servant in peace ... for my eyes have seen your salvation, which you have prepared for all peoples.'"[5]

Cepari records that the ambassadors had visited the Holy House of Loreto and traveled through a large portion of Lombardy before making their way to Mantua, where they were greeted by Duke William and his son, Don Vincenzo. Many nobles traveled to Mantua to be present for the celebrations, including Don Ferrante and Rudolfo.[6] Aloysius seems to have taken no part in the festivities, as he was making his retreat at the Jesuit college under the direction of Father Antony Valentino. He spent his time in prayer and meditation and in spiritual reading. His devotion and simplicity edified many who saw him, and he used this retreat as an opportunity to make a general confession of his whole life. In his account of the life of Aloysius, Father Cepari records the deposition given under oath by Father Valentino to the vicar of the Bishop of Reggio. Prior to coming to Mantua, Valentino had served as rector and master of novices in the Venetian province of the Society. When asked whether he was aware that Aloysius had led a life of perfection, adorned by numerous spiritual gifts, the priest responded:

Yes, my Lord, I am aware, not merely from what I have heard our Fathers say, but much more from a young man who was his valet, Clement Ghisoni, who wrote out his lectures, and was almost his fellow student, from whom I have learnt a great deal about the penance, love of retirement, the extraordinary acts of virtue, and holy life of this young man. I know it too from a still better source, because I

[5] Christopher Devlin, *The Life of Robert Southwell: Poet and Martyr* (New York: Farrar, Straus, and Cudahy, 1956), 83. See Lk 2:29–31.
[6] Cepari, *Life of Saint Aloysius*, 79.

had at that time to see much of him, as I was engaged in giving him the *Spiritual Exercises*, with a view of his being more sure about his vocation, as it was his father's wish that he should be. On this occasion I heard his general Confession. [In] spite of much consideration, I cannot recall anything which I could put down as a mortal sin; on the contrary I could record many marvelous things, thanks to his holy and very virtuous life. This I certainly can affirm, that his Confession impressed upon me a high regard for his holiness, innocence and great purity, and I have always spoken of him in this sense.[7]

Father Valentino was called away before the *Exercises* were completed, and another Jesuit, Father Lelius Passionei, completed the retreat with Aloysius. The young man went to confession several times, and Passionei also, deposed under oath, testified that he admired Aloysius' remarkable goodness, devotion, humility, and other virtues.[8] Aloysius asked for a copy of the Jesuit *Constitutions*, which he studied very closely, delighted by what he read. Before leaving Mantua, he also asked for a copy of Ignatius' *Meditations on the Passion* so that he could make use of them after his return home.[9]

After his return to Castiglione, Aloysius rededicated himself to his practices of prayer and penance. At the time, he was actually beginning to grow weaker because of his austerities.[10] Donna Marta became so concerned that she encouraged her husband to allow their son to enter the Society of Jesus. There can be no doubt that Aloysius was becoming a victim of his own zeal, but he thought he was right in acting as he did. Having no one to direct him, he let his fervor be his guide.[11] But from his stay in Castiglione, we also get a glimpse of a more sensitive, loving side of the prince. Aloysius devoted himself to his younger brothers and sisters with a most tender affection, teaching them their catechism and prayers. To help in this, he kept a ready supply of sugarplums and small toys.[12] Among his younger siblings, his favorite was his brother Francis, who would later succeed Rudolfo as Marquis of Castiglione and who would be a strong supporter of

[7] Quoted in ibid., 80; translation adapted.
[8] Ibid., 81.
[9] Ibid.; Meschler, *St. Aloysius*, 105.
[10] Meschler, *St. Aloysius*, 106.
[11] Cepari, *Life of Saint Aloysius*, 82.
[12] Ibid.

his brother's beatification and the publication of Father Cepari's *Life*. In her *Book of Unlikely Saints*, Margaret Monro presents this change in Aloysius as being another sign of his spiritual growth and maturity. She writes that the Aloysius who was emerging in the midst of these difficulties was "a more genial, simple-hearted Aloysius, more childlike, less everlastingly on the defensive, readier to be happy in simple ways. Aloysius was born old. He now begins to become young enough for the Kingdom of Heaven."[13]

Once the family was together again in Castiglione, Aloysius finally began to see that his father had no intention of letting him leave anytime soon. He was careful not to irritate his father, waiting patiently to see if Ferrante would bring up the subject himself.[14] When the prince did finally question his father, the marquis shocked him by denying that he had ever given permission to let his son enter the Society of Jesus and that Aloysius was too weak at that time to even consider entering a religious community. He would allow him to go when he was twenty-five—Aloysius was then seventeen.[15] He did give his son the option of leaving without his consent, but he promised that, should this happen, he would be disowned.[16] The young man began to sob, shocked and wounded by his father's harsh reply, and he began to beg him to give his consent.[17] The marquis absolutely refused, and the prince left his father.

Aloysius returned to his room in tears and tried to figure out what he should do. He sat and began to write to the Jesuit general to ask his advice, but the marquis entered and began to demand an answer from his son: Would he leave without his father's consent or not? Feeling robbed of any chance to make this situation right, he replied in writing to his father:

> Though nothing could happen more painful to me, or which would rob my soul more thoroughly of its peace, than to see my entry into religious life delayed, still to satisfy you, my father, whom, after God, I would wish to please above all others, I am willing to make this

[13] Monro, *Unlikely Saints*, 41–42.
[14] Cepari, *Life of Saint Aloysius*, 81; Martindale, *Vocation of Saint Aloysius*, 118.
[15] Martindale, *Vocation of Saint Aloysius*, 118; Monro, *Unlikely Saints*, 43.
[16] Meschler, *St. Aloysius*, 107.
[17] Cepari, *Life of Saint Aloysius*, 83.

concession. And this all the more, as the Father General bade me to try to gain your approval for my leaving, as far as that is possible, with a safe conscience and without offending God. I consent to wait two or three years longer, provided these conditions are kept. If you refuse either of these two, I cannot with safe conscience displease God to please my father, and I would rather, against your will, be a wanderer through the world, if the Fathers of the Society will not receive me, than in any way sacrifice my duty to God. The conditions are, first that I shall spend the time of this interval before entering the Order in Rome, where my vocation will be more secure, and where I can with greater ease attend to my studies; secondly that you now give your consent, that I should enter the Society after the lapse of this period, and write in this sense to the General, so that no difficulties will later arise.[18]

The marquis was surprised by his son's attitude and tone, and waited two days before accepting Aloysius' conditions. In truth, Don Ferrante was also frightened by the prospect of angering his son any further.[19] It was becoming more clear to everyone (including the marquis, although he would never admit it) that the prince's call to the Society of Jesus was truly a gift from God and that Aloysius would rather die a hundred times than ever renounce it.[20] For his part, Aloysius wrote to Claudio Aquaviva to explain the situation as it now stood and to convey his grief and frustration at seeing his hoped-for abdication and departure delayed even longer.

In accord with his promise to his son, Don Ferrante began to consider where his son was to stay in Rome. His first choice was their relative Giovanni Vincenzo Cardinal Gonzaga, son of Ferdinand, the Count of Guastalla. The marquis asked the Duke of Mantua to write to his cousin the cardinal, which the duke promised to do, on account of his affection for Aloysius. Sadly, however, because a dispute arose between the marquis and the duke over protocol, the letter was never written, things remained unsettled, and nothing more was done.[21] Yet, surprisingly, this development did not trouble

---

[18] Quoted in ibid., 83–84.
[19] Ibid., 84.
[20] Meschler, *St. Aloysius*, 108.
[21] Cepari, *Life of Saint Aloysius*, 85.

Aloysius. He discerned the hand of God in this difficulty, realizing that should he have taken up residence with the cardinal, it might possibly have been years more before he would have been able to free himself from the cardinal's service.[22]

Because his first plan had come to no avail, Don Ferrante suggested that his son take up residence in the Roman Seminary, then in the care of the Jesuits, having a private room for his use and a small number of servants (befitting his rank). This would allow Aloysius to dedicate himself to his studies under the direction of the Jesuit priests until the time of his entrance. This, however, was against the laws of the Society and would not have been in keeping with the spirit of a religious house.[23] The marquis asked another of their relatives, Scipione Cardinal Gonzaga, for his assistance in obtaining a dispensation from the rules for his son. The cardinal received a negative reply to his inquiries and dutifully reported back to Ferrante that nothing could be done. The marquis, however, was determined to see this plan through and asked Aloysius to enlist the aid of Eleanor of Austria, the Duchess of Mantua, who was a great supporter of the Jesuits. Aloysius refused, pointing out to his father that he had already asked her for assistance in obtaining the emperor's permission to abdicate the marquisate.[24]

At this point, Aloysius redoubled his prayers and penances, asking God to remove all the obstacles standing in his way. One day, after spending four or five hours in prayer and meditation, Aloysius felt the time was right, and, rising from his knees, he went to his father's chamber, where the marquis was again confined to bed by gout.[25] With all the seriousness and firmness he could manage, he said, "Father, I place myself entirely in your hands, do with me as you please. But I declare to you that I have been called to the Society of Jesus by God, and by your opposition to this vocation, you are resisting the Will of God."[26] As soon as he finished speaking, without waiting for a response, he left the room. The marquis was deeply impressed by his son's words, and on reflecting on all the events of

[22] Ibid.; Meschler, *St. Aloysius*, 108.
[23] Meschler, *St. Aloysius*, 108.
[24] Ibid., 109; Martindale, *Vocation of Saint Aloysius*, 120.
[25] Cepari, *Life of Saint Aloysius*, 86.
[26] Ibid.

the past months and years, he came to realize how much his resis-
tance had hurt his son. He also came to understand that his motives
were not as pure and disinterested as he might have pretended.[27] He
was overwhelmed with emotion. Fear and remorse filled his heart,
but he also mourned the loss of his beloved son. Overcome by these
emotions, he turned his face toward the wall and wept.[28]

After a while, the marquis called his son and said to him, "My son,
you have wounded my heart. I love you and have always loved you
as you deserve. I have fixed all my hopes for the family on you. But
since God calls you, as you tell me, I do not wish to stop you. Go,
my son, where you wish, I give you my blessing."[29] The marquis
again broke out in tears; Aloysius thanked him very simply and then
quietly left the room. When he reached his own room, he shut himself up alone, and there, prostrate on the ground, he began to thank
God with many tears for the inspiration to speak to his father and for
having blessed all his efforts with success.[30] This was Ferrante's final
surrender, and after this exchange, no more obstacles were placed in
Aloysius' path.

[27] Meschler, *St. Aloysius*, 109.
[28] Ibid.; Cepari, *Life of Saint Aloysius*, 86–87.
[29] Quoted in Cepari, *Life of Saint Aloysius*, 87; translation adapted.
[30] Ibid., 87–88; Meschler, *St. Aloysius*, 110.

Chapter 10

Abdication

The news of Aloysius' imminent departure spread quickly through Castiglione. The townspeople wondered at the thought of their prince abandoning his rights and titles for the life of a cleric. Aloysius was, understandably, eager to enter into his new way of life as soon as possible.[1] When the local people would ask Aloysius why he had chosen to leave them, Aloysius would reply, "I assure you I want to go and secure a crown in heaven, and it is too difficult for the ruler of a state to save his own soul. One cannot serve two masters, the world and God; I wish to secure my salvation, and I advise you to do the same."[2] But, despite his eagerness, the prince was required to wait a few weeks more. At the time, his mother, Donna Marta, was away from Castiglione visiting Princess Catherine—the youngest daughter of King Philip II of Spain and the new Duchess of Savoy—who had traveled to Turin with her new husband on August 10 of that year. While Aloysius waited for his mother's return, he was also required to obtain the consent of a large number of relatives who would be affected by his abdication.[3] It had been the express order of the emperor that all those members of the Gonzaga family be present at the abdication who, in case the marquis' family lose the right of succession because of a lack of suitable heirs, might inherit the rights of the marquisate.[4] Because most of the involved relatives lived in the courts of Mantua, the

---

[1] Virgil Cepari, S.J., *Life of Saint Aloysius Gonzaga*, ed. Francis Goldie, S.J. (New York: Benziger Brothers, 1891), 88; Maurice Meschler, S.J., *St. Aloysius Gonzaga: Patron of Christian Youth* (Rockford, Ill.: TAN Books, 1985), 111.

[2] Quoted in Cepari, *Life of Saint Aloysius*, 88; translation adapted.

[3] Meschler, *St. Aloysius*, 112.

[4] Cepari, *Life of Saint Aloysius*, 89.

marquis traveled there to make the final arrangements before Aloysius joined him.

During the time of waiting, Aloysius wrote three letters to his father.

My Illustrious Lord Father,
My Lady tells me to send you the enclosed news-sheets that Signor Giovanni Ordandino has received from a nephew of his at Venice, which I do, more because Her Ladyship asks me to and to give Your Lordship something to read, than for any authenticity or savour they may contain, save for the news of the plague, if it is true, which please God it may not be. Pietro del Turco has heard from Florence that Don Giulio del Caccia has been made governor-general of the state of Siena. This is all that now occurs to me, as we are all well except that Lord Rudolfo has a little toothache: may His Divine Majesty please to keep you too in health, and to conclude I kiss your hands.
At Castiglione, September 29, 1585.[5]

The following day he wrote again:

My Illustrious Lord Father,
I send your Lordship the list of things that have to be got here. Master Tullio considers that the season being so far advanced makes *rasetta* [a thin cloth] useless for everything except stockings, for which it will do; also it would serve for a traveling cloak, if he likes. Further he thinks that he had better carry out the list I send, since I have to go in clerical dress. However, if Father Prospero [Malavolta, rector of the Jesuit college at Mantua] does not think I have to change my clothes before [actually] entering religion, there would be little or nothing more left to do. For my part, I do not mind one way or the other what they judge best in Mantua. After all, as the Council says, it isn't the cowl that makes the monk. For the rest, what concerns me personally, I will go on waiting, and hoping that Your Lordship will arrange for things to be done quickly, as the season of year demands [it was autumn and the roads would soon be very bad, if not impassable], and so, kissing your hands, I pray for you from the Lord the

[5] Aloysius Gonzaga to his father, Sept. 29, 1585, in *Lettere di S. Luigi Gonzaga*, ed. Oliviero Iozzi (Pisa, 1889), quoted in C.C. Martindale, *The Vocation of Saint Aloysius* (New York: Sheed and Ward, 1946), 121; translation adapted.

full restoration of your health. Your Most Illustrious Lordship's very obedient son,

Castiglione, September 29, 1585.[6]

Aloysius Gonzaga

The third letter soon followed:

Most Illustrious Lord Father,
Lord Rudolfo received Your Lordship's letter this morning, which I answer in his name because he finds himself in bed with a slight temperature [brought on by his toothache]. He has carried out your orders except going to make the country visit owing to his indisposition. But Signor Antonio will not fail. Yesterday I sent the list of the things which are waiting for Master Tullio to set to work on. Anything else Your Lordship will hear from others; so I will not go on to say more save to kiss your hands and pray to our Lord to preserve you.

At Castiglione, October 1, 1585.[7]

A few days later, as the carriage carrying Aloysius rolled out of the castle at Castiglione, the people ran to take a last look at the prince, sorrowful that they would never see him again.[8]

During his two-month stay in Mantua, Aloysius stayed in the palace of San Sebastiano, where he followed his regular routine, spending a great deal of time at the Jesuit college. Despite his eagerness to leave behind his old life and enter into his new life as a religious, he was forced to wait because of the question of an allowance insisted upon by the marquis. Don Ferrante had arranged for his son to receive four hundred ducats annually for his private use, and this detail had been included in the document presented for the emperor's approval. Father Malavolta, rector of the Jesuit college, informed Aloysius that the rules of the Society did not permit this money to be given to Aloysius directly. Everything was to be placed at the

---

[6] Aloysius Gonzaga to his father, Sept. 29, 1585 (*sic*), in Iozzi, *Lettere*, quoted in Martindale, *Vocation of Saint Aloysius*, 121–22; translation adapted. Father Martindale notes that September 29 (the date appearing on the second letter) is most likely a slip for September 30, for the letter dated October 1 says that he sent the list "yesterday".

[7] Aloysius Gonzaga to his father, Oct. 1, 1585 in Iozzi, *Lettere*, quoted in Martindale, *Vocation of Saint Aloysius*, 122; translation adapted.

[8] Meschler, *St. Aloysius*, 112.

disposal of the superior so that the spirit of poverty could be maintained.[9] The marquis refused to agree to this provision and demanded that the allowance be canceled. Sadly, it seems that one of the reasons for this was the financial strain the family regularly experienced because of the marquis' gambling problem and his great debts.[10] For his part, Aloysius was willing to have the allowance canceled, but the lawyers noted that any change in the terms of the prince's abdication might make the whole document invalid. Lengthy discussions ensued, and Aloysius became increasingly frustrated, expressing that, as far as he was concerned, they could add as many provisions and clauses to the document as they wished if only they would make haste and get everything finished.[11]

Finally, all the details were completed, and on the morning of November 2, 1585, a meeting was held in the palace of San Sebastiano. Among those present were Vincenzo, the son of Duke William; Prosper Gonzaga (the closest relative); and the other noblemen and ladies who were required to be present as witnesses. Immediately before the ceremony of abdication began, as the marquis was discussing the details with the duke, Aloysius had an argument with some of the assembled noblemen who were ridiculing him for his desire to become a religious, trying to make him change his mind during these final moments.[12] Finally, the ceremony began. As the long document was being read by the notary, Hannibal Persia, tears rolled down Don Ferrante's cheeks. Only Aloysius, who was usually so serious, looked happy. Don Prosper later recalled that he never saw Aloysius as happy as he was on that day.[13] After he had signed the document, he turned to Rudolfo, who could hardly hide his pleasure, and said, "Which

---

[9] Ibid., 113; Cepari, *Life of Saint Aloysius*, 90.

[10] Meschler, *St. Aloysius*, 113. In a letter of April 1, 1584, to Marcellus Donati, secretary of the Duke of Mantua, Don Ferrante wrote the following: "I assure you that I have spent these three years traveling about from house to house, and with the additional expense of my wife and children with me. By so doing, I have considered the reputation of those masters rather than my own welfare. Now that I am home again, I find myself reduced to such an extremity, that this expense will produce what happens in a storm. When the sun is out, the damage is more easily seen than while the tempest rages." Quoted in Cepari, *Life of Saint Aloysius*, 371.

[11] Meschler, *St. Aloysius*, 113.

[12] Ibid., 114.

[13] Cepari, *Life of Saint Aloysius*, 91.

of us two is happier? I am sure it is I."[14] Aloysius was free to enter the Society of Jesus, and Rudolfo, the second son Don Ferrante and Donna Marta, was the heir of the Marquisate of Castiglione.

Did those who were gathered together for the ceremony of abdication have any sense of the true meaning of what was happening? Were they able to discern the plan of God in Aloysius' abdication? Certainly Aloysius did. Faith allowed the prince to look back on all that had taken place in his life and to see that his life had not been made up of a series of random events. Rather, he could discern what Pope Benedict XVI has called "a road that leads to a particular goal".[15] Although Aloysius could have no way of knowing with certainty what the future would hold for him, he did have a perspective on the past and the future that empowered him with a prophetic voice. In his act of abdication, he was offering to his family and to the world a lesson in the difference between what is truly life-giving and what will destroy the future God has planned for us.

Following the ceremony, Aloysius excused himself and, retiring to his room, spent nearly an hour offering prayers of thanksgiving for the grace he had just received.[16] When he had finished his prayers, Aloysius summoned Father Luigi Cattaneo, who had accompanied him from Castiglione, to ask him to bless a Jesuit habit he had

[14] Martindale, *Vocation of Saint Aloysius*, 124.

[15] Joseph Cardinal Ratzinger, *God and the World: A Conversation with Peter Seewald*, trans. Henry Taylor (San Francisco: Ignatius Press, 2002), 61.

[16] Martindale provides a transcription of the following letter to Claudio Aquaviva, attributed to Aloysius but now considered inauthentic, which purports to have been written on the day of the abdication: "My Lord and Father Most Reverend in our Lord, this very day I have stripped off the dress of the 'old man,' and have put on the *vestem novi hominis*—that of the 'new man,' whereof I inform Your Reverence and assure you that I do not know how to thank God for so great a grace most blessed, all the more so as today He has deigned to give me a new consolation, permitting me to follow Him in poverty; for my father is no more prepared to assign to me what he had promised and to which he had bound himself. However he will pay for my journey and incidentals. I also pray the blessed God that He will do all for the best and, if He also thinks it expedient, that my Lord Father find himself in a situation to fulfill his promise in favor of the Society. However, I have letters *ad hoc* both from the Superiors of the college here and from my Lady Mother which I will present to Your Reverence, whom *genibus humiliter flexis ex toto corde* [kneeling humbly and with all my heart] I pray for the love of God to receive me out of charity into the harbor of escape and safety and *quam-primam* [sic] for I will make efforts not to prolong overmuch the visits that I must pay during my journey, and to conclude I kiss your hands: Mantua, November 2, 1585." See Martindale, *Vocation of Saint Aloysius*, 125.

commissioned in Mantua.[17] Taking off his lay clothing, including his undershirt and silken hose, he put on the habit and presented himself in the hall where his relatives had assembled for dinner. The assembled guests were so surprised and moved that no one spoke. The marquis was so overcome with emotion that he wept silently through the remainder of the meal. Aloysius kept up a lively and cheerful conversation, and Cepari records that he spoke with such authority and passion that all who listened to him remembered his words and attitudes for years afterward.[18]

The next day, November 3, Aloysius took leave of Duke William and his childhood friend, Vincenzo, and their wives. That evening, he knelt before his father and mother and asked for their blessing. Aloysius' servant, Clement Ghisoni, later recalled that despite the sorrow and tears of all those present, the young man remained calm and recollected.[19] Indeed, Aloysius had no cause for sorrow. Finally, after years of struggle and suffering, he had gained his heart's desire.

The morning of November 4 saw the former heir of the Marquis of Castiglione, a beloved son and brother, leave the palace as a poor pilgrim, in imitation of his spiritual father, Saint Ignatius Loyola. Among those who were to accompany Aloysius to Rome were Father Luigi Cattaneo; his former tutor, Pietro del Turco; Dr. Giovanni Battista Bono; his valet, James Bellarini; and a handful of other attendants. Rudolfo accompanied him as far as the River Po, where Aloysius embarked for Ferrara.[20] In Ferrara, he said farewell to the duke Alphonsus d'Este and the duchess Margaret Gonzaga. From there, he traveled to Bologna, intending to present himself at Florence to the grand duke Francis. His party was stopped, however, at Pietramala, in Tuscany, because of fear that the group might be carrying the plague. Because they had brought no certificate of health with them, the party returned to Bologna, where Aloysius wrote to apologize to the grand duke for not having been able to visit.[21] He

[17] Cepari, *Life of Saint Aloysius*, 92. See also the letter to his father of September 29, 1585, in Martindale, *Vocation of Saint Aloysius*, 121–22. Pious tradition has recorded that Aloysius had this habit secretly made, but this letter, preserved in the Trivulziana Library in Milan, would indicate that this tradition is incorrect.
[18] Cepari, *Life of Saint Aloysius*, 92.
[19] Ibid.
[20] Ibid., 92–93; Meschler, *St. Aloysius*, 117.
[21] Meschler, *St. Aloysius*, 118.

took this opportunity to fulfill the vow his mother had made at the time of his birth to visit the Shrine of the Holy House (Santuario della Santa Casa) of Loreto.

* * * * *

For centuries, the Holy House of Loreto has been honored as having been the house of the Blessed Virgin and Saint Joseph in Nazareth.[22] Records concerning the building date back to the fourth-century writings of Saint Epiphanius (d. 403), and it is recorded that Saint Louis of France (d. 1270) visited the house, where it was enshrined in the crypt of the church constructed by Saint Helena around the year 330. According to tradition, the House disappeared from Nazareth on the night of May 10, 1291, and was found in Tersatto, Italy, on land that had been barren the day before. The house reportedly remained at Tersatto for three years before disappearing again on December 10, 1294. The house's final resting place was the small town of Loreto, where a hermit on Mount Urso, Paul of the Woods, received a vision of the Blessed Virgin, who identified the house and its origins. In 1310, the house was given official canonical recognition by Pope Clement V (1305–1314).

Inside the house is a wooden statue of the Madonna and Child that measures two feet, eight inches high. This statue, before which Aloysius prayed, was removed by Napoleon's troops in 1797 and was housed for a time in the Louvre. Through the influence of Pope Pius VII (1800–1823), it was returned to the shrine in 1801. The original statue of Our Lady of Loreto was destroyed in a fire in 1921. The present statue is an identical reproduction and was crowned in the Sistine Chapel by Pope Pius XI. Aloysius retained a devotion to the Blessed Virgin through the rest of his life, and it might have been at this time that he purchased a copy of the statue of Our Lady of Loreto, which he kept until his death.[23] Today, this copy is kept in the Franciscan Convent in Vienna.[24]

---

[22] For a fuller treatment of the history of the Holy House of Loreto and its basilica-shrine, see Joan Carroll Cruz, *Relics* (Huntington, Ind.: Our Sunday Visitor, 1984), 172–77.

[23] Martindale, *Vocation of Saint Aloysius*, 127.

[24] This small statue is located in a niche not far from the cloister entrance. A document authenticating the statue states: "This miraculous image belonged to Blessed Aloysius Gonzaga, and is a true copy of the original at Loreto which was also venerated by him. It then

The basilica that shelters the house was begun in 1468. By the time Aloysius visited the shrine in 1585, the house had been enclosed within an encasement of white marble. It is unknown how many pilgrims have visited the shrine through the centuries, but it is thought that more than two hundred of those canonized or beatified by the Church have been to the Holy House, including Saint Ignatius Loyola and Saint Charles Borromeo.

* * * * *

During his visit, Aloysius spent nearly an entire day in the Santa Casa, where he attended a number of Masses and received Communion. He spent the hours reflecting on the hidden years the Holy Family had spent within its walls and offering thanks for the many graces and privileges he had received.[25]

Aloysius' identity and intentions soon became know to the other pilgrims visiting the shrine, and many were edified by the sight of the seventeen-year-old prince who had abandoned wealth and power for a life of poverty and simplicity.[26] On the third day, Aloysius attended Mass and received Communion for a final time before taking leave of the house, setting out on the last stage of his journey to Rome.

Father Meschler offers us a picture of how the young man spent his time during the journey:

> When he rose in the morning, he spent a quarter of an hour in meditation. Then he recited with the chaplain the Little Hours of the Breviary, and finally the Itinerary [his usual daily devotions]. On the way he usually rode alone, occupying himself with vocal prayers or meditation; sometimes, however, he would converse with

---

passed to Prince Hannibal Gonzaga and from him to Princess Isabella Gonzaga; then to her son Philip, Count von Dietrichstein; subsequently to Isabella Ferrarin, and after the death of all these to the reverend Franciscan Fathers. This image has touched the sacred [relic of the] tongue of Saint Anthony of Padua and many other holy relics in Rome. Many wonderful miracles have already been wrought by it. It is about two hundred years old and has at all times been much revered. Given by me in the year 1706. [From] Mary Frances von Schardin, Baroness of Innig." See Cepari, *Life of Saint Aloysius*, 372.

[25] Ibid., 94.

[26] Ibid. See also Margaret Monro, *A Book of Unlikely Saints* (Freeport, N.Y.: Books for Libraries, 1943), 45.

the chaplain on spiritual subjects. He wore a crucifix under his tunic, in order to be constantly reminded of God. His thoughts frequently ran upon the austerities that he hoped now to be allowed to practice, and he pictured to himself the happiness of being sent on the missions to India, like others of his Order. While the horses were being fed at mid-day, he recited Vespers and Compline with the chaplain, and then took a little nourishment. When he arrived at the inn where he and his suite were to spend the night, he at once returned to his room, knelt down before his crucifix and spent an hour or two in prayer. After he had taken the discipline, he recited Matins and Lauds for the following day.[27]

Finally, after several days' travel, the party reached its destination. Upon entering the city, the group first visited the palace of Scipione Gonzaga, the Patriarch of Jerusalem. After a short rest, Aloysius walked to the professed house of the Fathers of the Society of Jesus,[28] the Gesù, to present himself to Claudio Aquaviva, the general of the Society. When Aquaviva met him in the garden, Aloysius fell to his knees and asked the general to accept him as son and subject.[29] Aquaviva kissed the young man's forehead, greeted him warmly, and helped him to rise. Aloysius then gave his new superior a letter from his father.

Most Illustrious and Most Reverend Sir,
My profound respects. In the past I considered it to be my duty to refuse my son permission to enter your holy Society, for I feared that owing to his youth he might embark upon his enterprise without firm resolution. Now I think that I am sure that it is God who is calling him, and so I should feel it on my conscience were I to refuse him the permission that he has longed to receive, and has prayed for from me so urgently and so often. So, freely and willingly, with my mind at peace and full of God's good consolation, I send him and commend him to Your Reverence, who will be to him a more helpful Father than I can be. I have nothing here to add concerning the person of my son. I merely say, that I am giving into Your Reverence's hands the most precious thing that I possess in all the world, and my chief

[27] Meschler, *St. Aloysius*, 119.

[28] Ibid., 120.

[29] Ferrante Gonzaga to Claudio Aquaviva, Nov. 3, 1585, quoted in Martindale, *Vocation of Saint Aloysius*, 129.

hope, that I placed entirely in him, of maintaining and giving glory to my Family: my Family henceforward will regard, as its greatest protection, his prayers and those of Your Reverence, to whom I offer all my respects, and for whom I beg from the Lord all the happiness that you can desire. Your Reverence's most devoted servant,

Mantua, November 3, 1585.[30]

The Prince Marquis of Castiglione

Following Aloysius' audience with Aquaviva, he visited the cardinals Alexander Farnese, Louis d'Este, Carlo Michele "Alessandrino" Bonelli, and Ferdinand de Medici, who was later to become Grand Duke of Tuscany. Cardinals Farnese and Medici were especially kind to the young man, inviting him to stay with them as long as he wished.[31] Declining their invitations, Aloysius then set out to see the seven great stational churches in Rome: St. Paul-Outside-the-Walls, St. John Lateran, St. Mary Major, St. Lawrence-Outside-the-Walls, Santa Croce, St. Sebastian-Outside-the-Walls (also known as St. Sebastian "at the Catacombs"), and, finally, St. Peter's Basilica.[32]

Aloysius' visit to St. Peter's was also the occasion of his audience with Pope Sixtus V (1585–1590), to whom he presented a letter from his father, the marquis. Word of his visit to the Holy Father preceded him, and by the time he arrived at the Vatican, the corridors had filled with courtiers who had come to stare at this Gonzaga who had, as Father Martindale says, "taken all the hereditary force of that family, and had turned it full against what they had always used it for—self-enrichment, self-aggrandizement, self-worship".[33]

On entering the pope's presence, Aloysius, according to the custom of the time, kissed his feet and presented his father's letter. The pope asked him a number of questions about his intentions and how Aloysius had come to choose the Society of Jesus. He also asked the prince if he had seriously considered all the sacrifices and hardships he would face as a religious. He replied that he had; Pope Sixtus granted his approval and offered his blessing.[34]

[30] Martindale, *Vocation of Saint Aloysius*, 129.
[31] Cepari, *Life of Saint Aloysius*, 96.
[32] Ibid.
[33] Martindale, *Vocation of Saint Aloysius*, 132.
[34] Cepari, *Life of Saint Aloysius*, 96.

The following morning, a Sunday, Aloysius heard Mass and received Communion in the chapel of Saints Abundius and Abundantius,[35] located beneath the high altar of the Gesù, after which he heard a sermon.[36] He dined that day with Scipione Cardinal Gonzaga and the Fathers of the Society in their refectory at the invitation of Father Aquaviva. The cardinal was amazed by Aloysius' modesty and manners, remarking on both his prudence and simplicity.[37]

On the morning of November 25, 1585, the Feast of Saint Catherine of Alexandria, who was to be a special patron for Aloysius throughout the remainder of his life, he, with Cardinal Gonzaga and their attendants, went to the Jesuit novitiate at Sant'Andrea on the Quirinal. The cardinal said Mass, and Aloysius received Communion from his hand. Upon entering the Jesuit's house, Aloysius turned to his attendants and urged them to be always mindful of their salvation. He thanked Dr. Bono for having accompanied him, and he ordered his majordomo to go to Livorno and present his letters and respects to the Duke of Tuscany. He also asked his valet to give a special message to his mother.[38] Aloysius then asked Father Cattaneo, the chaplain of the group, to say to the marquis, in his name, "[F]orget your people and your father's house" (Ps 45:10). When asked for a message for Rudolfo, he answered, "Tell him, 'He who fears the Lord will do what is right'" (see Sir 15:1). Finally, Aloysius expressed his sincere thanks to Scipione Gonzaga for his hospitality and kindness. The cardinal began to weep, saying that he envied Aloysius, because he had chosen the better part. As he left, the old prelate told the Jesuits that he was leaving an angel among them.[39]

The master of novices and rector of the Jesuit community took Aloysius to the room which was to be his during his period of probation. In keeping with the customs of the Society, Aloysius would spend these days in silence and solitude. It was, no doubt, a time of great joy and consolation for him. Upon entering his room, the new Jesuit proclaimed, "This is my resting place for ever; here I will dwell,

---

[35] The relics of the fourth-century martyrs Abundius, a priest, and Abundantius, a deacon, were enshrined in a chapel built in their honor in the crypt of the Gesù in 1583, two years before Aloysius' arrival in Rome.

[36] Cepari, *Life of Saint Aloysius*, 98.

[37] Ibid.

[38] Martindale, *Vocation of Saint Aloysius*, 133.

[39] Ibid., 133; Cepari, *Life of Saint Aloysius*, 99.

for I have desired it" (Ps 132:14). As soon as he was alone, he fell to his knees and thanked God as tears of joy fell from his eyes. Father Cepari tells us that "he offered and dedicated himself entirely as a sacrifice and perpetual holocaust to the Divine Majesty, and begged for the grace to dwell worthily in the house of God, and to persevere [until] death in His holy service."[40]

Was Aloysius right or wrong in his determination to follow his call into the "house of God"? Thoughts of sentimentality aside, Aloysius appealed to an argument that Margaret Monro notes is not freely given or gladly heard in our society today: Aloysius Gonzaga appealed to the fact that he had a "direct personal call from God to follow an exceptional line of action".[41] Like so many of the saints who had gone before him—and here we might think of Saint Francis of Assisi or Saint Joan of Arc—Aloysius was chosen by God to undertake a mission that required more of him than mere public or even filial duty. But, Monro goes on to ask, what kind of God would want Aloysius to do such a thing? He had obligations to his family, to his subjects, and to the Church that he could have very well and quite successfully fulfilled as Marquis of Castiglione. Her answer is, rightly, the sort of God who was Incarnate in Jesus.[42]

Aloysius put into action the words of Jesus with all their vibrancy and all their demand, and, for the rest of his life, he would remember the date of his entry into religious life with special devotion.[43] He was the 828th novice to be received into the Roman novitiate of Sant'Andrea. In a folio kept in the archives of the novitiate, entitled *Ingressus Novitiorum ab anno 1569 usque ad 1594*, the following entry is recorded:

Don Aloysius Gonzaga arrived on the 25th of November. He brought with him two cloaks of black cloth, two cassocks, a short and a long one of the same material, one Zimarra [a sleeveless overcoat for indoors] of black cloth, one coat of course cloth of Terni, two doublets, one of Mocajale [a kind of material made from hair], the other of Fustagna [a material that is rough on one side and smooth on the other], two pairs of breeches of Saja [a thin cloth] with hose of

[40] Cepari, *Life of Saint Aloysius*, 99.
[41] Monro, *Unlikely Saints*, 50.
[42] Ibid., 53.
[43] Cepari, *Life of Saint Aloysius*, 99; Meschler, *St. Aloysius*, 124.

the same material, one felt hat, one red under-jacket, twelve shirts, twelve pairs of shoes, twelve pocket-handkerchiefs, nine towels, two pairs of linen stockings, two birettas, one trunk, one picture representing our Savior on the Cross.[44]

It is worth noting that although the inventory of the other novices was valued at ten or twelve *scudi*, the possessions of Aloysius were valued at forty-eight *scudi*, according to the estimate of the brother who took charge of the clothes.[45]

[44] Cepari, *Life of Saint Aloysius*, 372–73.

[45] Ibid., 373. The picture of the Crucifixion included in the list of Aloysius' possessions is preserved in the sacristy of the Cappelletta of Saint Aloysius in the Roman College.

Chapter 11

Rome

The Rome which Aloysius now called home was a dirty, plague-stricken, and dangerous place. Felice Peretti di Montalto assumed the papal throne as Sixtus V on April 24, 1585, only a few months before Aloysius' arrival in the Eternal City.[1] He would serve as Rome's bishop for five years, and his pontificate would be marked by continuing reform and defense of the Church. Pope Sixtus imposed strict discipline upon the clergy of Rome, and, through a series of repressive measures, virtually succeeded in eliminating the crime that plagued the city and the Papal States. He was able to refill the papal coffers through commercial and agricultural reforms, and it was during his reign that the Lateran Palace was completed. Sixtus V also oversaw the completion of the great dome of Saint Peter's Basilica, the construction of the papal residence at the Vatican and a new Vatican Library, and the placing of four great obelisks in the city, including the one in Saint Peter's Square.[2]

Beyond all these achievements, Pope Sixtus V was also a willing supporter of the continuing reforms of Trent. On December 20, 1585, he reestablished the custom of the *ad limina Apostolorum*, which required bishops to make detailed reports of their dioceses to the Holy Father. He was also responsible for the establishment of the fifteen pontifical congregations that oversaw administration of the Church and the Papal States. A Franciscan by religious profession, he honored his former religious community in a number of ways and tended to favor the mendicant orders in their theological and pastoral disputes

---

[1] See J. N. D. Kelly, *Oxford Dictionary of Popes*, rev. by Michael Walsh (New York: Oxford University Press, 2006), 271–73.

[2] R. Po-chia Hsia, *The World of Catholic Renewal, 1540–1770* (New York: Cambridge, 1998), 155.

with the Jesuits. Despite this bias, he was nevertheless a great supporter of the Society's missions in South America, Asia, and England. Sixtus was a vigorous and eloquent man who was born to rule, and he devoted himself wholeheartedly to the renewal of the Church in Rome and around the world.[3]

While the contributions and reforms of this influential pope were far-reaching and significant, there were many others working within the city of Rome and its environs to further the reforms of Trent and to relieve the sufferings of the poor. Among them, we can recognize a group of Roman saints who stand out because of the legacies they left to the Church both in terms of their support and implementation of the reforms and, in some cases, in the religious communities they founded. These were the "movers and shakers" of the Rome that Aloysius now called home.

Saint Philip Neri

Philip Neri was born in Florence in 1515. Considered to be one of the Church's most attractive saints, "his natural gifts of perspicacity, sensitivity, and common-sense realism were crowned by joy, based above all on his perpetual realization of God's presence."[4] The man who would be known as the Apostle of Rome entered the city in 1533, after having spent some time near the great Benedictine Abbey of Monte Cassino, where he developed a love for the liturgy, the Desert Fathers, and stability in the common life.[5] While working as the tutor for the sons of a Florentine customs agent, Philip undertook an intensive study of the thought of Saint Thomas Aquinas. His biographers record that he frequently visited the Seven Pilgrim Churches and spent entire nights in vigil in the catacombs.[6]

---

[3] For a fuller account of the life and work of Pope Sixtus V, see D. R. Campbell, "Sixtus V, Pope", in the *Catholic Encyclopedia* (Washington, D.C.: Catholic University of America Press, 2003), 13:197–99.

[4] Paul Burns and David Hugh Farmer, eds., *Butler's Lives of the Saints: New Full Edition; May* (Collegeville, Minn.: Liturgical Press, 1996), 144. Philip was known for his eccentricities, which he cultivated to avoid a "cult of personality" among the people and to disarm nobles who came to him for direction. See Enzo Lodi, *Saints of the Roman Calendar*, trans. Jordan Aumann (Staten Island, N.Y.: St. Paul's, 1992), 128.

[5] Burns and Farmer, *Butler's; May*, 144.

[6] See, for instance, Hsia, *Catholic Renewal*, 130.

Ordained a priest in 1551, Philip felt called to give himself over to the service of the poor. Inspired by the witness of Saints Ignatius Loyola and Francis Xavier, whom he numbered among his friends, he began working among the poor at the Hospital of San Giacomo, ministering to both the bodies and the souls of the patients. It was here that he came to know Saint Camillus de Lellis, who had sought out Philip's advice and support in his own efforts to establish his Servants of the Sick. Desiring a life in community, Philip associated himself with the priestly fraternity at San Girolamo. His days were marked by the daily celebration of the Mass, hearing confession, preaching, presiding at Eucharistic devotions, and serving those who came to San Girolamo for food and lodging. These ministries would become the principal works of the congregation he was to found.[7]

Philip gathered around him a number of directees who accompanied him on his visits to the Seven Pilgrim Churches and who came together for the recitation of vespers. This group formed what became the nucleus for the Congregation of the Oratory (the Oratorians). One of the most important aspects of Philip's Oratory was that it attracted men from every walk of life. Regardless of a man's former wealth or rank, it was Neri's expectation that all would serve in the hospitals and collect food, clothing, and money for the poor. Another of his innovations was his use of musical and dramatic presentations with sermons as a means of attracting crowds to the Oratories, an effort that laid the groundwork for the musical genre that would come to be known as the *oratorio*.[8] For Philip, the Christian life was characterized by a spirit of joy, and he often told his followers, "A servant of God ought to always be happy."[9] It was his own spirit of cheerfulness that attracted many men and women, great and poor alike, to this dynamic, if not eccentric, man.

Not everyone favored Philip's innovations. Both Pope Paul IV (1555–1559) and Pope Saint Pius V (1566–1572) called him to appear before the Holy Office (the Inquisition). Church authorities at one point even decided to close the Oratory, but the congregation was saved through the intervention of Saint Charles Borromeo. While

[7] Owen Chadwick, *The Reformation* (New York: Penguin, 1990), 279.

[8] Ibid., 437; Richard P. McBrien, *Lives of the Saints: From Mary and St. Francis of Assisi to John XXIII and Mother Teresa* (New York: HarperCollins, 2001), 213.

[9] Lodi, *Saints*, 129.

these trials caused Philip much pain, he endured it all with patience, humility, and even humor.[10]

It was during the pontificate of Pope Gregory XIII (1572–1585) that the Congregation of the Oratory received official approval as a community of secular priests. This new form of clerical life provided Neri's followers with a way of focusing their zeal, contributing significantly to the renewal of the priesthood in general.[11] Gregory was the same pontiff who approved the reforms of the Carmelite Teresa of Avila. He went so far as to offer the Oratorians a gift of eight thousand crowns to aid in the building of their community's mother church, the Chiesa Nuova. The years immediately following the official approval of the Congregation of the Oratory saw the foundation of new houses in Naples and in a number of other Italian cities, as well as a steady increase in the number of candidates.[12]

Philip's greatest gift to the people of Rome was his very presence. His days were spent in offering God's mercy to the many penitents who came to him and to teaching and encouraging those struggling with their faith. Philip advocated reading the Bible and frequent reception of the sacraments. He spent what was to be the final day of his life celebrating Mass and hearing confessions. Historians credit him with introducing to Italy the practice of the Forty Hours' Devotion in honor of the Blessed Sacrament.[13] In tribute to his zeal and vision, one of his contemporaries said of him, "With the Word of God he miraculously enkindled in many men a holy love of Christ. He had nothing else in mind but to put them on fire with the desire for prayer, for frequentation of the Sacraments and for works of charity."[14]

Saint Philip Neri suffered a stroke on the night of May 25, 1595, and died the next day. Following his canonization in 1622 (in the same ceremony as Ignatius Loyola, Francis Xavier, Teresa of Avila,

[10] Burns and Farmer, *Butler's; May*, 146.

[11] Michael J. Buckley, "Seventeenth-Century French Spirituality", in *Christian Spirituality: Post-Modern and Modern*, ed. Louis Dupré and Don E. Saliers in collaboration with John Meyendorff (New York: Crossroad Publishing, 1989), 44.

[12] Antonio Gallonio, *The Life of Saint Philip Neri* (San Francisco: Ignatius Press, 2005), 151.

[13] Keith P. Luria, "The Counter-Reformation and Popular Spirituality", in Dupré, Saliers, and Meyendorff, *Christian Spirituality*, 115.

[14] Burns and Farmer, *Butler's; May*, 147.

and Isidore the Farmer), the Congregation of the Oratory came to spread beyond Italy, and today, houses of Oratorians can be found all over the world.

Saint Alexander Sauli

Alexander Sauli has long been considered the ideal of a Tridentine bishop. Born in Milan in 1534, he received a good education and served as a page in the Milanese court under Emperor Charles V. A devout young man, he gave up a promising secular career to join the Clerks Regular of Saint Paul (the Barnabites), the community founded by Saint Antony Zaccaria (1502–1539). Proving that his former wealth and status would be no obstacle to his success in the order, he was ordained in 1556 and was appointed to teach philosophy and theology at the University of Pavia. As time passed, he gained a reputation for his skill as a preacher who urged his hearers to return to the sacraments and who promoted the Forty Hours' Devotion. Alexander was, in fact, so highly respected that he eventually became the confessor of both Saint Charles Borromeo and (the future) Pope Gregory XIV (1590–1591). In 1567, he was named provost general of the Barnabites; and, in his lifetime, he was celebrated as its "father, lawgiver, and model".[15]

In 1570, Pope Saint Pius V appointed Alexander as Bishop of Aleria in Corsica. Alexander, a firm and zealous reformer, worked there for more than twenty years, building a cathedral and seminary, preaching, and caring for his people, even as he faced plague and threats of violence to his person. During his time in Aleria, he visited Rome on several occasions and became a friend of Philip Neri, who regarded him as the model of a reforming bishop. In 1591, he was appointed to serve as Bishop of Pavia but died on October 11, 1592, before being able to claim jurisdiction of his new diocese.

Although little known to many today, Alexander is remembered as having been both a capable administrator and a gifted, caring pastor. Among his writings are a large number of pastoral and catechetical

[15] Paul Burns and Peter Doyle, eds., *Butler's Lives of the Saints: New Full Edition; October* (Collegeville, Minn.: Liturgical Press, 1996), 73.

works, including the *Doctrine of the Roman Catechism*. This good and faithful shepherd was beatified in 1742 and canonized in 1904.

Saint John Leonardi

John was born in Lucca, Tuscany, around the year 1542. A pharmacist by trade, he left that profession and was ordained a priest in 1572. Following his ordination, he served in hospitals and prisons throughout the city and brought together a group of young laymen to share in his work. This new community lived in common and shared lives of prayer and ministry. John developed a special interest in Christian education according to the ideals of the Council of Trent, and he believed that the Church could be reformed only through a return to basic Christian values. He also recognized that this reform must begin with the young.[16] Although he met strong opposition, he founded the Order of Clerks Regular of the Mother of God (the Matritani) in 1574. In 1583, the Bishop of Lucca gave his support to this work and, under Pope Gregory XIII, the community was organized as an association of secular priests with simple vows of poverty, chastity, and obedience. John also benefited from his friendship with Saint Philip Neri and Saint Joseph Calasanz, the founder of the Piarist Fathers.

In 1595, Pope Clement VIII (1592–1605) officially recognized the community as a religious congregation. It was at this time that John was asked to reform a number of monasteries, and he also became involved in establishing a new Roman seminary for training priests bound for the foreign missions. Under Pope Urban VIII (1623–1644), this seminary became the Collegium de Propaganda Fide.[17]

Father Leonardi published a manual on preaching in 1574 and wrote a large number of books on theology and educational works that addressed the duties of both parents and children. Ultimately, his work became an important part of the Tridentine reforms.[18]

John Leonardi died on October 9, 1609, of plague, contracted while caring for the sick. Today his congregation has fifteen houses in

[16] Ibid., 52.
[17] McBrien, *Lives of the Saints*, 415.
[18] Burns and Doyle, *Butler's; October*, 53.

Italy as well as one other European foundation and a community in Nigeria. Saint John was beatified in 1861 and canonized in 1938.

Saint Camillus de Lellis

This patron of the sick was born in 1550 in Bocchianico di Chieti, Italy. The son of a noble family, he had a distinguished military career, and at age seventeen, he joined the Venetian forces in their fight against the Turks. Noted for his exceptional height (six feet, six inches), he was a large man with a quick temper and a gambling addiction.[19] Because of an ulcer that developed on his leg, he traveled to Rome and was a resident for a time in the San Giacomo Hospital for Incurables. He did return to military service, but after he had gambled away his inheritance, his military equipment, and weapons, he was discharged. Camillus even lost his shirt, which was taken off his back in the streets of Naples in 1574.[20]

Reduced to extreme poverty, he took a job as a laborer at a Capuchin friary in Manfredonia. Under the guidance of the guardian of the community, he began to lead a life of penance; and, in 1575, he asked to be accepted as a member of the community. His ulcer, which had still not healed, prevented his entrance, so he returned to San Giacomo in Rome to devote himself to the care of the sick.[21]

Camillus became both a devoted, skilled nurse and a successful administrator, eventually being named bursar of the hospital. As his work progressed, he became ever more convinced that the patients needed more than just medical care. He recognized a lack of compassion in those who nursed the sick. The nurses with whom he worked often neglected the patients and gave bad witness by the immoral quality of their lives.[22] With the approval of Philip Neri, who was his spiritual advisor, Camillus separated himself from the Hospital of San Giacomo, and, with two companions, he set out on his own. He

---

[19] P. Mario Vanti, *St. Camillus: The Saint of the Red Cross* (Milwaukee, Wis.: St. Camillus Campus, 1998), 6.

[20] Paul Burns and Peter Doyle, eds., *Butler's Lives of the Saints: New Full Edition; July* (Collegeville, Minn.: Liturgical Press, 2000), 100.

[21] Vanti, *St. Camillus*, 9–10.

[22] Burns and Doyle, *Butler's, July*, 100.

wanted to establish a company of men who "would consecrate themselves to the sick purely out of love of God and would wear a cross
as their badge".[23] The companions began working in the Hospital of
Santo Spirito in Rome, and they earned great respect because of the
quality of care they provided their patients and for the virtue of their
lives. In the midst of all this activity, Camillus was ordained a priest
in 1584.

The following year, Camillus rented a larger house and drew up a
rule of life for the men who had come to serve with him. His vision
for the company was that they would dedicate themselves to serving
plague victims, prisoners, and those suffering in private homes. For
a religious habit, the men wore a simple black tunic with a large red
cross on the breast and on their capes. Pope Sixtus V granted provi-
sional approval to the company in 1586. The new Congregation of
Servants of the Sick (the Camillians) received formal approval from
Pope Gregory XIV in 1591. That same year, Camillus and twenty-
five others made solemn vows, adding to the three vows of poverty,
chastity, and obedience a fourth vow of "perpetual physical and spiritual assistance to the sick, especially those with the plague".[24] In
1595 and 1601, some of the brothers traveled to Hungary and Cro-
atia to care for those wounded on the battlefield, becoming the first
recorded medical field unit. Camillus was so zealous in his care and
concern for the sick-poor, that he is recorded to have said: "If there
were no poor people in the world, it would be necessary to dig to the
center of the earth to look for them and rescue them, to show them
compassion and do them good."[25]

Camillus recognized the value of modern methods of hygiene and
medical care. He insisted that the order's hospitals have proper venti-
lation, suitable food, and isolation for those suffering from infectious
diseases. He urged his nurses to recognize Christ in the sick, and he
adopted as his guiding principle Christ's words, "[A]s you did it to
one of the least of these my brethren, you did it to me" (Mt 25:40).

Camillus de Lellis served as superior general of the order until
1607. This quick-tempered, volatile man came to be known for his

---

[23] Ibid.
[24] Ibid.
[25] Lodi, *Saints*, 185.

care and tender concern for his patients; to him, service of the sick
was service of Christ himself.[26] Saint Camillus died on July 14, 1614.
Canonized in 1746, he was named patron of the sick in 1886 by Pope
Leo XIII (1878–1903) and patron of nurses in 1930 by Pope Pius XI.
The Order of Servants of the Sick spread quickly after his death, and
two female branches were established in the nineteenth century.

Saint Joseph Calasanz

Joseph Calasanz (or Calasanctius), the holy founder who was honored as being a "perpetual miracle of fortitude and another Job", was
born in 1556 to an aristocratic family near Petralta de la Sal in Ara-
gon, Spain.[27] Educated at the Universities of Valencia and Lérida, he
earned a doctorate in law before transferring to Alcalá to study theology. In 1583, Joseph was ordained a priest and, over the next few
years, held a variety of administrative posts in various parts of Spain
before being named vicar general of the Diocese of Trempe.

From the beginning of his ministry, Joseph was interested in
improving the quality of education available in poor communities.
In 1592, he resigned his benefices, divided his patrimony among his
sisters and the poor, and traveled to Rome. In the Eternal City, he
befriended Camillus de Lellis and, with him, cared for the sick during
a plague that ravaged the city in 1595. His particular interest in education inspired him to become a member of the Congregation of
Christian Doctrine, which taught adults and children on Sundays
and holy days. He recognized that there were really no educational
opportunities for abandoned and homeless children and that no religious orders were even attempting to provide for their needs.

Joseph asked the parish schools to accept homeless children at no
fee, but the teachers refused, insisting that they would do so only
if their salaries were increased. After the Roman Senate refused to
make these salary increases, Joseph asked the Jesuits and Dominicans for help, but both orders were already overextended by the

---

[26] Vanti, *St. Camillus*, 17.

[27] Prospero Cardinal Lambertini (the future Pope Benedict XIV [1740–1758]) to the Congregation of Sacred Rites in 1728.

responsibility of caring for their own institutions. This led him to make a decision that would have a profound and lasting impact on the future of education: Joseph decided that he would open a school himself. The school he established in the parish of Santa Dorotea in 1597 became the first free school in Rome. There, together with two companions, he received more than one hundred children in the first week. These numbers increased rapidly, and by 1599, he and his companions had to find a new location for their community and school. By this time, Joseph was acting as unofficial superior of a fledgling religious community that would eventually become the Order of Clerks Regular of the Mother of God of the Pious School. (Today they are more commonly known as the Piarists or Scolopi Fathers.) Despite his noble intentions, Joseph was harshly criticized in certain circles because of a commonly held belief that, if the poor were educated, there would be no one left to do their jobs in society.[28] This unrest would increase over the years, contributing to the dissent that erupted within the order at the end of the holy founder's life. While the community's spirituality was largely influenced by the writings of Ignatius Loyola, it was their unique fourth vow to educate the poor, and their emphasis on poverty formed the true basis of the Piarists' spirituality.[29] The order's members had a great reverence for the Blessed Sacrament and to the Blessed Virgin, under the title "Our Lady of the Pious Schools".

By 1602, Joseph and his followers had more than seven hundred students and benefited from the patronage of Popes Clement VIII and Paul V. During this period, the community also began accepting students from wealthier families, and, in 1612, with papal approval, Joseph transferred the work to the Torres Palace, near the Church of San Pantaleone. Following the move, the number of students increased to more than twelve hundred and included a number of Jewish boys whom Joseph had invited to attend. Other schools were founded, and the Piarists came to enjoy the support of a number of Roman prelates. Even with this patronage, however, Joseph insisted

[28] McBrien, *Lives of the Saints*, 346.

[29] Paul F. Grendler, "The Piarists of the Pious Schools", in *Religious Orders of the Catholic Reformation: In Honor of John C. Olin on His Seventy-Fifth Birthday*, ed. Richard L. DeMolen (New York: Fordham University Press, 1994), 264.

that the Piarists themselves seek out the funds necessary to maintain and educate their students. The religious went door-to-door, begging for wood for the school and for grain, wine, and olive oil to feed the teachers. In this way, the Piarists were somewhat distinct from other orders founded during this period, who did not make begging an integral part of their efforts to raise funds to support their works.[30]

For a time, the Piarists were united with the Matritani, the congregation founded by Saint John Leonardi; however, in 1617, Pope Paul V again separated the two orders and granted the Piarists papal approbation. The new congregation elected Joseph as superior, and in 1621, Pope Gregory XVI (1831–1846) gave them full ecclesiastical recognition, approving their Rule the following year.

While the Piarists were the first of the Reformation-era orders of men to be dedicated solely to education, Joseph would often use what time he could spare to care for the sick and needy outside the school.[31] He urged his followers to give themselves wholeheartedly to their ministry, writing, "All who undertake to teach must be endowed with deep love, the greatest patience, and, most of all, profound humility. They must perform their work with earnest zeal."[32] Although he was highly regarded by many in Rome, divisions developed among the ranks of the Piarists themselves. Mario Sozzi, a Piarist priest who had begun to work independently of the order, encouraged this division and made unjust accusations against Joseph to the Holy Office. Although there were some in the ranks of the hierarchy who came to his defense, Joseph (who was then eighty-five years old) was arrested by the Inquisition, and only the intervention of Alessandro Cardinal Cesarini the younger saved him from imprisonment.[33] Sozzi used the arrest as an opportunity to seize control of the congregation, claiming that Joseph was senile. The founder was suspended from office, and Joseph suffered constant humiliations at the hands of Sozzi and his associates. Finally, in 1645, a committee of cardinals was appointed to examine the issue, and Calasanz was

[30] Ibid., 263.
[31] Ibid., 262.
[32] Lodi, *Saints*, 246–47.
[33] Paul Burns and John Cumming, eds., *Butler's Lives of the Saints: New Full Edition; August* (Collegeville, Minn.: Liturgical Press, 1998), 247.

reinstated as superior. Sadly, however, in 1646, Pope Innocent X (1644–1655) suppressed the Piarists, reducing the congregation to a society of priests under the direction of the diocesan bishop.

Joseph, who was now ninety, suffered all this patiently and quietly. He forgave all those who worked against him and died peacefully on August 25, 1648. The congregation was restored in 1656, and their right to have solemn vows was restored in 1669. Today, the Piarists have houses throughout the world, and, since 1948, Joseph, who was canonized in 1767, has been honored as patron of Christian schools.

Saint Robert Bellarmine

Robert Cardinal Bellarmine was born in 1542 in the town of Montepulciano in Tuscany. Called "the greatest little man on earth", he is remembered as having had one of the most engaging minds and personalities of the age.[34] The nephew of Pope Marcellus II (1555), he received a superior education, and by the time he was eighteen, he had mastered, in addition to the usual core curriculum, the violin, debate and rhetoric, and the art of writing Latin verse.[35] His parents hoped he might become a medical doctor, but, after Robert spent three years studying under the Jesuits in Montepulciano, he decided to enter the Society. In 1560, he was clothed as a novice of the Society in Rome, and by 1563, he was working as a teacher, first in Florence, then in Mondovi. Having studied theology in Padua and Louvain, Belgium, he was ordained in 1570.

Robert taught at the University of Louvain from 1569 to 1576, where he became noted for his pedagogical skill and mature mind, and he was the first Jesuit commissioned to give lectures on the teaching of Saint Thomas Aquinas.[36] When he was not engaged in the classroom, he was occupied in a study of the writers of the Protestant Reformation. This laid the foundation for what would become

---

[34] Paul Burns and Sarah Fawcett Thomas, eds., *Butler's Lives of the Saints: New Full Edition; September* (Collegeville, Minn.: Liturgical Press, 2000), 155.

[35] Ibid.

[36] John F. Fink, *The Doctors of the Church: An Introduction to the Church's Great Teachers*, vol. 2, *Doctors of the Second Millennium* (Staten Island, N.Y.: St. Paul's, 2000), 161.

his own style of "controversial theology", which focused on those questions and controversies facing the Church.[37] Bellarmine was a skilled preacher who recognized that sermons were a powerful means of promoting Christian teaching and spirituality.

In 1576, Robert returned to Rome, where he taught "controversial theology" at the Jesuit's Roman College, the Gregorianum.[38] The lectures he gave formed the basis for his great theological treatise *Disputationes de Controversiis Christianae Fidei adversus huius Temporis Haereticos* (Disputations on the Controversies of the Christian Faith against the Heretics of the Age). This work, which was published in three volumes between 1586 and 1593, was so highly regarded that many believed it had been the work of a team of scholars. In the decades that followed, it became essential reading for those engaged in theological study.[39]

During his time at the Roman College, Robert served as one of the spiritual directors for the Jesuit students, including Aloysius Gonzaga, with whom he formed a strong bond. Besides Aloysius, Father Bellarmine also counseled those Jesuit men who were destined for England, where many of them would die for their faith. In 1592, he was appointed rector of the college.

In addition to his responsibilities within the Society, Bellarmine was involved in the publication of a new edition of the Latin *Vulgate* and worked on the commission responsible for revising the Church's liturgical calendar in accord with the mandates of the Council of Trent. He also worked on the new catechism *A Short Christian Doctrine*, which remained in use for more than three hundred years. Pope Sixtus V called upon him to aid in the theological and political disputes between the so-called Catholic League and Henry of Navarre, the Huguenot king of France (1589–1610).

In 1594, Robert was appointed as provincial of the Jesuit Province of Naples. Earning a reputation as a devoted and conscientious leader, Bellarmine was summoned back to Rome by Pope Clement VIII, who in 1599 named him a cardinal. Although he adopted the dress and many of the customs of a Roman prelate of this age, he remained

[37] Burns and Thomas, *Butler's; September*, 155.
[38] Ibid., 156.
[39] Ibid.

a Jesuit at heart. He lived simply, giving away surplus food to the poor and refusing gifts which would have compromised his neutrality and poverty.[40]

In 1602, Bellarmine was appointed Archbishop of Capua. Again, he proved himself to be a capable administrator and pastor. Loved by his clergy and people, he worked for their benefit, becoming personally involved in the welfare work of his diocese. In 1605, Robert was nearly chosen to be the successor of Pope Leo XI, who died after only twenty-six days in office.[41] The man elected, Pope Paul V, immediately appointed him as prefect of the Vatican Library and asked him to serve on a number of the Roman congregations. Accepting these posts, Robert resigned as Archbishop of Capua and returned to Rome. He would stay in the Eternal City for the rest of his life.

Because of his many skills and brilliant mind, Cardinal Bellarmine found himself involved in the great theological controversies of his day. Among these was the case of Galileo Galilei (d. 1642), whom Bellarmine numbered among his friends. Galileo accepted the theory of Nicolaus Copernicus (d. 1543) that the earth and other planets revolved around the sun. This theory contradicted the then-commonly held teaching that the earth was the center of the universe. During the first stages of Galileo's trial, Bellarmine was able to prevent his friend's condemnation by the Holy Office, but he also urged Galileo to protect himself by acknowledging the difference between hypothesis and proven fact.[42] In the end, Bellarmine was himself unable to avoid the rigid, literal interpretation of Scripture that was the basis for the condemnation of Galileo.[43] Robert was no longer alive when Galileo was finally condemned by the Holy Office in 1633.

In his final years, Bellarmine dedicated himself to writing a number of devotional works, including *De Ascensione Mentis in Deum* (*The Mind's Ascent to God*) and *De Arte Bene Moriendi* (*The Art of Dying Well*). His personal life was permeated with a spirit of joy, and he

---

[40] Ibid.

[41] Chadwick asserts that Bellarmine would have been elected pope, had he not been a Jesuit. See Chadwick, *Reformation*, 315.

[42] Fink, *Doctors of the Church*, 166.

[43] Burns and Thomas, *Butler's; September*, 158.

remained faithful to his Jesuit vocation. Although he was small of stature, he was a man of great presence who attracted many to himself with his quick wit and brilliant mind.[44]

Robert Bellarmine retired to the Jesuit novitiate in Rome at Sant'Andrea in 1621. Following his death on September 17, 1621, he was celebrated for his contributions to his order, to the cause of the Catholic Reformation, and to the life of the Church at large. Canonized in 1930, he was named a Doctor of the Church in 1931.

* * * * *

Throughout this period, the Jesuits, for their part, supported the works of these reformers and founders and were involved in the life of the Church in Rome in a number of ways. To understand the culture and attitudes of the Society in which Aloysius placed himself, we must seek to understand more fully how and why the Jesuits stood out from the other religious communities of their day.

From its inception, the Society was undeniably formed by the *Spiritual Exercises* and the spiritual vision of Ignatius Loyola. A second, but no less influential, document was what is generally referred to as the Formula of the Institute. The result of deliberations primarily among the original companions, it sought to establish a common vision for the Society that would succeed in obtaining the much-desired papal approval.[45] The original document was revised in 1550 and incorporated into the bull *Exposcit Debitum*, which confirmed the Society of Jesus. The most notable change contained in the 1550 version was specification that the Society's primary purpose was for the "defense and propagation of the faith".[46] This goal was to be achieved through ministries of

> public preaching, lectures, and any other ministrations whatsoever of the Word of God, and further by means of the *Spiritual Exercises*, the education of children and unlettered persons in Christianity, and

[44] Ibid.

[45] John W. O'Malley, S.J., *The First Jesuits* (Cambridge, Mass.: Harvard University Press, 1993), 5.

[46] Ibid.

the spiritual consolation of Christ's faithful through hearing confessions and administering the sacraments. Moreover, the Society should
show itself no less useful in reconciling the estranged, in holily assisting and serving those who are found in prisons and hospitals, and
indeed in performing any other works of charity, according to what
will seem expedient for the glory of God and the common good.[47]

Although schools were omitted from this list, the Jesuits were already
involved in the apostolate of education by this time, and the Society's emphasis on the value of education would only increase in the
coming decades.[48]

The *Constitutions of the Society of Jesus* later developed in detail
the ideals contained in the Formula. Only six months after the ratification of the Formula, Ignatius was elected superior, and the responsibility of composing a set of constitutions fell to him. Assisted
by his secretary, Juan Alfonso de Polanco, Ignatius presented the
first version for approval in 1552. The *Constitutions* were eventually approved by the First General Chapter of the Society of Jesus
(1558–1559), which was convoked to elect the successor to Ignatius
Loyola. Ignatius had continued to modify the document until the
time of his death.[49] Although the *Constitutions* are primarily a collection of laws and ideals, they also served indirectly as a discernment
tool for those contemplating entrance into the Society.[50] It is worth
remembering, however, that because of the nature of the Society
and the diversity of its ministries, the members often spoke of "our
way of proceeding" (*noster modus procedendi / nuestro modo de proceder*),
a term which was said to have originated with Ignatius and made
reference to ideas and charisms that transcended the formal documents of the Society, distinguishing Jesuit life and ministry from that
of other religious orders.[51]

The experiences of the Jesuits during the first decades of their existence led to new visions and directions for the Society, but behind

---

[47] *The Constitutions for the Society of Jesus*, trans. George E. Ganss (St. Louis: The Institute of
Jesuit Sources, 1970), 66–67, quoted in ibid.
[48] See John W. O'Malley, S.J., "The Society of Jesus", in DeMolen, *Religious Orders*, 149–52.
[49] O'Malley, *First Jesuits*, 7.
[50] Ibid. We may recall that Aloysius had carefully studied the *Constitutions* during his stay
in Mantua after making the *Spiritual Exercises* a part of his discernment of his own vocation.
[51] Ibid.

these more transient aspects of Jesuit identity lay more general-
ized patterns of "organization, membership, and self-determination
that [were] crucial for understanding the Jesuits' pastoral vision and
enterprise".[52]

The Jesuits opened their first school for extern (non-Jesuit) students at Messina in 1568.[53] With the establishment of their first university at Padua in 1542, and other universities throughout Europe,
including the Roman (or Urban) College in 1551, the Jesuits came
to be considered a teaching order.[54] A testament to the Society's zeal
for education was their involvement with the college in Goa, India,
which began in 1543, the year after the establishment of the university
at Padua. As we have seen, the Society's priests dedicated themselves
to educating and forming leaders for the Catholic Church by means
that quite effectively challenged and even halted the advancement of
Protestant and secular ideologies.[55]

According to the *Constitutions*, there were essentially two types
of schools that the Society might operate. The first was a college
where the humanities and Christian doctrine were taught. The second model was the university, where the higher disciplines of logic,
metaphysics, ethics, the sciences, mathematics, and theology formed
the curriculum.[56] The Roman College (*Collegio Romano*) combined
these two models, and the school's founders hoped to model the
Collegio's curriculum on what the early Jesuits had experienced at
the University of Paris.[57]

Although the Society's earliest academic endeavors were inspired
by a concern to educate their own members, the responsibility of
training diocesan clergy soon became one of their concerns as well.
By the beginning of the 1560s, the Roman College had become
the international meeting place for Jesuit priests and clerics. Students
from Italy, Spain, Portugal, France, Flanders, Germany, Bohemia,

[52] Ibid., 51.

[53] Christopher Chapple, "Quest for Identity: The Ideals of Jesuit Education in the Sixteenth Century", in *The Jesuit Tradition in Education and Missions: A 450-Year Perspective*, ed.
Christopher Chapple (Scranton, Penn.: University of Scranton Press, 1993), 20–21.

[54] Chadwick, *Reformation*, 262.

[55] Ibid.

[56] O'Malley, *First Jesuits*, 215.

[57] Ibid., 216.

Dalmatia, Greece, and elsewhere were studying at the Roman College.[58] Ignatius sought to ensure that the college's professors were the best the Society had to offer, and his successors continued to share his vision for the future of the school. In time, non-Jesuits were also admitted to the Roman College (and later the German College, as well), but in the minds of the Jesuit superiors, its special character was its importance in forming Jesuit clerics.[59]

Another key institution for the formation of new members of the Society was the novitiate. The Roman novitiate of Sant'Andrea, the house on the Quirinal that was used by the Society's novices in Rome, including Aloysius, was presented to the third general of the Society, Saint Francis Borgia, in 1566 by the Duchess of Tagliacozzo. The previous year, the Bishop of Tivoli had given the small parish Church of Sant'Andrea to Borgia, who established a residence there for sick priests previously residing at the Gesù, the house of the finally professed Jesuits in Rome. It was here that another Jesuit novice, Stanislaus Kostka (whose life shares many parallels with that of Aloysius), died on August 15, 1568. By the time Aloysius entered the novitiate in 1585, the complex had significantly expanded and housed hundreds of Jesuit novices destined to serve the Society and the Church throughout the world.

Saint Stanislaus Kostka

Stanislaus Kostka was born in the castle of Rostkowo, Poland, in October 1550.[60] Born in a time when nearly half the population of

[58] Ibid., 233.

[59] Ibid., 234.

[60] In reading accounts of the life of this young saint, it is easy to recognize the hagiographical conventions used by devotional writers of the past centuries. Numerous anecdotes contained in the traditional lives of Saint Stanislaus are also to be found in the life of Saint Aloysius and other young saints, including a third Jesuit youth, Saint John Berchmans. So closely were Stanislaus and Aloysius identified with one another that a vita of Stanislaus dating from 1870 includes a novena (see Appendix C) that could be offered to either saint, depending on the preference of the reader. Despite the use of these conventions, Saint Stanislaus should nonetheless be honored for his simple, heartfelt piety and for his devotion to Mary and the saints, in whose intercession he found the consolation and courage he needed to face the vicissitudes of a difficult, lonely childhood and the challenges of religious life. Saint Stanislaus is commemorated in the *Roman Martyrology* on August 15.

Poland (which included Lithuania and fragments of other countries) was Greek or Russian Orthodox and when members of a number of Protestant sects were winning large numbers of converts in the country's relatively tolerant atmosphere, Stanislaus was raised as a Catholic and was noted for his childhood piety. The son of a member of the Polish Parliament, he was educated by a private tutor until he was fourteen, at which time he was sent to study in the Jesuit college at Vienna. Stanislaus felt very much at home in the college where, accompanied by his older brother, Paul, he was highly regarded for his hard work and sharp mind. In 1564, the brothers and their tutor left the college and took up residence in the home of a Lutheran family. Despite Stanislaus' objections to living in the home of "heretics", the brothers stayed in their new lodgings. Outside the Jesuit school, the boy became an object of derision to his peers and suffered a great deal at the hands of his own brother, whose teasing soon turned to bullying. Disregarding his rank and his brother's attitudes, Stanislaus dressed modestly and was especially resentful of having to attend dancing lessons, preferring to keep his own company instead. The boy received Communion as often as he could, and when he was not attending classes or in church, he could be found studying or praying in his room.

After living what seems to be a fairly miserable existence for nearly two years, the young man suffered a sort of breakdown.[61] Believing himself to be near death, he asked for the last sacraments. Dismissing the boy's request, the Lutheran landlord refused to allow the Blessed Sacrament to be brought into his home. Stanislaus prayed to his patron, the virgin-martyr Saint Barbara, and, according to his own testimony, his prayer was answered when two angels brought Holy Communion to him in his sickroom.[62] At this time, he was also comforted by a vision of our Lady in which he was told that it was not time for him to die and that he should enter the Society of Jesus. Having already considered this possibility himself, he went to the Jesuit provincial in Vienna and asked for admission. Fearing that he might anger Stanislaus' father, the provincial refused. Undeterred by

[61] Burns and Cumming, *Butler's; August*, 156.
[62] *The Life of St. Stanislaus Kostka of the Society of Jesus, Patron of Novices* (Baltimore: Kelly, Piet, 1870), 33–35.

the provincial's answer, the boy decided to go to Rome to seek the permission of the superior general himself.

On August 10, 1567, Stanislaus set out for Rome on foot—a 350-mile journey. Although his brother and tutor tried to find him, they were unable to track him down. In Dillingen, he was kindly received by Saint Peter Canisius, who recognized the boy's virtues and encouraged him in his endeavor. Having proven himself to Canisius, he was sent on his way, finally reaching Rome on October 25. The general of the Society, Saint Francis Borgia, admitted him immediately. Stanislaus was clothed in the Jesuit habit on October 28; he was seventeen years old.

Jan Kostka, Stanislaus' father, was infuriated by his son's actions and ordered him to return to Poland. Attacking his son for choosing a profession that was beneath his station, Jan went so far as to threaten to have the Jesuits chased from Poland. Standing firm in his resolution, Stanislaus refused to give in to his father's demands and stayed in Rome. Known as a model religious, his observance of the Rule was exemplary, and he was held in high regard for his devotion and piety.

Stanislaus' life as a member of the Society was to be a joyful but brief time for him. Suffering from the heat and pestilence that ravaged Rome in the summer of 1568, he became seriously ill on August 10 and died early on the morning of the Feast of the Assumption, August 15. Claiming to see the Blessed Virgin surrounded by angels, he died peacefully at the novitiate of Sant'Andrea, surrounded by his Jesuit confreres.

As devotion to the young Jesuit spread, Stanislaus came to be a significant part of the Jesuits' mission in Poland. Honored as the second patron of Poland, he was canonized with Saint Aloysius in 1726.

* * * * *

The Jesuit novitiate lasted for two years (rather than the single year common for many other religious communities) and was distinctive because of its emphasis on external ministries and time of pilgrimage. Following the second year, the novice took the vows of poverty, chastity, and obedience and entered the scholasticate, where he received intensive training and education in one of the Jesuit's colleges in the hopes of being allowed to profess final vows and enter into full membership in the Society.[63] It was only at this time that he would be allowed to make the distinctive fourth vow, binding the Jesuit to serve the pope and making him eligible to hold an administrative position in the Society.

[63] Chadwick, *Reformation*, 261.

Chapter 12

Early Formation

The initial stage of the postulancy of a newly arrived Jesuit in Aloysius' day was a period known as the "first probation". Its purpose was
to provide the young man with an opportunity to examine more
closely the possibility of his vocation and help him make a more definite decision before entering the novitiate. The postulant read the
Rule of the Society and received instruction about the Jesuits' customs and way of life. For Aloysius, this period of probation was very
short. Because he had made the *Spiritual Exercises* in Mantua not
long before, and because his struggles with his father had proven his
resolve, he was allowed to enter the novitiate sooner than his peers.[1]

As he transitioned into the novitiate, Aloysius was struck with
some sort of illness. His early biographers concur with Cepari's conclusion that this indisposition might have been brought about by
"the change of air and of life, or perhaps by the penances which he
still continued to practice, or perhaps by the greater ardor and application of mind with which he applied himself to his mental exercises".[2] Father Martindale acknowledges the value of these opinions,
but he believes that this illness might have arisen from another source.

> I cannot but think that, while this may be so, the sudden *removal* of a
> strain had no less to do with it. Abruptly to find that you have no more
> to fight, that you really have reached the haven of your desires, may
> induce a reaction as exhausting as any effort. This seems to me more

---

[1] Maurice Meschler, S.J., *St. Aloysius Gonzaga: Patron of Christian Youth* (Rockford, Ill.:
TAN Books, 1985), 131; Virgil Cepari, S.J., *Life of Saint Aloysius Gonzaga*, ed. Francis Goldie,
S.J. (New York: Benziger Brothers, 1891), 105.

[2] Cepari, *Life of Saint Aloysius*, 105.

likely, because either actually during this retreat, or at the beginning
of his novitiate, Aloysius found that he had lost all the cheerfulness, all
the sweetness of religion, that had usually been his.... For, say what
you will, his life and each day were now perfectly and paradoxically
different from anything he had hitherto preferred.[3]

While Aloysius seems to have experienced a great sense of calm
and contentment, he also had to face the fact that, for the first time,
he was not his own master. Although he had practiced a great deal
of self-discipline and self-denial in his former way of life, this was
not same kind of asceticism demanded by life lived in a religious
community under a superior. He had chosen to do hard things, but,
as Father Martindale notes, *he* had chosen them for himself and had
performed them with a great deal of tenacity and even stubbornness.[4]
Now, he was subject to a way of life and rules that were not of his
own making. But, as we might expect, he overcame this difficulty
and distinguished himself by his openness and willingness to learn.
For the first time in his life, Aloysius Gonzaga was being asked to be
ordinary. Although he struggled with conflicting feelings of despon-
dency and conceit and even wondered if he would ever be of use to
the Society, he persevered and was soon rewarded with a renewed
sense of peace and tranquility.[5]

The novitiate in any religious community is an extended period
of intensive discernment and formation intended to prepare novices
to make their religious vows. This time is set aside to give them the
freedom to practice and acquire the virtues and perspectives that will
allow them to live a happy, productive life in their community. For
the Jesuits, the virtues of detachment, humility, trust in God, and zeal
for souls epitomized those values instilled in the novices of Aloysius'
day. It was expected that the novices would have a solid foundation
for the rest of their lives by the time they made their first profession
of vows. For his part, Aloysius had already made significant strides
in these virtues and habits, but he nonetheless underwent the same
tests and trials that other novices endured.

[3] C. C. Martindale, *The Vocation of Saint Aloysius* (New York: Sheed and Ward, 1946),
138–39.
[4] Ibid., 139.
[5] Ibid., 140; Cepari, *Life of Saint Aloysius*, 106.

More than a decade before Aloysius was received into the community of novices, another young man, seventeen-year-old Robert Southwell, later destined to become a celebrated poet and priest who would give up his life in the Jesuits' English mission, entered the novitiate at Sant'Andrea.[6] Having chosen to commit his life to God as a member of the Society of Jesus rather than pursuing the contemplative ideal of the Carthusians, Southwell faced the prospect of never being allowed to return to his native England as he entered into the "strange, buried life" of the Jesuit novitiate.[7] Among the spiritual writings of this future martyr, we find these words: "Do not be sad or angry whatever they tell you to do, even though they want you to spend your whole life in the kitchen or in the pantry or in abject drudgery. They would never tell you to do it unless it were God's will."[8] Christopher Devlin, Southwell's biographer, writes:

> In the peace and interior stillness of Sant' Andrea [Southwell] listened for the voice of the Holy Spirit. The stillness, however, was not the perfect and gracious silence of a Carthusian monastery. "Stillness", indeed, is not the dominant impression a visitor would get from a Jesuit noviceship. It consists largely, as far as mere time is concerned, in a relentless rush from one duty to another, during which vocal silence is counterbalanced by a good deal of noise from

[6] Robert Southwell was born around the year 1561 in the village of Horsham Saint Faith in Norfolk. After studying in the Jesuit colleges at Douai and at Paris, he entered the Jesuit novitiate at Sant'Andrea in Rome on October 15, 1578. Ordained in 1584, he was appointed to the English mission in 1586. Southwell's years in England were spent in prayer and writing and in a clandestine ministry to recusant Catholics in London and, later, in Warwickshire. In 1591, Southwell composed his celebrated *Humble Supplication to Her Majesty*, an attack on the government's claims that the persecution of Catholics was not limited to matters of religion. Betrayed and subsequently captured in 1591, Father Southwell underwent severe tortures, which he himself described as being "each one worse than death". Imprisoned for more than three years, he was finally convicted of the crime of being a priest and was condemned to be hanged, drawn, and quartered. He was executed on February 21, 1595. Saint Robert Southwell, celebrated poet and defender of the rights of Catholics in Elizabeth's England, was beatified in 1929. Canonized with thirty-nine other martyrs of England and Wales in 1970, his commemoration is celebrated on February 21. For a fuller treatment of the life of Robert Southwell, see Paul Burns, ed., *Butler's Lives of the Saints: New Full Edition; February* (Collegeville, Minn.: Liturgical Press, 1997), 212–16.

[7] Christopher Devlin, *The Life of Robert Southwell: Poet and Martyr* (New York: Farrar, Straus, and Cudahy, 1956), 40.

[8] Robert Southwell, in ibid., 40.

other instruments—knives, plates, broomsticks, buckets, not to mention heavier objects. And silence-time itself at Sant' Andrea would be
amply compensated by the pious but piercing din of an Italian recreation. It was the human, not the superhuman or inhuman, element in
the noviceship that provided its severest test.

The shock that awaited sixteenth-century neophytes, most of whom
were of high breeding, was the very absence of those noble weapons
by which they had hoped to achieve heroic sanctity in a short time—
enormous flagellations, nocturnal vigils, protracted fasts. Instead they
had to settle down to a humdrum, rhythmic life: eating plenty, sleep-
ing soundly, and achieving a smiling and modest efficiency at half-a-
dozen tasks, among which those of scullion and pantry-boy loomed
large. The kitchen was generally recognized as the battle-ground on
which most sixteenth-century novices won their spurs.[9]

As for Aloysius, no one doubted his maturity. His words were few,
and he never spoke without thinking, so, for him, life in community would have had its own unique challenges. Expectations that he
would recreate and freely converse with his confreres in the novitiate would have been a trial for him.[10] By placing himself under obedience, he was forced to lead a more prudent, even moderate life. By
living a life of obedience to the common demands of the novitiate, he
was able to set out on a path of perfection that effectively freed him of
any self-will. He came to recognize that his smallest actions held a great
value when they were performed for the love of God.[11]

Aloysius would allow no one to defer to him because of his family
or rank. Father Cepari makes this very clear:

Having been born and educated as a prince, and being of a very delicate and weak constitution, he nevertheless adapted himself immediately in such a manner to common life, and to the discipline of the
house, that he did not appear different from the others in any point.
Never would he accept attention or any kind of privilege that his
superiors offered of their own accord; and he applied himself with as
much ardour to the lowest and vilest domestic duties as though he

[9] Ibid., 41.
[10] Paul Burns and Kathleen Jones, eds., *Butler's Lives of the Saints: New Full Edition; June*
(Collegeville, Minn.: Liturgical Press, 1997), 155.
[11] Cepari, *Life of Saint Aloysius*, 104.

had been accustomed all his life to be a servant, instead of having been waited on in everything.[12]

Aloysius threw himself into his new life. This should be no surprise because, although he was now bound by obedience, he nevertheless remained true to himself. He had always given himself completely to everything he did, and life in the novitiate was no exception. His literalness and his commitment to excellence manifested themselves in the way he dealt with the minutiae of Sant'Andrea. And yet, his superiors did find ways to challenge him more directly. Seeing his habit of walking about with his head bowed, his novice-master ordered that he be given a very stiff collar to wear with his habit so that he could not bend his head forward. It is recorded that he willingly, even joyfully, accepted this little trial and even joked about it when talking to his Jesuit brothers.[13] When he realized that his habit, his biretta, and his breviary were of a nicer quality that those of his confreres, he gladly gave them away, so that he could be like the others.[14] His greatest trial as a novice came only two-and-a-half months after he embarked on his life with the Society, when, on February 13, 1586, Don Ferrante died.

After Aloysius had departed for Rome, a remarkable change took place in the marquis. Although he had always been regular in his religious observances, he gave up gambling and devoted himself to pious exercises and devotions. Confined to bed by gout, he asked that his attendants bring him the silver and ebony crucifix Aloysius had used, and each evening he and a servant, Ghisoni (who had been Aloysius' valet), recited the Penitential Psalms and other prayers while he held the crucifix and wept.[15] He never failed to credit the prayers of his son for the graces he received.[16] After Father Cattaneo returned from Rome, the marquis asked him to travel with him to the shrine of the Madonna of Mantua, where he made a general confession.[17] Recognizing that the end was drawing near, Ferrante asked to be taken

---

[12] Ibid.

[13] Ibid., 105; Meschler, *St. Aloysius*, 141.

[14] Cepari, *Life of Saint Aloysius*, 106.

[15] Ibid., 109.

[16] Meschler, *St. Aloysius*, 133.

[17] The shrine of the "Basilica of Madonna delle Grazie" of Mantua in Curtatone. Following a plague that devastated Mantua in 1399, Francesco Gonzaga, Lord of Mantua, made a

to his physician in Milan. Understanding that there was no hope, he asked his kinsman Venerable Francesco Gonzaga, the Conventual Franciscan general, to send a friar to him so that he might again confess and receive absolution. Finally, on February 13, he passed away in the arms of Father Francesco, having consoled his family by telling them that they should be glad, rather than grieve, because God had called him in a state of grace.[18] His body was transferred to Mantua and buried in the Church of Saint Francis.

Aloysius received the news of his father's death with great calm. He wrote to his mother:

> Most Illustrious Lady,
> Most Honored Mother in Christ,
> The peace of Christ be with you. The death of my father was very bitter to me for the moment; "I felt very much cast down." But after having given way to the grief which nature demanded, I now rightly rejoice at the thought that really I have, from today, reason to call him father, and to thank God that He has taken him to His heavenly bliss; as we may hope from His boundless mercy.
>
> With holy resignation and interior joy let us submit ourselves to the Will of His Divine Majesty.
>
> So I conclude, begging your blessing.
> Rome, April 1586.
> I am, illustrious Lady,
> Your most obedient son in Christ,
> Aloysius Gonzaga, S.J.[19]

---

vow that he would build a church to house the already famous image of the Madonna and Child that had been venerated there since before the year 1000. Francesco entrusted the new shrine to the care of the Franciscans of the Strict Observance in 1407. Pope Martin V (1417–1431) visited the shrine and granted an indulgence to its pilgrims. Pope Pius II also visited there in 1459 and offered a second indulgence. In 1810, the community of friars tending the shrine was disbanded. A restoration of the shrine was begun in 1825 and completed in 1858. See Cepari, *Life of Saint Aloysius*, 375–76.

[18] Ibid., 110.

[19] Aloysius Gonzaga to his mother, Apr. 1586 (Letter XV), in ibid., 374–75; translation adapted. There is debate over whether the dating of this letter is correct. Cepari relates that Aloysius wrote to his mother on the day he received word of his father's passing. If this is indeed the letter that he composed at that time, it seems very unlikely that he would have learned of the death a month and a half later; therefore, we can assume that the dating of the letter itself is incorrect. For more on this debate, see Martindale, *Vocation of Saint Aloysius*, 144–45.

On April 10, he wrote a second letter to Donna Marta:

> Most revered mother in Christ.
>
> The consolation which I by a letter, enclosed in one from the Father Minister of Mantua, meant to wish to offer you, and of which the sorrow at the loss of my father of happy memory makes me feel the need, all urge me to recall to you, as I do by this [letter], what I urged in my last: resignation to the Divine Will.
>
> As he was always submissive to it in life, now that God has called him by so happy a death, we may trust too that he has by that same holy Will happily reached the life to which we all aspire.
>
> And so should we not rejoice rather than grieve when those we love arrive there, in full hope in God that it has been so ordained by His fatherly providence, which the Lord has towards all? He will not fail to pray very specially for those who commend themselves to him, for you yourself and your family. And since I have not omitted before, I will not cease to beg His Divine Majesty to console and govern you.
>
> Nor do I fail to receive the recompense of consolation in the news of how well all has gone with Signor Rudolfo, my brother. Besides what I advised him by letter some days back, I think I ought not to cease reminding him how useful I think the service of Doctor Sallust, who offered his services to me by letter, would be for him; and this for certain reasons, which as you and Rudolfo can examine them more closely at hand, so too if he remembers, he can do what the Lord dictates, from Whom in conclusion I beg for him every happiness.
>
> Rome, April 10, 1586.
>
> Your Ladyship's obedient son in Christ,
>
> Aluigi Gonzaga, S.J.[20]

Those around Aloysius were surprised by his serenity and self-control during this time.[21] Aloysius confessed to someone that the reality of his father's death by itself would have given him great sorrow, but when he thought about the fact that it came from the hand of God, he knew that he could not be troubled.[22] It seems fair

---

[20] Aloysius Gonzaga to his mother, Apr. 10, 1586 (Letter XVI), in Cepari, *Life of Saint Aloysius*, 409.

[21] Cepari, *Life of Saint Aloysius*, 108; Meschler, *St. Aloysius*, 135.

[22] Cepari, *Life of Saint Aloysius*, 108.

to assert that part of the reason Aloysius kept his feelings about his father's death to himself was the fact that he never liked talking about his family with those who asked.[23] He did love his father and truly mourned his passing, but he mourned as a man of faith, who saw the promise of the Resurrection in human death. His love and esteem for his father were shown in a very human way when he would often quote one of his father's expressions: "Whatever way of life you adopt, make the most of it."[24] This was certainly advice that his son had truly taken to heart.

Besides his general spirit of detachment, Aloysius continued to practice various penances, although not as many as he might have wished.[25] He once confided to a priest of the Society that the penances he then performed did not compare to those of his past life, but he took comfort in the knowledge that religious life was like a ship, in which it was not only those who labor at the oars, but also those who "stand idle in obedience", who speed along on the journey.[26] In his external ministry, the young Jesuit also, very willingly, took opportunities to seek out the most offensive patients in the Hospital of Santa Maria della Consolazione, where he was sent to work. At first Aloysius felt a natural disgust at the sights and smells that surrounded him, turning pale at the sight of stained linens. The acts of his canonization record that he had told one of his companions that he would picture Mary herself putting her Son, in the guise of the sick, into Aloysius' arms.[27] The testimony goes on to say that once, when Aloysius and his companion came to a bed whose sheets were stained with blood and pus, Aloysius turned white, then scarlet, and was unable to hide his revulsion. But he overcame himself and did what needed to be done. Afterward, his companion asked him what had happened. It was only then that he revealed that he grew sick and faint at the sight of blood.[28] This is why Aloysius used to grab the soiled bandages and linens with a pounce, demonstrating that it was an act of the will for him to overcome his bodily aversion to this

[23] Martindale, *Vocation of Saint Aloysius*, 145.
[24] Meschler, *St. Aloysius*, 136; Martindale, *Vocation of Saint Aloysius*, 145.
[25] Cepari, *Life of Saint Aloysius*, 111.
[26] Ibid.
[27] Martindale, *Vocation of Saint Aloysius*, 148.
[28] Ibid.; Meschler, *St. Aloysius*, 137.

type of work.[29] Aloysius had begun truly to see the presence of God in those around him, or, perhaps more appropriately, he had begun to meet them in God, and it was because of this that he was able to give so much of himself to them.[30]

Father Cepari dedicates a significant amount of space in his account of Aloysius' novitiate to reflecting on his ascetical practices. Although these penances might be distasteful to our modern sensibilities, they are worth recounting here for two reasons. The first is that they reflect a form of asceticism and devotion that was typical of religious life at that time. The second is that it is because of these practices that Aloysius (and with him, Stanislaus Kostka and John Berchmans, among others) was held up as a model for young religious for centuries. These practices offer us an added insight into the way in which Aloysius had internalized the virtues and habits of silence, modesty, custody of the eyes, and humility.

Noting his taciturnity in the face of humiliation, Cepari recounts the following instance. On the vigil of a certain feast, Aloysius had received the permission of the novice-master to take only bread and water at the main meal. Afterward, the superior, seeing that he had hardly eaten anything, ordered Aloysius to return immediately to the refectory and eat whatever was given him. He obeyed, but when the second meal was finished, someone said to him, "Well done, Brother Aloysius, yours is a good way of fasting, to eat a little at first, in order to return and eat a second time!" Aloysius replied, smiling, "What can I do? As the prophet says, '*Ut jumentum factus sum apud te et ego tecum semper*' (I am a beast in your sight, and I am always before you'" [Ps 73:22–23; my translation]).[31] Father Cepari also tells how Aloysius had a dislike for listening to talk he considered idle or unbecoming, showing his disapproval through his actions and silence. He always observed a strict custody of the eyes. Once, when the novices spent a free day in the country, they visited a house that they had not previously seen. When Aloysius was later asked how he liked the new location, he replied that he was surprised by the question, because he thought they had been to the same place they usually visited. He

[29] Margaret Monro, *A Book of Unlikely Saints* (Freeport, N.Y.: Books for Libraries, 1943), 64.
[30] Ibid., 61.
[31] Cepari, *Life of Saint Aloysius*, 111–12.

did concede, after reflecting for a few moments, that he had found a chapel in the new house that he had not found in the old.[32]

It also seems that Aloysius had lost, or at least denied, his sense of taste. He always sought to take the worst portion he could, and while eating, he always tried to meditate on some aspect of the reading rather than focus on the food being served. In his speech, he was very careful in choosing his words and expressing his ideas. Recall that he struggled as a younger man to restrain both his fiery Gonzaga temper and tendency to be judgmental. He would frequently pray the verse from the Psalms "Set a guard over my mouth, O Lord, keep watch over the door of my lips" (Ps 141:3), and in conversation he would often quote the Epistle of James: "[I]f any one who makes no mistakes in what he says he is a perfect man, able to bridle the whole body also" (Jas 3:2).[33] He always preferred silence, hoping to avoid offending God in any way. During the conversation that followed the morning and evening meal, Aloysius always preferred to talk of spiritual things. If he began to say something, and it occurred to him that it would remain best unsaid, he would sometimes stop in mid-sentence.[34]

When asked if going out to beg for alms bothered him, he replied that it did not: "Those who see me either know me or they do not. If they do not know me, I need not care for their opinion or feel humiliated. If they do know me, besides the edification I give, I lose nothing in their estimation, rather they hold me in higher consideration; and there is more fear of vainglory than of mortification, since to make oneself poor for the love of God, when one has been born rich, is considered worthy of honor even among those of the world."[35] When sent out to preach and catechize the poor in the streets of Rome, he did it with such joy and charity that he inspired many who saw him, and nobles and prelates would even order their carriages to stop so they could listen to him. On more than one occasion, he was able to impel his hearers who had been away from the sacraments for several years to go to confession and receive Communion.[36]

[32] Ibid., 112.
[33] Ibid., 113.
[34] Ibid., 114.
[35] Quoted in ibid., 116.
[36] Ibid.

Cepari tells us that there was only one thing in which Aloysius felt somewhat mortified: being publicly reprimanded for faults. And yet, this was not because he was embarrassed by having his faults proclaimed publicly. The mortification came from his having any faults at all.[37] In all things, he worked to be as obedient as possible, and even when he was made assistant to the brother in charge of the refectory, he performed his chores of sweeping, cleaning, and scrubbing in such a thorough way that this brother, who was by nature very exacting and demanding, was greatly impressed with Aloysius' humility and patience.[38]

Father Cepari concludes his reflections on Aloysius' novitiate with these words:

> From the very first month of his novitiate, he was so composed and modest in his external appearance, so severe in his treatment of his body, so given to mortification of his interior, especially in points of honor, so perfect in the observance of the least rules, so humble, so affable with others, so respectful towards superiors, and obedient to their commands, so devout to God, so detached in affection from everything of the world, so inflamed with charity and perfect in every virtue, that the novices all declared him to be a Saint. They kissed devoutly the things he had touched and used, and treated him with the greatest veneration. Others again, who were not novices, strove to get things that he had used, regarding them as holy relics. His copy of the Little Office [Office of Our Lady] which he had used in the world was taken by me [i.e., Cepari] at that time. It had already passed through the hands of two others, and I wished to keep it through devotion. It is still kept in Sicily. A Father who is a preacher kept as a relic the breviary which he used as a layman, and thus it was regarded by others also, so quickly were his sanctity and perfection recognized.[39]

---

[37] Ibid.
[38] Ibid., 117.
[39] Ibid.; translation adapted.

Chapter 13

Penance and Prayer

After a number of months in the novitiate at Sant'Andrea, the novices were allowed to spend some time at the Gesù, the house for the professed members of the Society in Rome. Although they had rooms apart from the professed, they took turns serving Masses, reading at table in the refectory, and doing those kinds of work which novices have done for centuries. After Aloysius had been in the novitiate for about three months, he received orders to go to the professed house. Excited by the prospect of being able to benefit from the example of the older Fathers living there, he was also pleased to be able to serve Mass frequently as an expression of his devotion to the Blessed Sacrament.[1]

Early each morning, Aloysius and the other novices went to the sacristy so that each could begin taking his turn in serving six or seven Masses. In the time between these Masses, Aloysius would remain on his knees in a corner of the sacristy where the relics were kept, meditating, reciting prayers, or reading.[2] At midday, some of the novices would be sent to help the cook, while others served in the refectory or read aloud. Aloysius performed all these tasks simply, and his reading was especially clear and distinct. It happened on one occasion, however, that he was not well understood because of a great deal of background noise in the refectory. The prefect of the novices (a novice selected to act as head of the novice class) promptly took him

[1] Virgil Cepari, S.J., *Life of Saint Aloysius Gonzaga*, ed. Francis Goldie, S.J. (New York: Benziger Brothers, 1891), 118. Cepari also records here that Aloysius' devotion to the Blessed Sacrament was so well known that there were some in Rome who, desiring to have a portrait painted of Aloysius after his death, considered having him depicted in the act of adoring the Blessed Sacrament.

[2] Maurice Meschler, S.J., *St. Aloysius Gonzaga: Patron of Christian Youth* (Rockford, Ill.: TAN Books, 1985), 144.

aside after the meal and lectured him on the spiritual loss his hearers had suffered because of his bad reading. Rather than make any kind of excuse, Aloysius asked for pardon and promised to make amends, even offering to begin reading all over again.[3]

The novice-master at the Gesù was Father Jerome Piatti, S.J. (d. 1591), a man whom Cepari describes as being "holy and spiritual, thoroughly conversant with religious perfection".[4] Piatti knew of Aloysius before his arrival in Rome and was very pleased to have this particular novice entrusted to his care. He had already formed a very high opinion of Aloysius, and he did not hesitate to praise Aloysius in a letter to his friend, Father Mutius Vitelleschi, who was studying theology in Naples at the time Aloysius began his novitiate.

Dearest Brother in Christ,
Pax Christi.

I cannot make a better reply or one more pleasing to you in return for a letter which I have just received from you, my dearest Vitelleschi, than by giving you an account of a distinguished novice who entered Sant' Andrea five days ago, on the feast of Saint Catherine. He is a youth, by the name of Aloysius Gonzaga, son of a Marquis whose estate borders the duchy of Mantua, and a near relation of the duke of that place, and, being the eldest son, he would have succeeded to the marquisate. But God was pleased to choose him for Himself, and about two years ago, when he was at the Court of King Philip of Spain, he resolved to join the Society. As his father was also at the Court, he openly declared to him his intention, and after submitting him to many trials, the Marquis at last consented. He returned shortly after from Spain, and wrote to his relative, Scipio Gonzaga, the Patriarch of Jerusalem, to speak to our Father General, and offer his son in his name. But as Aloysius was, as I have already said, the eldest son, with the right of succession, it was necessary for him to transfer his rights to another brother. This affair occupied several months, for it was necessary to obtain the consent of the Emperor. Finally however this business was settled, but when the good youth thought to enter at once into port, he was detained for some time by his father, who still made difficulties about the final permission, and wished to keep

<hr>

[3] Ibid., 144–45.

[4] Cepari, *Life of Saint Aloysius*, 120. Jerome Piatti, S.J. (also known as Platus), was best remembered for his book *On the Happiness of the Religious State*.

him for many years longer, either on account of the love he bore him, or because, as he wrote to Father General, he thought him still too young for such a step. And in this we can see how great the young man's constancy and fervor were, for although he had an extreme reverence for his father, he never ceased importuning him, and trying all possible means to obtain his consent. When he saw that his father was still unmoved, he wrote ardent letters to the General, imploring him to be allowed to depart without saying a word to the Marquis. This however the General would not allow. The affair thus dragged on till now, when, in what manner I know not, he finally obtained the necessary permission, and arrived in Rome in the dress of a priest, with some ten horses in his train. His coming was so widely known that wherever he passed people were aware that he was on his way to enter into the Society. The same was the case also in Rome, where he lodged a few days in the house of the Patriarch, Scipio Gonzaga.

His intention became known throughout the Pope's palace, and when he went to the Holy Father to ask a blessing on his plan, he was surrounded by the courtiers who, as they entertained very different ideas and plans themselves, regarded him as a miracle. Finally on Monday, the feast of Saint Catherine, he went to Sant' Andrea, accompanied by the Patriarch, who stayed to dine with the Father General.

His abilities are such that his rank is his least distinction; for although he is not yet eighteen years old and has spent so much time in Court, he is already well grounded in both logic and natural science. His prudence and his discretion of speech are such as to astonish us all; and it will be a sufficient proof of this to tell you that his father already made use of him in many ways at home; and in a letter by which he presented him to Father General, said that he was his dearest hope. But all this is nothing compared to his virtue and sanctity; for from the age of about eight he himself confesses he began to fear God; and this is clearly proved by the devotion he has, for during prayer he is constantly in tears, and he observes an almost constant recollection, as may be perceived by his face and manner of acting. His servants say that he used to meditate every day for four or five hours, besides what he did at night which they could not know, because for a long time of late, he would not allow any one to undress him, but shut himself up in his room, and attended to his devotions, without other restraint than his own fervor. And that you may not think that I am exaggerating these things, I merely tell you that Father Andrew Spinola, when talking with him, was so drawn to him, and so much admired his gifts, that when he spoke with me on the subject, he told me that I praised him very coldly, although you see in what manner I speak of him.

And the General and all our Fathers in Rome as well as in Milan and Mantua, where he stayed for a time, all have the same opinion of him.

I do not know if I ought to mention what follows, lest it should diminish your joy, as it has diminished ours; however I will tell you all, to urge you to pray for him. You must know then, that, of gifts of nature and grace, the only one that is wanting to Aloysius is health; for he is so delicate that only to look on him fills one with fear; and already, a day or two before he entered, he began to feel a pain in his chest. This which proves his fervor, he ascribes to the fact that after making his usual Friday fast of bread and water, he went the following day to pay his respects to the Holy Father and was obliged to wait fasting until nearly evening, and this was why he was so exhausted. However this may be, it is certain that, if he can be cured by great care, he will be tended with all possible solicitude and prudence, for so Father General has commanded, and this is being already done. And perhaps he will have a better chance under the wise care of the superiors of our Society, than when left without check to the guidance and impulse of his own fervor. So pray for him and be sure that, if God gives him life and health, you will see him do great things for the service of God and the Society.

I wished to relate these things at length, although I have omitted much that would edify, in order to give you a share in the joy which has been the one subject of our conversation during the past days, but I ask you, by praying that I may have the grace to be a true Brother and follower of those exalted souls that God calls every day to our holy Society. May God's blessing be with you.

Rome, November 29, 1585.

Your Brother and Servant in Christ,

Jerome Piatti[5]

Father Piatti later served as Aloysius' confessor and was able to obtain from him a detailed account of his personal history and his spiritual life.[6] Once, when he was speaking with another Jesuit about how the saints are so conformed to God's Will that they love and

---

[5] Quoted in Cepari, *Life of Saint Aloysius*, 120–24.

[6] Piatti's own recollections of Aloysius served as the foundation for much of Father Cepari's work and contributed greatly to the increase in devotion to Aloysius among the Jesuits.

desire only what God wills, Piatti said, "I perceive a clear example of this with regard to our Brother Aloysius. For as the saints in Paradise see how greatly God delights in his soul, their wills become like God's Will, and they are wholly engaged in advancing him with heavenly gifts and graces, in doing favors and praying for him. It seems to me that he is so favored by God and by them, and so full of supernatural virtues and graces, that they vie with each other as to who can do the most for him."[7]

* * * * *

After two months at the Gesù, Aloysius returned to Sant'Andrea, where he was supposed to remain for the rest of his novitiate. His most remarkable traits at this time could be said to be his serenity and cheerfulness, combined with his personal maturity.[8] Aloysius' sense of tranquility was a natural outgrowth of his self-mastery and desire to please God alone. His prayer and acts of obedience were manifestations of his union with God. He considered it impossible for anyone to achieve true renunciation of self-will and self-love without devotion to prayer and recollection. Aloysius also believed in the efficacy of prayer to overcome every difficulty. Finally, he realized how beautiful prayer was: it is conversation with God, a foretaste of Heaven. As he said, one need only try it in order to love it and so never abandon the practice of prayer.[9] It was these convictions and his understanding of prayer that gave him the strength and courage to persevere, even in the midst of struggle and temptations. Like all men of faith, Aloysius struggled with times of darkness and doubt. We have seen how he struggled with these as a novice, but more importantly, we have seen how he persevered.

The young novice's devotion to the Most Blessed Sacrament was a great source of strength and consolation to him. Of all his devotions, this was the one that had the most meaning for him and the one which seems to have been the most fruitful for him. Father Cepari records that he made use of one Communion to prepare him for the

---

[7] Quoted in Cepari, *Life of Saint Aloysius*, 124.
[8] Meschler, *St. Aloysius*, 148.
[9] Ibid., 148–49.

next and that he divided the week so that Monday, Tuesday, and Wednesday were dedicated to the Persons of the Trinity to thank each one for the graces he had received in his last Communion. Thursday, Friday, and Saturday were offered to the Trinity as he asked for the grace to be able to receive Communion worthily the next Sunday.[10] He would often take a few minutes during the day to make visits to the Blessed Sacrament, and his conversations about the Eucharist were always devout and sincere. This was so much so that some of the Jesuit priests would join him for recreation on Saturday evenings so that they might be inspired by listening to him. On the days on which he received Communion, he would go off to a quiet place and pass the morning in silence, reading the works of Saint Bernard of Clairvaux and Saint Augustine.[11]

Aloysius also had a particular devotion to the Passion of the Lord. Each day at noon he recited an antiphon in honor of the Passion, and he tried to place himself before the Cross of Christ, treating each day, as he himself said, as Good Friday.[12] Second only to his devotion to the Blessed Sacrament and the Lord's Passion was his deep love of the Blessed Virgin. Several times during his life, Aloysius was keenly aware of our Lady's patronage and intercession: she was "the Queen of his heart and the guiding star of his life ... he never tired of thinking of her, honoring her, praising and loving her".[13]

Finally, and perhaps not surprisingly, Aloysius had a special devotion to the Holy Angels. We have already noted his special devotion to Saint Catherine of Alexandria and Saint Mary Magdalen, but his devotion to the angels was well known among his companions, and he was even asked to submit a meditation on the angels for a book being written by Father Vincenzo Bruno.[14] This was the origin of

---

[10] Cepari, *Life of Saint Aloysius*, 119.

[11] Ibid.

[12] Meschler, *St. Aloysius*, 152.

[13] Ibid.

[14] Vincenzo Bruno, S.J., was rector of the Roman College in 1587, the year Aloysius repeated certain philosophy courses and made his first profession as a Jesuit. Aloysius would maintain contact throughout his short life with Father Bruno, who was among those to whom Aloysius confided the knowledge of his approaching death. Bruno's book, *Meditazioni sopra I principali Misteri della Vita, Passione e Risurrezione di Cristo N.S. e sopra le sette Festivitià principali della b. Vergine e sopra il commune de' Santi raccolte da diversi Santi Padri e da altri divoti autori* (Meditations on the Principal Mysteries of the Life, Passion and Resurrection of Christ

his "Treatise on the Angels, Especially the Holy Guardian Angels".
In addition to this treatise, a slip of paper on which Aloysius wrote
a short meditation for himself has also been preserved, which reads:

> Imagine yourself standing in the midst of the nine choirs of Angels,
> as they pray to God and sing that hymn of praise: *Sanctus Deus, Sanc-*
> *tus Fortis, Sanctus Immortalis* [Holy God, Holy Mighty One, Holy
> Immortal One]. Repeat this prayer nine times in union with them.—
> Recommend yourself three times daily to the special care of your
> Guardian Angel. Every morning and evening, and during the day,
> when you visit the church and pray at the altar, recite the prayer:
> "Angel of God ...".—Remember that you must follow the guidance
> of your Angel, like a blind man who does not know the way, and
> trusts entirely in the care of the person who leads him.[15]

Aloysius needed the comfort and strength he drew from his prayer
as he faced his own interior struggles with conceit and the memory
of his past life. Here we can begin to discern a sort of tension in
the writings of Aloysius' biographers. Although the young novice
sought after and, we believe, attained a significant union with God
as he lived an exemplary life as a religious, he was nonetheless a
sixteenth-century nobleman, and the sensibilities and values of his
former rank and station remained with him. By his own admission,
obedience was his greatest struggle—although this could not be
gathered from merely observing his conduct in the community.
This young man was the former heir of the Marquisate of Castiglione, the one who said of himself, "I am a piece of twisted iron;
I entered religion to get twisted straight." He understood that he
had much to learn, and he struggled to leave behind the values and
ideologies of his noble peers. The indifference which Aloysius was
eventually able to have toward his past was most certainly a grace
from God. When asked by a lay brother whether it was difficult for
a great nobleman to abandon the world, Aloysius answered that it

Our Savior and on the Seven Principal Feasts of the Blessed Virgin and on the Communion
of Saints Collected by Various Holy Fathers and Other Devout Authors) was first published
in Latin in 1597. Over the next three hundred years, it would be republished in numerous
editions in several different languages.

[15] Quoted in Meschler, *St. Aloysius*, 155.

was actually impossible unless the Lord put clay on his eyes, as he did the eyes of the man born blind. He must be made free to see the truth about himself.[16]

The aspect of obedience which seemed to bother him most was the demand that he be obedient even to those who were inferior to him intellectually. As Margaret Monro notes, "He was quick to recognize real superiority; his novice-master, Father John Baptist Pescatore, commanded both his affection and his respect on account of great gifts of mind and character. But this very penetration made Aloysius recognize a stupid order when he met one, recognizing too that behind it lay stupidity, not a higher intelligence putting him to a test his immaturity could not yet appreciate."[17] He seems to have overcompensated for this by being almost too literal in his obedience, even to the point of going against his common sense.

Aloysius tried very hard to be as perfect as he could, and one can only imagine the amount of patience his quest for perfection demanded of his superiors. Father Cepari records that one day, Aloysius went to his novice-master to ask his advice about something which was troubling him: however carefully he examined his conscience, he could discern nothing that amounted even to a venial sin. What troubled him was that he feared that this inability to discern a fault meant that he did not really know himself. Father Cepari uses this as an example of Aloysius' simplicity and purity of heart and omits the response of the novice-master.[18] What we can recognize is that he was making progress in virtue and was largely successful in overcoming his tendencies toward anger, impatience, and his Gonzaga temperament. It was an ongoing process of self-discovery and conversion that he never abandoned. This cannot have been easy, because he was a talented young man who was celebrated for his zeal, his quick wit, and his fierce sense of determination. He never tried to crush another in an argument, but spoke with simplicity. In fact, he knew how to walk away from nearly everything that could affect his peace of soul.[19]

* * * * *

[16] Cepari, *Life of Saint Aloysius*, 205. See also Margaret Monro, *A Book of Unlikely Saints* (Freeport, N.Y.: Books for Libraries, 1943), 62.

[17] Monro, *Unlikely Saints*, 62–63.

[18] Cepari, *Life of Saint Aloysius*, 130–31.

[19] Ibid., 132.

After his return to Sant'Andrea, Aloysius' novice-master, Father Pescatore, became seriously ill, and Father Aquaviva decided to send him to Naples in the hopes that a change of climate would be good for him. Pescatore invited Aloysius to join him, and the young novice readily agreed. Father Pescatore was a man who was renowned for his virtue and learning. He was also very fondly remembered by Father Cepari, who wrote of him:

> Whether he was sitting, walking, or standing his whole exterior was a perfect portrait of modesty: his face beamed with joyous serenity, which he communicated to those who beheld it. Never was he seen to change his countenance in any circumstances, nor to lose his tranquility, to become melancholy, or break out into unrestrained gaiety. He was always the same, showing that his passions were under control and that he possessed an imperturbable interior peace and calmness: nor was there ever seen in him the least sign of impatience or anger ... all his actions manifested his profound humility.[20]

Pescatore was especially solicitous of the needs of his novices, bearing their imperfections and struggles with great patience, stressing a realistic observance of the Ignatian Rule. Aloysius revered his novice-master, honoring him for the quality of his religious life.

As arrangements were being made for the trip, Aloysius learned that Aquaviva had asked Pescatore to take with him the three most delicate of the Roman novices and that Aloysius was selected because of his severe headaches. The other two, a Frenchman named Jean Pruinet and George Elphinstone, a native of Scotland, joined Aloysius and Father Pescatore when they set out on October 27, 1586. It was Elphinstone who later recounted the details of their journey to Father Cepari.[21]

The route taken by the group was quite scenic, dotted with ancient ruins and running nearly parallel to the Via Appia. Because of his illness, which seems to have been a symptom of tuberculosis, Father Pescatore traveled in a litter. Although Aloysius was hesitant to take the extra place in the litter, preferring instead to ride one of the two horses available, he was simply not strong enough to make the trip on horseback. Together, the two recited the Hours of the Divine

[20] Ibid., 143.
[21] Ibid., 144.

Office and passed the time discussing a variety of spiritual topics. Aloysius later said he gained more spiritual insight during these few days of travel than in his several months in the novitiate.[22] The group arrived in Naples on November 1.

At that time, the Jesuits had two houses in Naples. Their principal house was that used by the professed members of the Society, which had been established in 1579. The second house was the college, founded in 1554, which also housed the novitiate. Because the novitiate and college were in the same building, Aloysius was able to resume his studies, and he was provided with a worthwhile diversion that took his mind off of his intense, interior life.

Aloysius' metaphysics professor, Father Giovanni Camerota, S.J., later offered the following testimony as part of the investigation for Aloysius' beatification:

> I knew the Blessed Aloysius to be a person of great humility. He despised himself, yielded to all, and sought every opportunity to lessen himself in the esteem of others. He was given to extraordinary mortification, was very devout, spending much time in prayer and in union with our Lord God; he was very observant of the rules and of a very tender conscience; and together with holiness of life, he was gifted with a singularly acute intelligence, joined with great modesty and humility. All this I know, because of the opportunities I had of observing his actions and character during the time that he remained in Naples, and was my student. I esteemed him as being of great virtue and holiness, and this was the general opinion in the College of Naples, and shared in particular by that holy man, Father Pescatore, who is now dead and had been his novice master and his confessor. He spoke of him to me several times, as of a person of more than ordinary sanctity.[23]

Three years later, Father Camerota added this to his testimony:

> [Aloysius] was observant of the very least rules, like that of silence; he was a person of very few words. He so mortified his flesh that his superiors were obliged to restrain him. He was most devout, and

---

[22] Meschler, *St. Aloysius*, 160.
[23] Quoted in Cepari, *Life of Saint Aloysius*, 146; translation adapted.

during the time he was with me at Naples, he seemed to me to be continually occupied in prayer and in the contemplation of divine things, and to be always speaking with God. As to troubles in his soul he appeared to have none. As to humility he always desired to be held of no account, and he greatly rejoiced if he thought others saw him in this way. . . .

He was so humble that fearing to trouble me he waited a long time at my door, and then knocked so gently that I could scarcely hear him; but so far from disturbing me, it was a great consolation to me when he came either on account of difficulties in his lectures or for any other reason. He was most modest, and his modesty captivated everyone, and caused him to be loved and esteemed by all. His conversation was grave, of God and for God, short and in but few words.

Neither I nor others ever noticed in him anything that could be called venial sin, or even which betrayed any disordered passion. In 1596 I destroyed nearly all the letters I had received, but I preserved one that the Blessed Aloysius had written to me from Portici in 1587, sympathizing with me in my illness, and promising me his prayers; and, though many have begged this letter of me, I have never been willing to part with it, but preserve it for my devotion. I know that many of ours as well as seculars recommend themselves to his prayers, and especially the men employed in building our schools.[24]

During the same period of investigation, Father Vincenzo Figliucci, S.J., a distinguished theologian, shared this testimony:

I knew Aloysius in Naples, where he was studying metaphysics, from the end of 1586 to 1587. All that time he gave so admirable an example of virtue as to be recognized as the most eminent of our religious. He was constant and diligent in teaching Christian doctrine to the poor. When he was ill in bed his peaceful countenance showed how resigned he was to the Will of God, in Whom alone he trusted, and he always spoke of the happiness of the other life and of the things of God. And if indeed he conversed only a little, oftentimes when he spoke of God, he did it with such earnestness that one could see how united he was with God from his very abstraction of mind.

He showed great charity to his neighbors, and earnestly begged to be allowed to go to the aid of poor prisoners and to serve in the

---

[24] Quoted in ibid., 147; translation adapted.

hospitals; and he was the means of reconciling his brother novices when there was any slight misunderstanding. In prudence he was above his years, and he seemed to possess it to an almost superhuman degree, and showed it by speaking with the greatest consideration, as well as in all his exterior actions. He seemed to do nothing that was not premeditated and directed to its right end, and from this arose the singular calm he always enjoyed. He displayed in all his actions great candor of mind, interpreting favorably all the words and actions of others, confining himself to the bare facts, without circumlocution or fine words, never exaggerating but relating everything simply. He was never seen to give way to anger, and he had the movements of his soul under such control, that he appeared to enjoy perpetual peace.

Aloysius suffered constantly from headaches, but he bore them with such patience and outward composure that he appeared to be free of them. He suffered with the greatest patience the illness he had in Naples, leaving himself entirely in the hands of the infirmarians, and never allowing a word or a sign of impatience to escape him. He was very remarkable for the virtue of humility, avoiding all praise whether on account of his noble birth or of the singular gifts he had received from nature, and he was always among the first to seek any humble or mean job with a readiness of will and even gladness. He cared not to hear news of what was happening in the world but seemed like a man dead to himself. He was a model of custody of his feelings, and showed it in his exterior behavior, which struck everyone. He delighted in mortifying himself continually as far as he could. He was most observant of the rule of silence, so that, I think, he never broke it. He loved poverty, and there arose in him the desire to wear the most worn-out clothes that were to be found in the house. He obeyed the slightest sign of his superiors with the utmost simplicity and readiness.[25]

As far as it was possible, Aloysius always tried to conceal his rank and status. It is related that when word reached Naples that Pope Sixtus V had named his kinsman Scipione Gonzaga (already Patriarch of Jerusalem) a cardinal, Aloysius showed no change in his countenance, despite the fact that he felt a great affection for him because of the assistance he had offered Aloysius during his time of discernment. In fact, Aloysius seems to have been somewhat annoyed with the

[25] Quoted in ibid., 147–49; translation adapted.

messenger who came to the college for the sole purpose of telling him the news. One witness, Father Antony Beatilli, S.J., related that Aloysius, "having heard the news without even raising his eyes from the ground, [showed] by the slight blush that rose to his cheeks that he felt annoyance rather than pleasure".[26]

The superiors of the college hoped that their new charge would have a positive influence on the other novices, so it was decided that Aloysius should be placed in the largest room, a place where a number of the students slept. Because of this new arrangement, Aloysius suffered many sleepless nights, and his headaches grew significantly worse. When his superiors learned this, they decided to place him in a new room. Unfortunately, this room was located directly under a passageway that led to a number of occupied rooms. As a result, the new room was even noisier than the previous one, but Aloysius did not complain. In addition to the headaches, he now began to suffer from erysipelas and fevers.[27] This illness, which was referred to by Fathers Camerota and Figliucci, confined Aloysius to bed for more than a month, and he came very close to death. Realizing that the climate of Naples was ultimately unsuitable for Aloysius, his superiors recalled him to Rome as soon as he had recovered. He returned to the Eternal City on May 8, 1587.

[26] Ibid., 149.
[27] Erysipelas is an infection of the blood that causes inflammation of subcutaneous tissue and redness and irritation of the skin.

Chapter 14

The Scholastic

When Aloysius returned to the Roman College in May 1587, he was warmly greeted by his Jesuit confreres. Aloysius was very pleased to be back in Rome and to be able to resume his studies. It was at this time that Father Cepari came to know Aloysius personally, and from this point on, his account of the saint's life assumes a more personal tone. He recalled: "From this time till the day of his holy death, I, with many others of the same college, lived on familiar terms with him, and I was thus an eyewitness of the greater part of the things here related; and more than this, from that time I carefully noted them with a view to writing them down."[1]

Aloysius continued his study of metaphysics and showed his competency in logic and the natural sciences. Because of his skill, he was chosen to participate in a sort of public debate in the presence of Cardinals della Rovere, Vincenzo Lauro, and Scipione Gonzaga. As was to be expected, Aloysius won the esteem of his hearers for his thoughtful defense, and many present were amazed that he had been able to advance so far in his studies, particularly in light of his weak health. The audience had no way of knowing that Aloysius had, in fact, tried to get out of participating in the discussion. Finding that all his requests to be excused fell on deaf ears, he then wondered if it might be permissible for him to give incorrect answers so that he might avoid the praise of the audience. One of his philosophy professors dissuaded him, and, ever obedient, Aloysius answered with all his skill. Unfortunately, however, one of the professors responsible for

---

[1] Virgil Cepari, S.J., *Life of Saint Aloysius Gonzaga*, ed. Francis Goldie, S.J. (New York: Benziger Brothers, 1891), 151.

attacking the thesis Aloysius was to defend began by complimenting the noble heritage of his opponent and the entire Gonzaga family. This seems to have been a bit too much for Aloysius to stomach because he answered that particular professor somewhat curtly for the remainder of the debate.

Finally, in the fall of 1587, Aloysius completed his philosophical studies. Having been trained by a number of prominent professors, he always had a preference for the works of Saint Thomas Aquinas, which he admired for their clarity, order, and accuracy. This young man, who was now eighteen years old, possessed many great qualities and was blessed with numerous abilities. His professors enthusiastically testified to his intellectual abilities and his sound judgment.[2] Aloysius was a dedicated student and never hesitated to ask for help from his professors when he needed it. His skills were especially apparent in the debates that were a common pedagogical tool at the time. His statements and replies were always clear and concise, and he always made his point with minimal difficulty. But Aloysius also avoided any tendency toward priggishness. He argued with modesty and gave his opponent ample time and space to make his own responses. Finally, his time in the classroom was always preceded by a visit to the Blessed Sacrament.

Aloysius was allowed a special concession by his superiors. Because of his weak physical health, and because he would not have been able to do so himself, he was allowed to use a professional scribe to take dictation at the lectures he attended. He very willingly lent out his copies of the lectures to others, and he never asked for them back, trusting that they would be returned in good time. He did eventually receive permission to transcribe the lectures for himself, arguing that use of a professional scribe might be perceived by some as being an unnecessary vanity or extravagance. Although he was unable to keep up with the pace of the masters' lectures, he was able to listen attentively and record the most important and salient points, looking through his companions' notes to fill in anything that might have been lacking in his. He enjoyed working hard, and he kept for his personal use only a Bible and an old copy of the *Summa* of Saint Thomas, going to the library to consult any other books he might

[2] Ibid., 154.

need. In time, Aloysius even gave his copy of the *Summa* to another student who did not have one for his own use.

* * * * *

After being in the Society for more than two years, Aloysius (having already made a retreat and the *Spiritual Exercises*) pronounced his simple vows of poverty, chastity, and obedience on November 25, 1587, the Feast of Saint Catherine of Alexandria. The profession ceremony took place in the chapel of the Roman College in the presence of the rector, Father Vincenzo Bruno, S.J. On February 25, 1588, Aloysius received the tonsure in a ceremony in the Basilica of Saint John Lateran. He soon received the minor orders in quick succession: porter on February 28, lector on March 6, exorcist on March 12, and acolyte on March 20.

On the occasion of his religious profession, Aloysius wrote the following to his mother:

> Honored Mother in Christ,
> I received some days back a letter from you which gave me much joy in the Lord, because of its good news of yourself and your family, but I could not help feeling deeply what you hinted at regarding my brother; and as I hope our Lord will direct this affair, I commend it to him. I beg of you to salute my brother in my name, and recommend to him what is due to him and his family, that is dependence on those to whom he owes it and according to the directions of our Father. I inform your Ladyship of the gift I made of myself to the Divine Majesty by my vows on the feast of Saint Catherine, and begging you to thank God for this favor, also ask you to obtain from Him that I may keep them and go forward in the way in which he has called me, that after this life, we may enjoy him together in Heaven, where He is so anxiously waiting for all His own. I also accept the offer you made me in your last [letter] of some more money for writing [?], so I ask you for another twenty-five crowns. I recommend myself to you in our Lord, from whom I beg for you every increase in His Grace.
> Rome, December 11, 1587.
> Your Ladyship's most obedient son in Christ,
> Aluigi Gonzaga, S.J.[3]

* * * * *

[3] Aloysius Gonzaga to his mother, Dec. 11, 1587 (Letter XVII), in ibid., 409–10.

For generations, Aloysius Gonzaga, together with a handful of other saints, was held up as a model for all religious, but most especially for those in the early years of their religious life. In the case of Aloysius, this effort to make him a sort of icon of religious zeal and perfection obscured the true dynamism of his personality and his struggles to overcome the expectations attached to his Gonzaga name as well as his own interior dispositions and passions. While many today have little patience for overly pious or saccharine representations of anyone (especially saints), it is nevertheless worthwhile to learn these stories so that we might discern the truths they contain.

Among those virtues for which Aloysius was held in particular esteem was that of humility. Our Christian tradition has certainly placed this virtue before almost every other. In his Rule for monasteries, the great Saint Benedict (d. ca. 550) observes that it is only by ascending the "ladder of humility" that the monk could attain that "perfect love of God that casts out fear" (cf. 1 Jn 4:18; my translation). He writes: "Through this love, all that he once performed with dread, he will now begin to observe without effort, as though naturally, from habit, no longer out of fear of hell, but out of love for Christ, good habit and delight in virtue. All this the Lord will by the Holy Spirit graciously manifest in his workman now cleansed from vices and sin."[4] Although we may never know if Aloysius ever read Benedict's Rule, we do know of his great love for the writings of Saint Augustine and Saint Bernard of Clairvaux, and we can trust that he would have certainly recognized and appreciated the truth of these words.

Father Cepari records that after Aloysius' death, some of his spiritual writings were discovered, and the following meditation on humility was among them:

> The first principle is that you are made for God, and obliged to tend towards Him because of your being, redemption and vocation. From this you will conclude that you are bound not only to abstain from every evil deed, but even from those that are indifferent and useless; and on the contrary to make every endeavor that all your actions, interior and exterior, may be virtuous, so that you may always draw nearer to God.

[4] Benedict of Nursia, *The Rule of Saint Benedict*, ed. Timothy Fry (Collegeville, Minn.: Liturgical Press, 1982), 38.

Afterwards, in order to descend more to particulars in serving God, you must establish within yourself these other three principles.

First, that by the vocation of the members of the Society of Jesus, and yours in particular, you are called to follow the standard of Christ and of His Saints: hence it follows, that in every office, duty and exercise, you will consider it as belonging to your vocation; and on your side will avoid or embrace it as much as it is conformable to the example of Christ and of His Saints. For this reason you will make yourself well acquainted with the life and actions of Christ by meditating on them and with those of the Saints by consideration and reflection.

The second, to regulate your affections is, that you will lead a religious and spiritual life, inasmuch as in your interior you seek to guide yourself according to the rules of eternity and not of time, so that in all your affections, desires, and joys, you may have a spiritual motive, and the same in what displeases you: being convinced that in this consists spirituality.

The third is, that as the devil continually attacks you by vanity and self-esteem, and as this is the weak side of your soul, you must the more strenuously and constantly endeavor to resist him by humility and self-contempt, both interior and exterior. For this end you will propose to yourself some rules to attend especially to the study of this virtue, which have been taught by our Lord and confirmed by experience.

For the Practice of Humility

The first means is to understand well that though this virtue is particularly suited to human beings, because of the lowliness of their origin, nevertheless, "it does not grow in our garden," but we must beg it from Heaven, from Him, "from Whom is every best and perfect gift;" therefore, although you are proud, endeavor with the greatest possible humility to ask this virtue from the Infinite Majesty of God, the first and principal author of it, and then by the merits and intercession of the profound humility of Jesus Christ, "who, though he was in the form of God... emptied himself, taking the form of a slave" [cf. Phil 2:6a, 7a].

The second means is to have recourse to the intercession of those Saints that have excelled in this virtue.

1) Remember that if here below they were worthy to obtain in a special way and degree this virtue, so in Heaven, where they are more pleasing to God than they were on earth, they will be all the more worthy and deserving; and as they have no more need to

humble themselves for their own sake, as by this virtue they have gone up to the heights of Heaven, ask them in prayer to obtain it for you from God.

2) Consider that here on earth the one who has distinguished himself in any profession naturally tries to help others in the same calling. Thus candidates for the army try to secure the good word of a successful general at Court; and it is the same with literary men, architects, and mathematicians—those who themselves have achieved excellence in these arts are the patrons of those who aspire to achieve it. So in Heaven those, who have been pre-eminent in any virtue, are specially ready to assist all who desire to acquire it and with this object address themselves to them. Therefore, do not forget to have recourse in the first place to the Blessed Virgin, Mother of God, who excelled in this virtue above any other pure creature. Next, among the apostles, to Saint Peter who said of himself: "Go away from me, Lord, for I am a sinful man!" [Lk 5:8b] and to Saint Paul who, though he had been taken into the third heaven, thought so humbly of himself that he said: "Christ Jesus came into the world to save sinners—of whom I am the foremost" [1 Tim 1:15b]. The first of these two thoughts will make you understand what powerful advocates these Saints are with God for obtaining this virtue for you. The second will convince you that they are not only able, but willing to do it.[5]

In another surviving manuscript entitled "Divine Affections", Aloysius again records his thoughts on humility.

You should recommend your desires to God, not as they are in yourself, but as they are in the breast of Jesus. For since they are good, they will be in Jesus, before they are in you, and He will express them infinitely better than you can to the Eternal Father. When you desire any virtue, you should have recourse to those Saints who have been especially distinguished for it. For example, for humility, to Saints Francis, Alexius,[6] etc.—for charity, to Saints Peter and Paul, to Saint

---

[5] Aloysius Gonzaga, reflection on humility (n.d., from personal papers), quoted in Cepari, *Life of Saint Aloysius*, 160–62; translation adapted.

[6] Tradition relates that Alexius (or Alexis) was the son of a Roman senator who left his bride on the night of their wedding, choosing to live as a hermit in Edessa. After seventeen years, he returned to Rome and lived the remainder of his life under the steps of his father's home, unrecognized by his family or wife. At the time of his death (which was held to be around the year 417), a document was found on his body that revealed his true identity. Although scholars generally agree that the story of Saint Alexius is no more than a pious

Mary Magdalene, etc. If you wanted to obtain promotion in the army from an earthly prince, you would address him through the General of his forces or through one of the colonels, rather than through the Master of the Household, or any other domestic official. In the same way, if you wish to obtain fortitude from God, you should go to the martyrs; for penitence, to the confessors; and so with the rest.[7]

Aloysius knew the value of humility, and he did everything he could to live a life hidden from the eyes of the world. But we should not think that it was his desire for hiddenness that made him humble. Rather, Aloysius understood who and what he was: the child of a loving God, without whom he would not be, and a sinful human creature who, because he loved God, wanted to grow into the man of faith, the saint, that God had made him to be. The young Jesuit recognized that true humility is not to be equated with enduring humiliations. Rather, real humility is the ability to see ourselves as God sees us: we are His beautiful, broken children, in need of healing and redemption. For Aloysius, this understanding of who and what he was, was rooted in his faith in a God who was his all. He never did or said anything that would draw attention to his lineage or his family or to his own personal gifts and attributes. We can only imagine what sort of interior struggles he must have endured as he battled what he himself referred to as his "vanity and self-esteem". Part of his knowing himself was his awareness that he had unique gifts and talents. But rather than seek to use these to his own advantage, he made the sacrifice of offering them to and for the good of others.

Aloysius sought as much as possible to avoid any concessions that might be made for him on account of his health. His fear was that they might really come from some regard for his Gonzaga name. He wanted only to live as other religious.[8] On one occasion, he was offered a private room at the Roman College. His superiors had

---

legend, his cult was widespread in both the East and the West, and he is honored as the patron of the Alexian Brothers, a religious congregation of men dedicated to serving the sick and elderly. The liturgical Feast of Saint Alexius was abolished in 1969. For a full account of the legend of Saint Alexius, see Jacobus de Voragine, *The Golden Legend: Readings on the Saints*, trans. William Granger Ryan (Princeton, N.J.: Princeton University Press, 1993), 1:371–73.

[7] Aloysius Gonzaga, "Divine Affections" (n.d., from personal papers), quoted in Cepari, *Life of Saint Aloysius*, 163; translation adapted.

[8] Cepari, *Life of Saint Aloysius*, 164.

wanted to provide him with a private, quiet space where he could rest as he needed. Because there were more than two hundred priests and religious residing at the college at the time, the only individuals who typically had the luxury of a private room were the priests, professors, and college officials. Aloysius, trying to avoid any kind of preferential treatment, even on account of his health, went to the superiors and asked to be allowed to live in a common room. A compromise was finally reached when he was assigned to a room with one other student.

Beyond this, Aloysius never sought out what was new or best. In fact, his preference was that he be given the worst of what was available. In this regard he even asked to be allowed to teach the lowest level of Latin grammar once he had completed his theological studies, arguing that his own Latin was poor and that he was suited for nothing else. In fact, his Latin was near perfect. He was motivated by a desire to form young souls in virtue and piety and also because he wanted to avoid, as much as possible, any chance of drawing attention to himself because of his intellectual gifts.[9] He never shied away from difficult work and volunteered to work with the lay brothers in the kitchen several times each week, and he even served as lamp cleaner at the college for a number of years. In his work in the kitchen, it was his responsibility to clear the dirty dishes after the midday and evening meals, clean the plates, and collect the leftovers for the poor. He also used his time after classes each day to sweep the corridors, using a long bamboo cane to clear away cobwebs. What makes these fairly insignificant acts have such a special meaning and serve as such good examples of Aloysius' humility is that, by his own testimony, he found great joy and satisfaction in being able to serve his confreres in such small, but meaningful, ways.

Flowing from his heroic humility was his obedience. We have already explored how difficult obedience could be for him at times. Nonetheless, he was able to overcome his vanity and self-will, and many witnesses attested to his nearly perfect submission to the wishes of his superiors and to the Jesuit Rule.

It is no surprise that Aloysius also had a great love of poverty. Considering his noble origins, it might seem to some that Aloysius'

9 Ibid., 166.

preference for poverty sprang from a romanticized ideal of religious life or of poverty in general. What made Aloysius' spirit of poverty sincere was that it was not the poverty of the miser or of one who could be called "cheap". Instead, his love of poverty sprang from his deep sense of gratitude for all he had been given by God and his brothers in the Society of Jesus. For this reason, he never sought to have anything more than those around him, and he was always willing to sacrifice for the good of another. As to his personal belongings, Father Cepari notes that he had no unnecessary clothing or books, no watch, nor any extra devotional items. Even his rosary was of no value. He kept only a religious picture of Saint Catherine of Alexandria and another of Saint Thomas Aquinas, and these he had been obliged to accept as gifts from others. This young religious had taken to heart the admonition that members of the Society were to ask for nothing and give nothing, believing that "one must be convinced that the worst things in the house will be given to him for his greater profit and advancement."[10]

In his prayer, as in the whole of his life, the *Spiritual Exercises* of Saint Ignatius held pride of place. He regarded the *Exercises* as a means not only of converting sinners but also of reviving religious fervor. Father Cepari records that each year during vacation time, he asked for a week during which he could revisit certain sections of the *Exercises*.[11]

For his own use during these times of retreat, Aloysius composed sets of notes, divided according to the four-week cycle of the *Spiritual Exercises*. These notes, in the form of sentences in Latin, were among those papers of his that were entrusted to Cepari after Aloysius' death. In his *Life*, Father Cepari transcribed a few of these, representing the themes of the first week:

> For the Exercises of the First Week
> The judgments of God are inscrutable, who knows whether He has yet pardoned my sins in the world?
> The pillars of Heaven have fallen and been broken to pieces, who can promise me perseverance?

[10] Ibid., 172.
[11] Ibid., 177.

The world is now in the depth of malice. Who shall appease the anger of the all-powerful God?

The greater number of religious and ecclesiastics forget their vocation: How will God continue to bear so great a loss to His kingdom?

The faithful all deprive God of His glory by the tepidity of their lives: Who shall restore it?

Woe to seculars, who defer penance until death is at hand. Woe to religious who have slumbered until the last hour.

By these considerations is sluggishness to be shaken off, and our resolution to do penance, to serve God faithfully and constantly renewed.

True repentance is awakened by deep grief for the contempt of such a loving God, who has been outraged by me.

This sorrow makes me grieve so deeply for mortal sins, that it excites great compunction even for all venial sins.

It goes so far, that not only does it acknowledge and venerate God's mercy in pardoning sins, but for the honor of Divine justice, it most earnestly desires to suffer all the punishment justly due to our sins.

God infuses into the hearts of the well-disposed this great hatred of self by which the resolution of severely punishing ourselves by external penances is excited and strengthened.[12]

His love for God showed itself in his untiring practices of prayer. In addition to his devotion to the *Spiritual Exercises*, he also frequently visited the churches and shrines of the city of Rome, venerating the relics they housed. One of his favorite shrines was that of the Madonna della Strada in the Church of the Gesù. Here he would frequently honor his "Mother and Mistress" by the recitation of the Rosary and other pious devotions.

* * * * *

In all of his penances and sacrifices, in his prayer and service, Aloysius' primary motivation was love. He loved God above all, and, out of love for God, he loved all those who were around him. This love manifested itself most especially in his eagerness to serve the sick (despite his natural repugnance of the sights and smells of illness). Aloysius willingly did small acts of kindness for those in hospitals,

[12] Aloysius Gonzaga, "For the Exercises of the First Week" (n.d., from personal papers), quoted in ibid., 177–78.

sweeping the floors, changing their linens, washing their bodies, and feeding them. He also received permission to visit the sick in their homes, where he tried to serve not only the physical needs of the infirm, but their spiritual needs as well. It could be said that in the sick he found a way to fulfill the missionary zeal that had once been a motivation for joining the Society of Jesus.

Aloysius was also very aware of the spiritual needs and well-being of his confreres in the Society. He tried to help his companions avoid idle or destructive talk, and, to assist him in this effort, he recruited a number of like-minded young religious. Together with these companions, having the blessing of his superiors, he set to work reforming the conversations of others, both his juniors in the community and also the priests and senior religious who were present during the times of recreation. As a token of the esteem in which the young Jesuit was held by his contemporaries, Father Cepari relates that, out of consideration for him, those present would automatically change the topic of conversation to spiritual topics when Aloysius was present, knowing that this would please him.[13] He also tried to assist the newly professed religious as they made their way from the novitiate into the ranks of the professed, striving to help them keep up good spirits and the zeal of the novitiate. "Yes" and "no" meant for him exactly what they expressed, and he himself said that duplicity, equivocation, and exaggeration were not only the enemies of simplicity, but incompatible with the spirit of a religious.[14]

Aloysius was also known to be particularly solicitous of those young religious he knew to be struggling with their vocation. During recreation, he would seek out a struggling brother, regardless of what others thought or said, and encourage him through his speech and presence. When he felt that his confrere was in a more secure place in terms of his vocation and religious commitment, Aloysius would then begin to encourage the brother to foster worthwhile friendships within the community. In this way, Aloysius also fostered a more general spirit of community among his confreres, a community of mutual support and true fraternity. With this endeavor to create a

---

[13] Cepari, *Life of Saint Aloysius*, 179.

[14] Maurice Meschler, S.J., *St. Aloysius Gonzaga: Patron of Christian Youth* (Rockford, Ill.: TAN Books, 1985), 186.

supporting and more zealous community, Aloysius was also gladly a part of things. As Father Cepari notes,

> He did not always keep the bow bent, without ever relaxing it, and this made him more pleasing to all. Prudently and wisely he suited himself to times, places, and persons, with sweetness of soul. Although he was grave in his actions, in his conversation he was never gloomy nor tiresome, but sweet, gracious and affable to everyone. He often would repeat some clever or witty saying, or tell some little example or story to amuse them within the limits of religious modesty. Such was the life led by Saint Aloysius, during the first two years and a half that he spent at the Roman College, and such were the effect which it produced.[15]

[15] Cepari, *Life of Saint Aloysius*, 182.

Chapter 15

Family Business

In 1589, Don Horace Gonzaga, Lord of Solferino, and the uncle of Aloysius, died at Mantua. Recall that Aloysius would have inherited these and other holdings had he himself assumed the marquisate, but, in light of his abdication, all bequests were to pass instead to his younger brother, Rudolfo, Marquis of Castiglione. Despite the fact that all had been arranged at the time of Aloysius' abdication, conflict erupted immediately following Horace's death.

The news of the death reached Rudolfo when he was in church, listening to a sermon. Immediately after the service ended, the new marquis, believing the lands of Solferino to be his possession, immediately led six hundred retainers to Solferino to take hold of the castle there. When Vincenzo, Duke of Mantua,[1] heard this, he sent word to Rudolfo that Horace Gonzaga had changed his will and left the fief to Vincenzo, and he ordered Rudolfo to surrender the castle. Rudolfo replied by declaring himself to be the duke's servant, but that as the fief was a free imperial one, it was not Horace's to bequeath to whomever he wished. Therefore, Rudolfo claimed, the holdings were his by right of succession. He, therefore, had no intention of surrendering the lands of Solferino. Vincenzo believed it was his duty to defend his own claims, and he immediately sent soldiers to force Rudolfo from Solferino. Hoping to prevent war, both Vincenzo and Rudolfo decided to defer the matter to the judgment of the emperor, who, as supreme judge, should determine who would be the new Lord of Solferino.

---

[1] Cepari, seemingly unaware of William's death in 1587, incorrectly states that William was the successor of Horace Gonzaga. Maurice Meschler observes that it was Vincenzo Gonzaga, William's younger brother, who succeeded Horace, and it was Vincenzo who entered into conflict with Rudolfo over the question of the castle in Solferino, in *St. Aloysius Gonzaga: Patron of Cristian Youth* (Rockford, Ill.: TAN Books, 1985), 180.

While it seemed that peace would be maintained and that the emperor would be allowed to decide the fate of Solferino, one of Vincenzo's captains took matters into his own hands and scaled the walls of the castle and claimed it for the Duke of Mantua.

In an effort to prevent all-out war, Donna Marta traveled to see the emperor in Prague. There, accompanied by her son Francis,[2] she laid Rudolfo's case before the emperor. The emperor sent a legate to serve as steward of Solferino until a final decision could be made. Finally, after some time, the affair was settled, and the emperor ruled in Rudolfo's favor.

Unfortunately, despite the emperor's ruling, peace did not prevail. Enmity had grown up between Rudolfo and Vincenzo, and the two kinsmen now considered one another enemies. Although there were many who wanted to see reconciliation, no peaceable solution could be found. Only after a number of futile attempts to secure peace did it occur to Donna Marta and Eleanor of Austria, Vincenzo's mother and the Dowager Duchess of Mantua,[3] that the young Jesuit would be the only one who could resolve the conflict.

Aloysius was aware of the tensions existing between his brother and the duke, as is apparent from a letter which he wrote to his mother at the end of 1588:

> Most revered Mother in Christ,
> Pax Christi.
> I received a few days ago a letter from you giving the answer of the Duke of Mantua about the castle of Solferino. It gave you an opportunity of exerting a mother's pity and love, while on me it lays the duty of begging His Divine Majesty to bring this affair to such a termination as He knows to be best. And meanwhile may He be with you in all these trials, in which as our most holy Lady is your guide,—for today, the feast of the Holy Innocents, she fled to Egypt,—I think you cannot have a greater consolation than to look at such a guide. It was for this very reason that our Blessed God and

[2] Francis, who was nine or ten years old at the time, was invited to stay in Prague, where he became a page in the court of the emperor. Francis would later succeed Rudolfo as marquis.

[3] Eleanor de' Medici, childhood playmate of Aloysius, married Vincenzo Gonzaga in 1584 and was thus the Duchess of Mantua at that time. Vincenzo's mother, Eleanor of Austria, was now the Dowager Duchess of Mantua.

His most holy mother chose to pass through the bitter waters of tribulation, that as they tasted so bitter to them they may be made sweeter for us.

I, by the Lord's favor, am pretty well, and as Christmas has come, the season of abundance of prayers, I remember all the more to pray for you. So I beg you to do for me, which is just what I need, as I, by God's goodness, want for nothing else; to Whom in conclusion I commend you.

Rome, December 29, 1588.

Your obedient son in Christ,

Aluigi Gonzaga, S.J.[4]

In September 1589, Donna Marta wrote to Claudio Aquaviva, superior general of the Jesuits, explaining the situation to him and asking that Aloysius be sent back to his family. When Aloysius was first approached about returning to Castiglione to seek reconciliation, he was understandably hesitant. He had no desire to become involved in political intrigue or to risk losing his hard-won peace. Only after taking the matter to prayer and seeking the advice of Father Robert Bellarmine, his spiritual director and confessor, did he finally consent. Bellarmine, in fact, encouraged Aloysius to do so, saying that he should go because it seemed to be God's Will for him.[5] Although he regarded his confessor's words as an oracle, he ultimately deferred the matter to his general, Father Aquaviva.

A short time later, Claudio Aquaviva received a second urgent request, this time from the emperor's brother, asking that Aloysius be sent to resolve the conflict. In light of this new appeal, Aloysius was ordered to leave Frascati, where he was staying during the September vacation, and return to Rome so that he might prepare to leave for Castiglione as soon as possible. Aloysius, always obedient, took only fifteen minutes to prepare for the trip to Rome. When he arrived there, he received his orders from Father Aquaviva to leave for Castiglione as soon as possible.

Before departing, Aloysius took the time to take leave of his relatives, the cardinals Gonzaga and della Rovere. While he was with Cardinal della Rovere, he fainted on account of his persistent

---

[4] Aloysius Gonzaga to his mother, Dec. 29, 1588 (Letter XIX), in Virgil Cepari, S.J., *Life of Saint Aloysius Gonzaga*, ed. Francis Goldie, S.J. (New York: Benziger Brothers, 1891), 411.

[5] Cepari, *Life of Saint Aloysius*, 184.

headaches and the stress of his hurried preparations to leave the city. The cardinal reproved him for not taking better care of his health. Aloysius responded that he, in fact, took too good care of his health, not doing nearly as much penance as he deserved.[6]

Aloysius left Rome on September 12, 1589, accompanied by a lay brother, James Borlasco. Borlasco was remembered as being a very prudent man, and his superiors gave him special instructions to watch out for Aloysius' health. In this regard, the lay brother was given full authority over the young cleric. The morning they were to begin their journey, the brother brought Aloysius a pair of riding boots. After Aloysius accepted them, Brother James made an offhand comment that they had once belonged to someone important. Aloysius, always afraid of being shown some sort of preference, began to look at the boots to see if he could find some excuse for not wearing them. Borlasco shrewdly figured out what his young charge was up to and took the boots away, quietly returning with a pair of boots a few minutes later. Aloysius gladly accepted this pair; in truth, the brother brought Aloysius the same pair of boots.[7]

Traveling with Aloysius and Brother James was a priest, Father Bernardino Medici, a friend of Aloysius' who was traveling to Milan to teach Scripture. During their journey, Aloysius did not omit his usual devotions, and he maintained his habit of discussing only pious topics. Father Cepari records that the coachmen and innkeepers they met along the way received him with devotion, showing great attention to his needs—a trait, he comments, which "is rarely seen in such people".[8] When the party stopped in Siena to stay in one of the Jesuit houses, Aloysius refused to allow his feet to be washed, believing it was being offered to him as a sign of preference for his past position.[9] Traveling further on, the party reached Florence, much to Aloysius' delight. It was there that Aloysius left Father Medici, proceeding on to Bologna, where he again stayed in a house run by the Society. Although the superior provided Aloysius with a guide who was to show him the famous sights of the city, he only wished to visit some of the principal churches. After seeing two or three of these, he was happy to return to the college.

[6] Ibid., 186.
[7] Maurice Meschler, S.J., *St. Aloysius Gonzaga: Patron of Christian Youth*, 192.
[8] Cepari, *Life of Saint Aloysius*, 187.
[9] This practice reflects a long-standing custom associated with receiving strangers.

Shortly before Aloysius and Brother James arrived in Mantua, they stopped for the night at a local inn. The innkeeper gave them a room that had only a single bed. Upon seeing this, the brother pulled the innkeeper aside and explained that they were religious and could not share a bed, as this was opposed to their custom. The innkeeper responded by saying that he would give them no other room because he wanted the other beds free in the event that some noble or other might stop for the night. Upon hearing this, Brother James became angry, asking the innkeeper if he took them for beggars. Aloysius, who overheard all of this, asked the brother to be quiet. Brother James responded by saying that Aloysius at least should be shown some respect. To this Aloysius answered, "Brother, do not be disturbed, for you have no reason to be; we make profession of being poor. If he treats us according to our profession, we cannot, we ought not to complain."[10] In the end, since no other travelers came to the inn that night, the brother got what he wanted.

As soon as Aloysius and Brother James arrived in Mantua, Aloysius went to visit Donna Eleanor of Austria. The dowager duchess was overjoyed to see him, and they enjoyed a meaningful visit together. From Mantua, he sent the following letter to Rudolfo:

Pax Christi.

Thanks be to our Lord, I have arrived safely at Mantua, with my Brother [i.e., Brother Borlasco], and am lodged through the kindness of the Fathers of the Society in their College. And today I will present myself and endeavor with God's help to disentangle and decide the business, which before all, I have wished to place in His Hands. It is for Him to do what is best, and this I hope He will. Towards evening, the lay brother, my fellow traveler, and I shall be at Castiglione, where we shall stay.

I conclude, asking you to present my respects to the Lady Marchioness, our Mother, whose hands I kiss.

The College of Mantua, 1589.

Your Devoted Servant in Christ,

Aluigi, Gonzaga, S.J.[11]

---

[10] Cepari, *Life of Saint Aloysius*, 188.
[11] Aloysius Gonzaga to his brother Rudolfo, 1589 (Letter XXI), in ibid., 412.

Aloysius immediately went to Castiglione with Brother James and another Jesuit, Father Antony Giunio, whom the pair had met by chance as Giunio traveled to Brescia. In passing, Father Giunio asked someone to run ahead and let the marquis know of his brother's arrival. The man went through the streets telling everyone he met that Aloysius had returned. Although it is not what he would have wanted, great numbers of people came out to meet Aloysius, and he was received with great joy and devotion: bells were rung and a round of cannon fire sounded from the fortress. Rather than being puffed up by this display, Aloysius was overwhelmed with confusion. When they finally reached the castle, Rudolfo came out to meet his brother.

Inside the castle, the servants and attendants addressed Aloysius as "Most Illustrious" and "Most Excellent", as they had done before his abdication and entry into religious life. This saddened him, because he realized that he would never be completely free of his past. His disappointment was further increased because Donna Marta was not in the castle at the time of his arrival. The following day, after sending his mother a message letting her know that he had come to Castiglione, Aloysius and his companion traveled the twelve miles to San Martino, where she was staying at the time. Mother and son spent the entire day together. Sadly, the joy of their reunion was overshadowed by the affairs that had brought Aloysius back to his hometown. Although Aloysius desired to have Brother James present during their conversations (it would seem that he hoped it would prevent any sort of emotional outburst from the marchioness), the brother did leave them alone. When Aloysius questioned him about this, he replied that as Donna Marta had asked the Father General to send her son all the way from Rome, she should be allowed to open her soul to him with all the freedom she needed. Not even Aloysius could find fault with such a reply.

Returning to Castiglione, Aloysius spent several days acquainting himself with the details of the dispute. Although he stayed with his mother and brother, he acted as guest in their residences, never asking for anything, including clothes warmer than those he had brought with him from Rome. To get what he needed, in accord with his vow of poverty, Aloysius wrote to the rector of the Jesuit college in Mantua. Donna Marta tried to press Aloysius to accept two warm vests, one for him and one for Brother James, but he refused. Undeterred, she went to the brother, who gladly accepted the vests. The following morning he took one of the vests in to Aloysius, who refused to take it from him. "Take it," he said, "since your mother gives it to you as alms for the love of God, and since you require it, I wish you would accept it." Aloysius submitted and wore the vest, remembering that he had been ordered to submit to the brother's judgment where his own health was concerned.[12]

As his business began to unfold, Aloysius made no assumptions of preference based on his former status as prince and heir of the marquisate. Instead, he waited for audiences in antechambers with others and would not allow himself to be announced ahead of anyone else. He also tried to avoid being waited on by the servants who surrounded him. As had been his custom before entering the Society, he refused any assistance in dressing and even made his bed himself, and all this in spite of the arguments put forth by the servants. He sought solitude as much as he was able and was diligent in offering up his daily devotions and in praying the Divine Office. Each evening, he spent three hours alone in prayer, and before going to bed, prayed the Litanies and made his examination of conscience.

Aloysius also made it a point to go out among the people of Castiglione, attending Mass and receiving the sacraments of reconciliation and the Eucharist in the parish Church of Saints Celsus and Nazarius. On the first feast that occurred during his stay, he considered giving a sermon, but decided against it, believing his first obligation lay in giving good example to his own family. Brother James, who witnessed all this and later spoke of these and many other details to Father Cepari and their Jesuit confreres, held Aloysius in great esteem.

The days passed quickly and were filled with meetings, and the pair of Jesuits had to make several trips to Brescia and Mantua. Finally, believing he had learned all he needed, Aloysius and Brother James relocated to Mantua where they took up residence at the Jesuit college. The time had come to begin negotiations with the Duke of Mantua. The task Aloysius had before him was not an easy one. Although he had a great deal of support for his mission, he had to navigate the intricacies of court politics. Aloysius was forced to wait

---

[12] Cepari, *Life of Saint Aloysius*, 191.

some time before he was able to have an audience with the duke. He spoke of this to his mother:

> My Mother in Christ,
> I send back the messenger to your Ladyship because I see that the audience with the Duke is delayed longer than I expected, as he is continually on the move between Mantua and Marmirolo. Signor Fabius [Gonzaga] told me the other day, that up to this time, since the arrival of his Highness, he had not had an hour in which he thought he could give me a quiet audience such as my business requires, and as the Duke promised. I do not fail to use the necessary diligence as I have Signor Fabius for procurator and Signor Prospero [Gonzaga] for solicitor. I do not dare to hurry them more, because I do not want seculars to preach patience to me, which I ought to teach to them. I therefore make this known to your Ladyship, and I beg you to inform Signor Alphonso, that he may not be surprised or anxious at my delay. As soon as I get an audience I will let you and my uncle know; and I recommend myself to both of you in our Lord.
> Mantua, October 26, 1589.
> Your Ladyship's Most Obedient Son in Christ.
> Aluigi Gonzaga, S.J.[13]

In Aloysius' first interview with the duke, after having first had recourse to prayer, he settled the entire matter. In the space of an hour and a half, Aloysius successfully brought to an end what others had spent months upon months trying to resolve. Aloysius had had to face a certain amount of animosity on the part of the duke, who was offended by the marquis' attitude toward him during their disagreement; nevertheless, Aloysius obtained all he had set out to achieve. It says a great deal about Aloysius' diplomatic prowess that, although he faced the duke's wounded pride and suspicions that he might act with a natural prejudice toward Rudolfo, Vincenzo deferred to his younger kinsman. Cepari records that there were some courtiers who insisted that the duke credit others of the princes and nobles who had worked to achieve reconciliation, hoping to downplay Aloysius' role in the matter. The duke responded that he wished to finish the business at once, since what he did, he did to

[13] Aloysius Gonzaga to his mother, Oct. 26, 1589 (Letter XXII), in ibid., 412–13.

please Brother Aloysius, and this is something he would have done for no one else.[14]

In a letter to his uncle, Fabio Gonzaga, written after Aloysius' audience with the duke, Aloysius reveals some of the necessary political maneuverings involved in this dispute and of the diplomatic sensitivity and tact being required of him.

> My illustrious and most honored Lord in Christ.
> Pax Christi.
> I beg your Lordship to see that his Highness gives his consent to receive my brother into his favor; to annul his banishment there cannot fail to be some plan according to the wishes of the Duke. I beg of you, since the Duke promised me to do this for the love of God, in Whose Name I asked this favor, not to seek to benefit him by means of any other Prince. I write this to your Lordship on account of a plan proposed to me, not from his Highness, but out of his own head by Signor Tullius, regarding the Emperor. As the Duke has not sought for this, it would only hinder and delay the affair so, that I could not before my departure have the consolation to know that the Duke had restored him to favor. If letters from members of noble families are required, they could be procured before my brother's arrival in Mantua, when the assurance of this favor has been given.
> I pray God to grant you every grace.
> The College of Mantua, November 5, 1589.
> Your obliged Servant in the Lord,
> Aluigi Gonzaga, S.J.[15]

For the sake of winning a complete reconciliation and in the hopes of clearing Rudolfo of a number of false charges brought against him by courtiers of the duke, Aloysius asked Tullius Petorzzari, secretary of state for the Duke of Mantua, to compile a list of all the complaints being leveled against Rudolfo. Aloysius took the list to Rudolfo in Castiglione, where the marquis cleared himself of all charges, replying to each point, to the satisfaction of the duke and his retainers. With this, Vincenzo was fully satisfied.

---

[14] Meschler, *St. Aloysius*, 196.

[15] Aloysius Gonzaga to Fabio Gonzaga, Nov. 5, 1589 (Letter XXIII), in Cepari, *Life of Saint Aloysius*, 413; translation adapted.

A short time later, Aloysius brought Rudolfo to Mantua where the duke received him with great warmth and where the two shared a fine meal. The duke urged Aloysius to remain with them, but he declined, preferring to return to the college and his Jesuit confreres.

It was with great joy that Aloysius was able to pen the following to his uncle, Fabio Gonzaga:

> Pax Christi.
> Thanks be to the Lord our God, who in His infinite charity and mercy, has deigned to bring this long and intricate business to a happy end by means of your Lordship, who has thus restored peace to our family and gained great merit in the sight of God. I receive this grace from His Hands and I beg Him to give you a reward in Heaven for it, and in the meantime every consolation here below as a pledge of eternal recompense.
> From the College of Mantua, 1589.
>> Yours devoted and obliged in the Lord,
>> Aluigi Gonzaga, S.J.[16]

* * * * *

Having brought about a peaceful reconciliation between his brother and the duke, Aloysius now set out to bring to an end a grave public scandal of which his brother was the cause. The marquis had fallen in love with a young woman of Castiglione who, although she was of noble lineage, was not his equal in rank. She was the only child of the man who had charge of the mint of Castiglione, and, as such, her father was very wealthy. Father Cepari records the incident in this way:

> One day when she chanced to be out walking, the Marquis caused her to be thrust into a close carriage, and carried off to one of his country houses. While mad and [sic] youthful love, and his absolute power and authority, prompted him to commit this crime, on the other hand his fear of God, and his good upbringing had so much weight with him, that he made up his mind not to retain the lady against his conscience

[16] Aloysius Gonzaga to Fabio Gonzaga, 1589 (Letter XXV), in Cepari, *Life of Saint Aloysius*, 414.

and with offence to God, but to take her as his lawful wife. He preferred to do himself and his noble house an injury, rather than to live
in sin and out of favor with Heaven. Accordingly he married her
secretly, in the presence only of the archpriest, who was his own parish priest, and of the necessary witnesses. He had obtained beforehand
the license of the bishop who gave the dispensation according to the
usual form on the twenty-fifth of October, 1588. The lady remained
with him as his wife.[17]

Rudolfo's reasons for keeping the marriage secret seem to have
been twofold. First, he did not want Donna Marta to have any
knowledge of the marriage. Second, he wanted to keep his uncle
Alfonso Gonzaga in the dark as well. Alfonso Gonzaga had no male
heirs, and, because of this, Rudolfo was to inherit his holdings in
Castel Goffredo. Alfonso did have a daughter, however, and Rudolfo
feared that his uncle would be angry that the marquis had married
someone other than his only daughter. The young lady was of an age
to marry, and her father had intended to obtain the pope's dispensation to allow her to marry her cousin, the marquis.

We know that Aloysius knew of the scandal as early as June 1588,
at which time he sent the following letter to his mother, addressing
both the tensions with the Duke of Mantua and Rudolfo's supposed
extramarital affair.

Honored Mother in Christ.
Pax Christi.
Your last letter tells me the good desire my brother had to come to
terms with the Duke of Mantua; and I beg you not to cease to help
towards this end. As to what you told me besides, I think the fittest
means is what Christ, our Lord, instituted on earth, namely marriage.
It seems to me it would be well to counsel it to my brother and if you
think it necessary Monsignor the Cardinal della Rovere and I will also
advise it, as to both of us it seems expedient. I know of no match here
except the daughter of Count Troilus di S. Secondo, who has been
proposed to marry the brother of a Cardinal of this Court, a great
friend of Monsignor della Rovere. But as the arrangement is already
begun, and especially as it is with a personal friend of the Cardinal, I

[17] Cepari, *Life of Saint Aloysius*, 197–98. The incident was omitted from the earliest editions
of Father Cepari's life of Saint Aloysius.

do not think it well to hinder it till we see the upshot. However he told me he did not think it would come off on account of the lady, who as she is from the north would be very unwilling to marry in these parts. If we wait, I think it would not be a bad match for the Marquis, my brother.

You could learn more about it there, and if you found it was a match which was pleasing to the Duke of Mantua, I think it better, because it would help to kill two birds with one stone. You and Signor Alphonso, my uncle, if you think it well, could take pains there to push the suit, while I, on my part, with the little I can do, will not fail to commend it to the Divine Majesty, from Whom in the first place we are to look for all good results. Besides, if needs be, his relatives, Monsignori the Cardinals Gonzaga and della Rovere will not fail to further it and to help in every way. With this in conclusion I commend myself to you with the Lord and beg you to salute in my name Lady Hippolyta,[18] my brother, the Marquis, etc.

Rome, June 20, 1588.

Your obedient son in Christ,

Aluigi Gonzaga, S.J.[19]

The clandestine marriage had taken place a year before Aloysius traveled to Castiglione. Since it had been kept a secret, everyone, including Aloysius, believed that the woman was Rudolfo's mistress rather than his wife. At his mother's request, Aloysius urged Rudolfo to break off his relationship with the woman and to marry their uncle's daughter.

Rather than tell Aloysius the truth, the marquis promised that he would end the relationship and do as Aloysius asked—a promise he never fulfilled. Aloysius feared that if the matter were not settled during his time in Castiglione, it never would be. He pressed Rudolfo to give his word of honor, which the marquis did. Satisfied with this, Aloysius traveled to Milan on November 25, 1589, while Brother James went to Venice. While in Milan, he resumed his studies and awaited his brother's arrival, which finally occurred in January. Arriving at the college on the morning of a feast day on which Aloysius had received Communion, the marquis was forced to wait

---

[18] Hippolyta was the wife of Don Alfonso Gonzaga.

[19] Aloysius Gonzaga to his mother, June 20, 1588 (Letter XVIII), in Cepari, *Life of Saint Aloysius*, 410; translation adapted.

until his Jesuit-brother had finished his act of thanksgiving; only then would Aloysius see him. It was at this meeting that Rudolfo confided to his brother that he and the young lady had been married fifteen months before.

Understandably, Aloysius was overjoyed at this news, but, although he was satisfied that his brother was in no way offending God, he would not agree to keep the marriage a secret without first seeking the counsel of some learned Jesuits in Rome. Rudolfo agreed to this, and Aloysius wrote to Rome and also asked the advice of some clerics in Milan. All those consulted agreed that Rudolfo had an obligation to make the marriage known and to end the public scandal, particularly since the scandal offended both the honor of God and the young lady in question. Rudolfo agreed to do this, and Aloysius took it upon himself to bring peace among their relatives. The next step was to be a difficult one for Rudolfo: he had to make the details of his marriage public:

> Most Illustrious and honored brother in Christ,
> Pax Christi.
> I thank you for the messenger you sent me. I have fully explained to him how much I feel before God, having consulted the judgment and opinion of competent persons, particularly of him whom you consulted in Milan, that you are in conscience bound under pain of grievous sin. Nothing more remains for me than to beg and most humbly entreat you for the love of God and by the bowels of Jesus Christ, and of the most Blessed Virgin, not to disappoint my hopes of you which you strengthened by a solemn oath to carry out one of the two plans, which I explained to the arch-priest. If you will do this I shall rejoice greatly to have in you a brother in Christ, whom I have always stood by, and whom I have wished to serve, and in future will never cease to serve.
> I have desired, if opportunity offered, to give my life for your soul's salvation. It was this desire for your salvation which induced me to leave Rome and to pass this winter in Lombardy to the detriment of my studies. All this seems as nothing to me if I win to Christ a brother so dear to me in Him. Should I however not obtain this from you, you must know, that I do not and will not recognize you as a brother in the flesh, for I have died to you as such more than four years ago. No, I should think it a great disgrace if, after renouncing every other thing and myself also for the love of Christ, I should now through

natural affection be ashamed of Christ and be blind to an offence
against Him. For Christ himself says: "Go and admonish thy brother.
If he hears thee..."

Thus I intend to act. However, I will wait twelve days, beginning
tomorrow, for your answer. If it be to the effect that you will do your
bounded duty, to which the example of the Duke of Mantua and of
your own uncle Alphonso should be sufficient to inspire you,[20] to
say nothing of any kindness I have done you, or of your obligation
to God, if I say, you act thus, then shall I return consoled to Rome.
If however you deal otherwise with God and myself, I shall proceed
in the affair, in the way I signified to the parish priest. I shall grieve
for the sad lot which has come upon me, and shall leave it to God
to remedy the evil by His holy and all-powerful Hand. I beg of you
again to be mindful of God, Who is always God, whether He waits
for our repentance or punishes the sins committed either against Him
or against those who wish to serve Him. Do not fail to do your duty.
Do not fail. I repeat again, do not fail. Take notice: I have repeated it
three times; for you will certainly repent, if you fail.

In the meantime, I shall pray that God may move your heart and
give you that happiness and abundance of graces that I desire for you
with all my soul.

Milan, February 6, 1590.

Your most affectionate brother in the Lord,

Aluigi Gonzaga, S.J.[21]

This letter was followed by another three days later:

Illustrious brother in Christ.

Pax Christi.

You have heard my proposition, which is so much easier, as of
two things which I required from you after my leaving Milan, I now
only bind you to one, which you owe me, not as brother only, but
as a Christian. In conformity with what I heard from you, I wrote to
Rome about my return which will take place shortly, though I do not
know the day, I know it will be soon. And as I am first to see you go

[20] In citing the examples of the Duke of Mantua and Alfonso Gonzaga, Aloysius presents
Rudolfo the example of one whose marriage was called into question and of another who
chose to marry beneath his rank.

[21] Aloysius Gonzaga to his brother Rudolfo, Feb. 6, 1590 (Letter XXVI), in Cepari, *Life of
Saint Aloysius*, 382–84; translation adapted.

to Germany, in case you take the more holy resolution, I think this
will be the sooner the better. Make haste therefore, for you may be
certain that I will keep my promise as far as I can. But do what is your
duty, I say again do not fail, as I feel certain you will not; therefore
commending you as earnestly as I can to God and asking for you, from
His Divine Majesty every happiness and abundance of his holy graces,
I conclude.

Milan, February 9, 1590.

>Your most affectionate brother in our Lord

>Aluigi Gonzaga, S.J.

I desire in every way that we should be friends in the Lord, but
from Him I have to look for the necessary strength to obtain this, even
if by religious force. And remember that of two things which you
promised me, to unveil the altar, and to send her away from you.[22] I
only bind you to one, and this too after your return from Germany.
Your departure has to take place before mine to Rome, which will
be very shortly.[23]

After only a short stay in Mantua, Rudolfo returned to Castiglione.
Aloysius, accompanied by a new brother-companion, Flavius Saraceni
of Siena, soon followed. Along the way, Aloysius pointed out to Saraceni that this was his second trip to Castiglione; the first trip was for
the business of the world, the second for the affairs of God.[24] Having
arrived in Castiglione, Aloysius convinced his brother to make the
marriage known to Donna Marta and to ask her to accept her new
daughter-in-law. This done, Aloysius himself announced the fact of
the marriage to the people of the town and sent letters to the Duke
of Mantua, Giovanni Cardinal Vincenzo, Scipione Cardinal Gonzaga,
and to other nobles and relatives affected by the marriage. Aloysius
received warm replies from all of these, but none pleased him so much
as that which he received from Don Alfonso (from whom Rudolfo
had especially wanted to keep his marriage a secret).[25]

---

[22] Here Aloysius again refers to his desire for Rudolfo to make the details of the marriage
known and to send his wife away from the castle until he had done so.

[23] Aloysius Gonzaga to his brother Rudolfo, Feb. 9, 1590 (Letter XXVII), in Cepari, *Life
of Saint Aloysius*, 414–15.

[24] Cepari, *Life of Saint Aloysius*, 199.

[25] Rudolfo did inherit Alfonso's estates in Castel Goffredo. In time, Francis Gonzaga, the
youngest of Aloysius' brothers and the successor of Rudolfo, exchanged the holdings at Castel
Goffredo for those of Medole.

Having succeeded in this endeavor, Aloysius was asked by Donna Marta to preach a sermon in the parish Church of Saints Celsus and Nazarius. The sermon, which he had hoped to keep a secret, was delivered on Saturday, March 3, 1590, to an overflowing congregation. In it, he exhorted all those present to receive Communion the next day, Quinquagesima Sunday, the last Sunday of *Carnevale*. His call was so effective that the priests and friars had to remain in the church all night hearing confessions, and several hundred people received the Blessed Sacrament that Sunday morning, including the marquis, his wife, and Donna Marta. Aloysius served the Mass.

His business now complete, Aloysius began his return trip to Rome, stopping first in Milan, where he would in fact stay for a considerable span of time. During the journey to Milan he stayed at the Jesuit house in Piacenza, where an old Jesuit, who had seen Aloysius years before surrounded by a number of attendants and servants, went to the youth's rooms to welcome him to the house. To his surprise and edification, he found Aloysius, brush in hand, cleaning his own shoes.

Having finally arrived at the Jesuit college in Milan, Aloysius wrote to his brother:

> Honored Sir, my brother in Christ.
> Pax Christi.
> The wish I have always had for your spiritual welfare and the consolation I so lately experienced in its regard at Castiglione, move me to write, at the Lord's dictation, what seems to me will be very useful and expedient for you, in the same Lord, to secure and preserve this welfare. And it is, that before your departure for Germany, during this holy season of Lent, until Easter, you prepare yourself to make a general confession, at least from the one I know you made five years ago at Mantua. For in this way you make sure, as far as can be in this life, that none of your offences against His Divine Majesty remain, which you may have left unsaid in those confessions that you made almost secretly and furtively during the time in which, through human respect, you did not dare to show yourself a servant of Christ. This I think will be all the easier as the difficulties are now removed, which you have got over, and nothing of them remains except the fruit of hope and the pledge, and a very certain one, as you may presuppose, owing to your confession, that you are in the grace of God. So I recommend it to you very much.

Henceforward to preserve this grace, the Lord it is Who, as He has deigned to move your heart far more than any words or endeavors of mine, will also instruct and direct you. Yet to fulfill the obligations I have towards you, and to cooperate with Providence to the end, as I have done up to now, I propose to you two means especially which occur to me.

One is to have in your heart that esteem and value of the grace of God, which as no matter what I might say I never could in the least part express, nor could anyone make you fully conceive, save the Blessed God, so I leave it to Him to teach it to you. This alone I will say, that as God is above all created things, honors, possessions, and anything whatsoever, so—if it were possible—should our internal esteem of His Divine Majesty surpass our esteem or idea of anything whatever. As however the limited capacity of our hearts does not allow this, we ought at least try that it should be as great as possible within us.

The second means is to act in conformity with the state of grace— "take thought for what is noble in the sight of all" [Romans 12:17b]. I remind you then of the worship and service of God, which I recommended you by word of mouth. And as it seems a special duty of religious to recommend the religious service due to God, I will descend to some particulars, which you can practice according to the measure of grace which the Lord may deign to give you.

Of these, one is to commend yourself to the Lord in prayer every morning, as by the *daily exercise* or by some such devotion, during which you might also ponder over some of the points you will find in the *daily exercise* at the end of the little book I sent you written by the late Cardinal Borromeo. There too are other souvenirs that you can read. I will not say more, but to urge you besides to go to Mass, as was agreed.

Then in the evening, I never would wish you to go to bed before looking into yourself to see whether you have offended God, so that in case you are conscious of mortal sin, from which may the Lord guard you! you may resolve as soon as possible to blot it out by means of the Sacrament of Penance. You should recollect that you always need this whenever you have anything to repent of. Nor should you therefore ever wait for a fixed period, like Easter, or any other time; for no one can be sure that he will be alive then.

Next, to provide "what is noble in the sight of all," I commend to you that respect we owe to our relatives and lords. I do not wish to say anything about this, as I feel sure how you have it at heart. Merely for the duty which is upon me, not for any need that I think you have of it, I commend to you that respect you owe to the Marchioness, our mother, as mother, and such a mother. Besides you know, as the head of your brothers, how you ought to keep them united and act towards them in a way that will lead them to always delight in that union. As to your vassals, I will not say more than that God has given them to you in charge in a special and particular way, perhaps to signify to you the special and spiritual care you should have of them, and how in the providence of God towards you, you should see the manner in which you should look after them. As to the rest, I leave God to instruct and direct you in the way of this life, till we reach our blessed country, where, that I may find myself with you and others, I have embraced the state in which I live.

Meanwhile, for the confession of which I spoke at the beginning of this letter, I propose for your spiritual director one of our own priests, as by the obligations of our Institute they are accustomed to such duties. Were you to go to Mantua, I would strongly advise Father Matthias who was confessor to the late Duke William. If you should not have to leave Castiglione, I have already spoken to the Father Rector of Brescia, who as he puts that college at your disposal, so he would always provide you with a confessor whenever you ask for one.

With this I conclude. And as what I have recommended depends for its execution more upon God's grace than on your own endeavors or on anything I might say, I offer you and promise in my prayers, such as they are, ever to commend you before the Divine presence that He may preserve you and guide you to that blessed end to which His elect aspire.

Milan, March 17, 1590.

Your Lordship's brother in our Lord,

Aluigi Gonzaga, S.J.[26]

He wrote the following to his sister-in-law a few days later:

Madam and sister-in-law.
Pax Christi.
I am thinking of beginning to avail myself of your aid for the spiritual advantage of the Marquis, which I proposed to myself when at Castiglione. Accordingly, I beg of you to recommend to him by word of mouth, what in the enclosed I urge by letter. Try then,

[26] Aloysius Gonzaga to his brother Rudolfo, Mar. 17, 1590 (Letter XXVIII), in Cepari, *Life of Saint Aloysius*, 415–17; translation adapted.

before he goes to Germany, to get him to set himself right, as I should wish him to be, by means of a general confession, in the way I have suggested to him.

I think you will have received some spiritual works which I ordered at Brescia to be sent to you.

With this, as a conclusion, I commend myself to you, and beg of our Lord to give you perfect happiness.

Milan, March 21, 1590.

Your ladyship's affectionate servant in the Lord,

Aluigi Gonzaga, S.J.[27]

Finally, when all was said and done, Aloysius convinced Rudolfo to make a general confession and to receive Holy Communion.

Sadly, the trip to Milan took a toll on Aloysius' health. During the journey, his hands, because of the severe northern winter, were swollen and chapped, and, although he was offered gloves and other remedies, he would not accept them. Not surprisingly, he became seriously ill. During his illness, he was nursed by Brother Augustine Salombrini, who delighted Aloysius with his piety and own quiet sanctity.[28] Later, after his recovery, Aloysius asked that Brother Augustine be assigned to him as his companion. When the time came for Aloysius to return to Rome, he asked that this kind brother be allowed to go with him.

During his stay in Milan, he attended lectures in theology at the college. Many remembered his simplicity and unobtrusive manner, being particularly taken by his spirit of gratitude.[29] He chose to spend what time he could spare doing odd jobs around the house and often sought out the company of the lay brothers, assisting them in their work. Aloysius found particular joy in accompanying the brothers who went out begging alms for the poor. During one of the begging trips, he was asked by a lady if he was a Jesuit. Replying that he was, she began to express her pity for a member of that Society who had once been a high-ranking noble—she was referring to Aloysius himself. He told the lady in reply that the religious in question was much

[27] Aloysius Gonzaga to his sister-in-law, Helen Aliprandi, Mar. 21, 1590 (Letter XXIX), in Cepari, *Life of Saint Aloysius*, 417.

[28] Cepari, *Life of Saint Aloysius*, 203.

[29] Meschler, *St. Aloysius*, 217.

less to be pitied than those who risk their salvation by living a life of luxury, enslaved by the world.

On another occasion, as he was walking to the Church of San Fidele to hear a sermon, he happened to meet a man who had once been one of his vassals. The man, bowing and addressing Aloysius as "Excellency", asked him to assist him in a legal matter. Aloysius returned his greeting with great humility and, taking off his biretta, replied, "I am now no longer anything but Aloysius of the Society of Jesus; I cannot assist you in any way other than by praying for you, and by advising you to lay your case before my brother."[30]

After Aloysius' death, Father Bernardino Medici, professor of Scripture in Milan, shared the following reflection of Aloysius with Father Cepari:

> Our good Brother Aloysius told me that he had a great esteem for steadfastness and perseverance in little things. He looked upon this as most important, and consequently in all his actions and regular hours kept always to the same order. He said nothing was more dangerous than to let oneself be guided by feelings. The only safe way was the way of understanding, knowledge and reason.... He had an ardent desire for tribulations, and he said to me that he looked upon it as a mark of great sanctity when he saw anyone suffering with a good conscience; that is, when he saw a man who was good, and to whom God sent occasions of suffering. He thought well of all, not that he condoned evident faults, but that he interpreted them favorably whenever possible. He admonished others for their faults, with the greatest prudence and charity, and begged to be told of his own. His conduct in all his affairs was marked by prudence, piety and charity; there was never any show of levity.
>
> The whole time I knew him I never saw a trace of any passion or inordinate emotion; nor did I ever see him commit the smallest voluntary fault or break any rule. He was preeminent in every virtue and yet there was nothing singular about him; and this I esteem the greatest of all his virtues.[31]

During the time Aloysius was residing in the college, another Jesuit priest, Achille Gagliardi, an esteemed spiritual master, came

[30] Cepari, *Life of Saint Aloysius*, 205.
[31] Quoted in ibid., 208.

to Milan to speak to the young Jesuits about prayer and spirituality. Hearing about Aloysius' gift of prayer, Gagliardi spoke with him
on several occasions and came to believe that the young religious
enjoyed "the closest union with God, daily walked in that mystical way, and was versed in that divine darkness, which is taught by
[Pseudo-Dionysius]. This practice he not only knew and delighted
in, but he had entered into it so deeply that the Father was filled with
consolation and amazement at seeing such heroic virtues and perfections in a youth, who had barely been four years in religious life."[32]

* * * * *

Shortly before Aloysius left Milan for Rome, he received, in prayer,
an interior illumination by which he understood that his time remaining in the world was to be brief. Inspired to give himself over more
completely to God, he took great consolation in this revelation of
his approaching death and renewed his efforts to be as detached as
possible from the cares of the world. Aloysius kept this revelation
to himself, sharing it only with his spiritual director and one or two
others in Rome.[33] Although he continued to apply himself diligently
to his theological studies, it was with less enthusiasm and joy than
before because, as Father Meschler notes, "he was soon to behold the
Eternal Truth and Beauty itself."[34]

---

[32] Ibid., 209.
[33] The room in which Aloysius received this revelation was converted into a chapel, and
the event is commemorated by a painting of an angel showing the young Jesuit a skull.
[34] Meschler, *St. Aloysius*, 219.

Chapter 16

Return to Rome

The prospect of returning to the Eternal City was a great consolation for Aloysius. This was where he had begun his religious life and where he would renew his friendships, becoming for the students of the Roman College a model of religious fidelity. Writing to a number of his friends about his return, he sent the following note to Father Cepari: "It will not, I think, be difficult to convince you how glad I am to be sent to the Roman College, again to see the Fathers and all my spiritual brethren there, and again to enjoy that intercourse, in the Lord, with you and so many of our acquaintances, from which I hope to derive even greater satisfaction than before. And I desire you to remember me to them in particular, while at the same time I recommend myself with my whole heart, mind and soul to the entire Roman College."[1]

To one of his former novitiate classmates, Aloysius explained that the prospect of returning to Rome was one "to which I shall respond with all the greater joy since if we have any country here on earth I acknowledge none but Rome, where I was born in Christ Jesus".[2]

Prior to receiving his final orders, Aloysius wrote to Rudolfo:

> Illustrious brother in Christ,
> Pax tibi.
> I had just finished the enclosed letter, when I received the one sent from your Highness. On the one hand it gave me great consolation, as I saw from it that my efforts with the relatives of your House have

[1] Aloysius Gonzaga to Virgil Cepari, n.d., quoted in Virgil Cepari, S.J., *Life of Saint Aloysius Gonzaga*, ed. Francis Goldie, S.J. (New York: Benziger Brothers, 1891), 211; translation adapted.

[2] Aloysius Gonzaga to Gaspar Alpieri, S.J., n.d., quoted in Cepari, *Life of Saint Aloysius*, 212; see also 385n23, and 378n10.

been successful. On the other hand, if I were to take its tone as the deliberate expression of your will, rather than as a mere outburst of feeling and lower appetite, which, when unsubdued by reason, will in such cases be easily excited, it would seem to show a certain lack of charity and concord. Nevertheless, the circumspection with which you will proceed in the future, and the respect which you will show to all to whom it is due, will in time overcome all difficulties, if your Highness will only take care always to rely on God's help and remain in His grace, from which I hope and indeed will promise you every blessing. As far as I am concerned, you may rest assured that nothing will ever come between us (for you know that in spirit I am always with you, though absent in the flesh), except whatever might separate you from God. As long as you take care to preserve the favor of His Divine Majesty, I shall never fail to render you all the friendly services that my vocation permits, as I do in the present instance by means of the letter I enclose for our lady mother. I wish you to deliver it yourself and ask her to show it to you, in order that you may see from its contents how much I have your welfare at heart. But indeed I think there is no need of further proof of this; as I have already said, nothing that I hear about you, short of an offence against God, will grieve me, whereas all good news of you will always be a great consolation to me.

I thought, also, now that my departure for Rome has been postponed until after Easter, that it could only be an advantage if, in addition to the letter which you intended to send me according to our agreement to take to Rome, you were to send a letter by post from Mantua, alluding to me and telling the most illustrious Cardinals in Rome of your journey to Germany, and also promising conscientiously to fulfill your duties as their relative. Thus you would oblige them all the more to give you a fitting recognition, and this mark of attention could not fail to promote the favorable issue for which I have been negotiating.

I should also be glad if you would pay the banker the 45 *scudi* in gold that I borrowed (in notes-of-hand) on the credit of Jerome Verduro in Rome; and I also beg you, if it seems good to you, to commission the Archpriest or some other person equally worthy of trust to pay, in case it becomes necessary, the remainder of the 100 of which I spoke, for the other purpose I mentioned. You can do this in the way that seems best to you. I intend to take advantage of the opportunity that presents itself to start after Easter, in the good company of our Fathers, on the journey to my home, Rome, and shall, in order to remain in this company, go by the way of Genoa. In passing through Tortona I shall pay my respects to her Highness the Duchess. I should be very glad if you could ascertain whether a letter I sent to Doctor Cuticio in Mantua, asking for certain books, has arrived. If he has not received them yet, I beg your Excellency to send them to me by Don Fabius Gonzaga; they must have been sent off to Rome by the attendant of the Lord Cardinal Scipio Gonzaga, so Father Hercules writes to me. If a favorable opportunity could be found to send a few other books to Rome as well, I should be very glad, and would send them to your Excellency as soon as possible. In conclusion I commend myself to you with all my heart. I have nothing more to add but the wish that you may fear God and keep his commandments (*timeat Deum et mandata ejus observet*), then you need fear nothing else, for God can do all things. May He protect you and grant you every happiness and blessing! This shall be my unceasing prayer.

Milan, March 25, 1590.

Your Excellency's most devoted brother in Our Lord,

Aluigi Gonzaga, S.J.

P.S. I shall be very glad if your Excellency can remember this long list of commissions and questions, and let me have an answer as soon as possible. It was quite right of you to open the letters, and if any more come into your hands I shall be glad if you will do the same with them. If you can get a copy of my letter of the 6th of February, do me the favor to send it to me.[3]

Finally, in May 1590, the official order for his return came from Claudio Aquaviva. Aloysius set off with a number of Jesuit companions, and, as one would expect, he maintained his usual devotions and penances as best he could during the journey. The others in the group tried to engage Aloysius in conversation and to provide small comforts for him out of consideration for his headaches and his weak health. This was something of a source of frustration for Aloysius, who exclaimed that he would have preferred to have traveled with companions who paid no attention to him at all.[4]

---

[3] Aloysius Gonzaga to his brother Rudolfo, Mar. 25, 1590, in *Lettere di S. Luigi Gonzaga*, ed. Oliviero Iozzi (Pisa, 1889), 54, quoted in Maurice Meschler, S.J., *St. Aloysius Gonzaga: Patron of Christian Youth* (Rockford, Ill.: TAN Books, 1985), 220–22; translation adapted.

[4] Cepari, *Life of Saint Aloysius*, 212.

The group stopped for a time in Siena, staying in the Jesuit college there. Aloysius expressed his desire to receive Communion in the room that had been used by Saint Catherine of Siena (d. 1380), a hope which he was able to realize, much to his delight. At the same time, the rector of the college asked Aloysius to preach a sermon to the young men who were members of the Sodality of Our Lady. He agreed to the request and, stepping into a side hall, prepared his sermon without the benefit of any books, using his prayer as his only guide and inspiration. Returning to his room, he wrote some brief notes, then delivered a sermon that was so moving and devout, that a number of those in attendance decided to enter religious life. The topic of the sermon was the text: "But be doers of the word, and not hearers only, deceiving yourselves" (Jas 1:22). After his departure from Siena, his notes were found in a copy of the writings of Saint Bernard. The page has long been venerated as a relic.

God speaks to the soul in three ways: First, by secret inspiration. *Cf.* Saint Bernard sermon 32 ... Of this mode of Divine communication the same Saint Bernard says that it is secret, and that we ought to keep it, not merely by retaining it in our memory, *nam sic scientia inflat; sed sicut servatur panis. Verbum enim Dei anis vivus est, et cibus mentis; quamdiu panis in arca est, potest a fure tolli, a mure corrodi, vetustate corrumpi; ita Verbum Dei etc. Trajiciatur igitur in viscera tua, transeat in affections et mores tuos.* [For, thus as knowledge it inspires, but it is preserved as bread. For the word of God is living and is the food of the mind. As long as the bread is in the tabernacle it can be carried away by a thief or gnawed by a mouse or decay because it is too old; so too the Word of God. Therefore it is passed into your innards, moves into your affections and your habits.] This is also what Saint James says: *Estote factores* [Be doers]. In the second book of Moses [i.e., Exodus] we read that the manna, which *non serabatur ad vescendum in die Sabbati* [which is not kept for eating on the Sabbath], was spoiled; so it is also with the Word of God, which spoils if it is kept for anything else than *ad vescendum* [for eating].

The second way: God speaks to us by the Holy Scripture, through the prophets in the Old Testament and through Christ in the New. So Saint Gregory teaches, and so Scripture itself says: *Saepe olim loquens Deus Patribus in prophetis, novissime autem in Filio suo.* [In former times, God spoke to the Fathers in prophecy, but in these latter days he speaks through his Son.] Of this speech of God, Saint James again says, *Estote factores* [Be doers (of the Word)]. It profits a Christian little to possess the Holy Scriptures if he does not live according to what

they prescribe. It profits us little to have the commandments given by
God in the Old Testament, if one does not live up to them; little to
know the beatitudes propounded by Christ in his discourses if, etc.;
little, to know how we ought to live ... little, to know of what perfection consists, if one is addicted to imperfections.... Thus the Holy
Scriptures are of no other use to such people, than that they carry their
death sentences, as Uriah carried that passed upon him by David to
Joab [cf. 2 Sam 11:14].

Thirdly, God speaks to us by his benefits. Thus Saint Bernard asks
... how God speaks to the soul and the soul to God. Of this speech
also the Apostle says: *Estote auditors et factores*; he is not content that
we should be hearers only, but also doers; for it is necessary not only
that we should acknowledge the benefits of God, which is equivalent
to hearing His Word, but that we should give them back to Him,
which is signified by *facere verbum ejus*. We see how all springs have
their origin in the sea and return to it. *Omnium virtutum et scientiarum
mare est Dominius Jesus Christus.* To Him, then, all gifts must return;
for as waters that do not run into the sea, but remain stagnant, form
into ponds and become putrid, so it is with the Divine gifts of health,
strength, talent, and eloquence. Students should offer their talents
especially to God, as Saint Augustine exhorts the young Licentius.

Now you have heard how God speaks to the soul in this threefold
manner, and that we ought to do what He says; it will therefore be
well now to consider *why* we ought to do it, and with what fervor.

The reason why we must do it seems to me to be this: It is sufficient that God has spoken. It sufficed that He said: "Let the world be
made," and the world was created; ought it not to suffice when He
says that we must be converted and go to Him by the way He wills?

Tell me, I beg of you: if your Grand Duke, who is now expected,
were on his arrival to summon some native of this town—be he poor
or rich—and promise to make him his adopted son, to give him a
share in the duchy that really belongs only to his own son, and further to care for him as his own son as long as he lived and make him
joint-heir of his states when he died; and supposing he laid down as
the sole condition of granting this favor that this adopted son should
so live as becomes the son of a duke, should leave the miserable hut
in which he had dwelt and come to the ducal palace; should take off
his wretched rags and put on rich garments; should give up his previous habits and his interactions with the common people, and only
frequent the society of the duke's son and the aristocracy;—which of
you, I ask, would then be satisfied to simply hear such an offer, instead
of accepting it immediately?

The Blessed Lord of Heaven is willing to adopt each one of us as His own; He promises to care for him in this world by His fatherly Providence, to such a degree that He will remember us more faithfully than a mother does her child, as He says by the mouth of Isaiah [49:15]:... [Can a woman forget her nursing child, or show no compassion for the child of her womb? Even these may forget, yet I will not forget you]; and after this life He will give us the eternal inheritance, as Saint Augustine says with regard to the words: *Cum dederit dilectis suis somnum....* He requires from us nothing more than that we leave behind the poor house of our fathers and mothers, either in reality or in spirit, according to each one's vocation, and living in the palace of the King of Heaven, which is ruled over by God and served by His angels; He wills that we should cast aside the miserable rags of self-love, and clothe ourselves with the festal garment of charity; we must give up the habits of common and vulgar people, i.e., renounce our imperfections and sins and acquire the habits of the Son of God, that is, gentleness, piety, justice, fear of the Lord, and other virtues. Which of us, then, will be content to only hear such a proposal and not agree to it? Truly, it seems to me that no one could do so but one who does not understand the Word of God or realize His promise!

Aristotle proves by much reasoning in the Tenth Book of Ethics that spiritual enjoyments are much greater than carnal. Then he asks why, in spite of this, we do not seek the former, and says it is because we do not know them. He gives an example of a king's son, who, as long as he is a little child, values his nurse's milk or an apple given to him by a servant more than his paternal inheritance, because he knows nothing about the latter, and the former are familiar to him; but let him arrive at a more mature age, and you will see how he despises those trifles and prefers his inheritance. So it is with us: because we do not know what God has prepared for those that love Him (1 Cor 2[:9]), we also value more the nurse's milk, i.e., earthly comfort, relatives, father, mother, etc., and prefer an apple of this earth to a lasting inheritance in Heaven. May God give us the grace to come to that maturity of spirit by which we shall value everything according to its real worth, since all the greatness of this world is nothing in comparison to what God promises us: *Super altitudines terrae sustollam te* [I will make you ride above the heights of the earth] (Isaiah 58:14[b]).[5]

* * * * *

[5] Aloysius Gonzaga sermon notes (Sodality of Mary, 1590), quoted in Meschler, *St. Aloysius*, 224–28; translation adapted.

After leaving Siena, the group finally made its way to Rome. Along the way, they would have been greeted by the new dome of Saint Peter's Basilica, which had been completed on May 14 of that year. Upon arriving in the Eternal City, he told his companions, "I have buried my dead, and no longer have any concerns with them; it is time now to think of the life to come."[6] In no time at all, it seems that Aloysius settled into life at the Roman College. Cepari relates that shortly after his arrival in Rome, the young scholastic went to the rector of the college, Father Bernardino Rossignoli, and gave him all his theological notes and papers, including his own compositions. When asked why, Aloysius explained that he did so because he felt a certain attachment to these creations of his own mind, and that they were the only things in the world for which he still felt any attachment. He wanted to be parted from them so that he might be free of everything.[7]

Father Cepari also relates that although Aloysius was remembered as having been affable and agreeable to everyone, manifesting a charity that showed no preference, during these final months of his life, he was even more amiable and engaging. His conversations at recreation almost always concerned the things of Heaven and in what perfection consists. When he was alone with anyone with whom he felt he could speak openly, he would share with them the consolations and union with God that he enjoyed. On one occasion, when at table, he heard something particularly profound read about the love of God, and he was so moved interiorly that he had to stop eating. Cepari remembers,

> We who were at table with him, noticed this, and, as we feared he felt ill, looked at him anxiously and asked if he wanted anything. But he was unable to speak, and seeing he was observed, only grew embarrassed, and remained with his eyes cast down and a tear or two stole from them; his face was burning and his breast heaving so much that we feared he should burst a blood vessel. All were filled with pity for him—and not till the end of supper did he by degrees regain mastery over himself.[8]

During this last year, Aloysius spent an hour each day in spiritual reading. His favorite books were a collection of the sermons of Saint

[6] Cepari, *Life of Saint Aloysius*, 213.
[7] Ibid.
[8] Ibid., 214.

Augustine, the life of Saint Catherine of Genoa, Saint Bernard's *Sermons on the Song of Songs*, and Bernard's *Epistola ad fratres de Monte Dei* (*Letter to the Brethren of Mont-Dieu*, also known as *The Golden Epistle*). Aloysius knew the letter so well that he almost had it memorized.

In November 1590, Aloysius began his fourth year of theology. Being assigned a room of his own, he asked for a small room and was given one at the top of a staircase. The room was so small and run-down that it would hold only his bed, a wooden chair, and a prie-dieu, which he also used as a desk. For light, the room (which measured about ten feet square) had only a skylight, and the ceiling was so low one could touch it with his hand. The scholastic who had the room after Aloysius remarked that it was a latrine, not a bedroom.[9] The Jesuits living in the house with Aloysius used to tease him by saying that at least Saint Alexius chose to live in poverty *under* a staircase.[10]

All those who knew him during his years in the Roman College, including his confessor, Robert Bellarmine, could find no fault with him. This is substantiated in the many statements made by superiors, confreres, and fellow students who knew him.

As the year 1590 came to a close, Aloysius composed a number of letters which offer us a valuable insight into his state of mind at this time.

To his brother the marquis, he wrote:

> Illustrious and honored Brother in Christ.
> Pax Christi.
>   I received a few days since a letter of yours of the beginning of September, which gave me much consolation, as I learned from it that you had sought so excellent a remedy for the sickness God had sent you, which was to have recourse to God Himself for health, and I have returned thanks to Him for restoring it to you. And as you tell me that the spiritual medicine you have used, has not only restored health, but will confirm it and preserve you from a relapse; I earnestly beg of you to use it not only in bodily infirmities, but also whenever you have any spiritual malady, because of this it has been instituted by Christ, our Lord, and from which I entreat His Divine Majesty to preserve you. I exhort you to make use of it as a preservative.

---

[9] C. C. Martindale, *The Vocation of Saint Aloysius* (New York: Sheed and Ward, 1946), 203.
[10] Cepari, *Life of Saint Aloysius*, 214.

Such medicines are not used merely in sickness, but at other times, to obtain the end which you tell me you expect from what you have taken. I am consoled that the lawsuit with the Duke of Mantua is at an end, for it will thus be easier for you to preserve the favor, first of the Divine Majesty, which I desire above all, and then of his Highness as lord and head of your family. Besides this, I hope and feel certain that between you and your brothers there will never be any quarrel or contention, other than might be the case of a father with his children, for their good and benefit. As my state of life does not allow me to entertain you with worldly news, I will tell you what my opinion is in this matter. It is, that though every law requires that positive justice (*jus*) should give way to natural, it seems to me that you will only do what is reasonable or perhaps obligatory, when in any difference or discord that may happen, you always prefer the natural laws of blood and fraternal affection to any law written by [lawyers]. I do not think it is needful to remind you of this, as I think you already have it sufficiently at heart, and in conclusion I beg the Divine Majesty to grant you the grace and peace I desire for you.

We have again here in Rome a Vacant See and we are praying for the election of a Sovereign Pontiff who may carry out the good desires with which the Lord had inspired him whom, for our sins, He called out of this world in a few days.[11]

October 4, 1590.

Your Lordship's most affectionate brother in our Lord

Luigi Gonzaga, S.J.[12]

Another letter, dating from December 1590, to one of Aloysius' Jesuit confreres, Antony Francis Guelfucci, has survived:

Dearest Brother in Christ.
Pax Christi.

I had intended not to write until I received letters from you, as we settled on when parting, but on the one hand my affection for you and the desire to enjoy a conversation with you by letter, as distance allows us no other means, and on the other hand the opportunity

---

[11] Pope Sixtus V had died on August 27, 1590. His successor, Pope Urban VII, who was elected on September 15, occupied the Chair of Peter for only twelve days, dying on September 27, 1590. Pope Gregory XIV (d. 1591) would be elected on December 5, 1590.

[12] Aloysius Gonzaga to his brother Rudolfo, Oct. 4, 1590 (Letter XXX), in Cepari, *Life of Saint Aloysius*, 417–18.

given me by Father Mancinelli's journey, have made me change my mind. So by this letter I salute you and embrace you in the Lord with all affection. God knows what consolation it has been to hear from Father Provincial the good news that for his comfort he told me he had received regarding you from your letter. May the same Lord in this precious time which He has granted to you for your spiritual profit, fill you with His gifts, and so increase His graces, that they may not benefit you only, but those also after your return here who most desire your company and have most need of spiritual improvement as is my case.

In the meantime help me with your prayers, and by recommending me to those of Father Pescatore, which I very, very much desire. I shall not fail to do the little I can in commending you to our Lord. May it please His Divine Majesty that we may help one another in His service.

In conclusion, again and again I commend myself to you and I beg you to commend me to Father Pescatore and to Father Mutius de Angelis.

Rome, December 12, 1590.
Your Brother and Servant in Christ
Luigi Gonzaga

P.S. Father Marius Fuccioli salutes you and says he has received your letter, and if you want anything you can make use of him, and I say the same of myself in all I am able.[13]

A third letter, this time to his mother, dated December 31, offers her some support as she endures the never-ending discord that plagued the family.

Illustrious Lady, my revered Mother in Christ,
Pax Christi.

As I know how much you desire and are consoled on receiving my letters for your satisfaction, I wish by this letter to take the occasion of this holy festival of Christmas to greet you and to wish you a happy feast as I have, with special fervor, begged the Lord in my prayers, such as they are, at this sacred time. It offers me an occasion to write

[13] Aloysius Gonzaga to Brother Anthony Francis Guelfucci, Dec. 12, 1590 (Letter XXXI), in Cepari, *Life of Saint Aloysius*, 418–19.

as suits my taste as all other worldly business, and whatever I have
once for all abandoned, is most tiresome to me and of the nature with
which I have least reason to be acquainted.

May God then, through the common joy of holy Church and
through the satisfaction that He had at the birth of His Only Son,
console your Ladyship and fill you with every grace. May He do this
through the intercession of His most holy Mother. Think of what
trouble and joy she felt at the same time: trouble for the temporal
poverty that she suffered in a stable, where she had not the means
to protect Jesus Christ, her Son, Who was born to her, from the
cold, nor even to provide for Him in the great need and necessities
in which she was. One can imagine that these took the place of the
pains of child-birth, from which she was freed by special privilege.
On the other hand, what great joy she felt at the sight and presence
of her Little Child, Whom she saw before her.

So as the Lord says of woman, *when she is in labor she is in sorrow, but
when she has brought forth her child, she remembers no more the anguish, for
joy that a son is born into the world,* so I think the most glorious Virgin,
when she considered the temporal needs of her Son, she had sorrow
and sadness like that of child-birth at not being able to provide for
Him as she would wish. When however she gazed on that same Son,
she was consoled and quite forgot every trouble, not merely because
a man was born, but because at the same time God was born into the
world. Thus too I will take courage, from the condition in which
I am, to advise your Ladyship what to do, to mirror yourself in the
example of the Virgin Mary; and if the cares and temporal anxieties
which you have to provide for your young orphan children sometimes gives you annoyance and trouble, just as the thought of how
to provide for the temporal wants of her child, Jesus, gave pain to
the glorious Virgin, so on your part console yourself, as she consoled
herself and received consolation from his example.

She is our real Queen, from whose example we should receive
better comfort than that offered by the Queen of Spain, in whose
service you are, or from anyone like her, who found herself in such a
condition. So if it is a comfort to the afflicted, to have companions in
like troubles, what greater consolation can your Ladyship have than
the company of Mary the Virgin, as she who shares them with you is
so great, and is in troubles and cares like those of your Ladyship?

I write just what occurs to me in the Lord, and to satisfy the desire
and consolation alike which you tell me you receive with my letters.
As to the rest, however, what concerns some individuals at home, of

which Cardinal della Rovere spoke to me, you will learn from him his opinion, to whom I entirely refer you, only adding that if that difference about which you spoke to me is to be ended without a lawsuit, as it seems to me also by no means fitting between brothers, but rather by means of arbitrators, I think they had better be chosen there than here, where owing to the great distance information could either not reach at all or be scanty. You could see who would be suitable for this, for example, perhaps the Duke Vespasian di Sabbioneta[14] or someone else whom you can better decide. I shall beg Jesus Christ that as in the Nativity the angels sang *Gloria in excelsis Deo et in terra pax hominibus bonae voluntatis*, so He may deign to grant true peace and a right will to those of your house, along with every fullness and abundance of His holy grace.

Rome, the last day of the year, 1590.

Your son, reverently in Christ,

Luigi Gonzaga, S.J.[15]

Finally, Aloysius wrote to his brother the marquis, expressing his pleasure that the family dispute had been resolved and encouraging Rudolfo to remember his obligations to those in his care.

Revered Brother in Christ,
Pax Christi.

It is a long time since I have paid you my respects by letter. So the opportunity that I have for doing this is all the more welcome. It is to recommend to you first of all an act of justice which is commended to me in aid and favor of some young women, de'Ferzadi, one of whom is already consecrated to God in a convent and the other who is perhaps going to enter. I beg you to interpose your authority that they may not be troubled or hindered from their good desires. Perhaps he who gives you this letter will make a more detailed request.

I recommend to you besides another work of mercy, but one to which I think you are bound, and it is that you remember to aid your vassals this year especially in their distress. If it is as dire as what it is here in this area and in this City, it is really extreme. Therefore, I greatly commend it to you who, I think, do not forget all the good

---

[14] Vespasian Gonzaga di Sabbioneta, Duke of Trajetto and Sabbioneta, was a fourth cousin of Saint Aloysius, descended from Louis III, Marquis of Mantua.

[15] Aloysius Gonzaga to his mother, Dec. 31, 1590 (Letter XXXII), in Cepari, *Life of Saint Aloysius*, 419–21; translation adapted.

advice and the frequent use of those preservative medicines, whether
of soul or body, of anything else, except to let you know in the end
the comfort I received at the news, in a letter from my mother, of the
agreement you have come to with your brothers about the disputed
property. In fact the agreement seems to be excellent and well fitted
to produce the union and concord that I pray for and desire from the
hands of our Lord God.

I am not going to write now to our mother, so I beg you to go on
purpose to pay her my respects in my name. This will be a consolation to her as you can at the same time give her good news about my
health. I likewise beg you to remember me to the Lady Marchioness,
your wife, to my brothers, to Monsignor the Archpriest, etc.

Rome, January 26, 1591.

Your affectionate brother in the Lord,

Luigi Gonzaga, S.J.[16]

These final letters, written by a young Jesuit to his family, reveal a
good deal about what was happening interiorly to Aloysius. Although
he had desired nothing more than to leave behind the cares and
responsibilities of his former rank and way of life, he nonetheless set
aside his own desire to be forgotten to come to the aid of his family.
We can discern, however, in his letters that Aloysius was becoming
more and more concerned with God alone, and his primary occupation was now the salvation of his own soul.

[16] Aloysius Gonzaga to his brother Rudolfo, Jan. 26, 1591 (Letter XXXIII), in Cepari, *Life
of Saint Aloysius*, 421.

Chapter 17

His Final Illness

The years 1590 and 1591 saw the whole of Italy ravaged by famine brought on by bad harvests and a fierce pestilence that decimated the population. We may recall that Aloysius urged his brother the marquis to be mindful of the needs of his subjects, as Aloysius himself was aware of the starvation and illness that plagued the city of Rome.[1] Complicating matters, people, fearing possible starvation in the country, began to flock to the cities, hoping for some reprieve. Sadly, many found none, and the estimate for the death toll in Rome alone (although the estimate is probably exaggerated) was sixty thousand.[2]

It is hard for us to imagine the effects of such famine and pestilence. A contemporary of Saint Camillus de Lellis (who ministered to the Roman poor at this time) records scenes of starvation, desolation, and desperation.

> It is horrible even to read of such a calamity; think then, what must have been their affliction, who saw men dying in the city under the benches of the butchers and other shops, reduced to feed on grass like cattle, and to eat even dead cats and dogs, and any filthy food they could find.... Anyone can imagine what must have been the condition of those wretched people, lying on the ground in the middle of winter, in damp underground vaults, without food, or fire, or, if they could sometimes light a fire, blinded and tormented with the smoke.... We will now pass from the vaults to the stables, for even there many starving and sick persons were collected, nearly buried in

---

[1] Aloysius Gonzaga to his brother Rudolfo, Jan. 26, 1591 (Letter XXXIII), in Virgil Cepari, S.J., *Life of Saint Aloysius Gonzaga*, ed. Francis Goldie, S.J. (New York: Benziger Brothers, 1891), 421.

[2] Maurice Meschler, S.J., *St. Aloysius Gonzaga: Patron of Christian Youth* (Rockford, Ill.: TAN Books, 1985), 238.

the dunghills, which had invited them by the little warmth they could find there.[3]

Giving themselves to the service of their fellow Romans, the priests and brothers of the Society of Jesus joined countless other religious in freely offering their services to the poor and starving masses. During the pestilence, both the Roman College and the novitiate at Sant'Andrea supported more than three hundred poor people each, and Claudio Aquaviva ordered the Jesuits to go out seek to the sick and poor and bring as many to the college as could be accommodated. A temporary hospital was erected near the professed house, and Aquaviva himself tended the needs of those who were housed there. Those Jesuits who were not well enough to serve the sick were commissioned to go into the streets and solicit alms for the poor. More than one of these fell victim to the plague, and Aloysius was among their number.

Despite his ardent desire to serve in the hospitals, his superiors feared exposing the frail young man to contagion, deciding that he would be allowed only to beg alms. He gave himself wholeheartedly to the task, going from door to door with his wallet. He went so far as to write to his mother and to Rudolfo asking them to send what they could for the poor of Rome. Donna Marta responded to her son's request with great generosity, in gratitude of which Aloysius wrote the following:

Pax Christi.

It was a great consolation to me to distribute the clothes to these poor, our brothers. May our Lord God, Who does not leave unrewarded anyone who does an act of charity, give you large recompense and reward in the heavenly country after which I seem now to aspire more and more, and may He by His grace grant it to us and quickly, for I feel now my days shall be shortened. God give you every joy and I kiss your hand.

Rome, February 23, 1591.

Your most affectionate son in Christ,

Aluigi Gonzaga[4]

---

[3] Quoted in Sanzio Cicatelli, *The Life of S. Camillus of Lellis: Founder of the Clerks Regular, Ministers of the Sick* (London: Thomas Baker, 1850), 1:90, 93–94.

[4] Aloysius Gonzaga to his mother, Feb. 23, 1591 (Letter XXXV), in Cepari, *Life of Saint Aloysius*, 422.

A few days later he wrote the following to his brother:

> Illustrious brother in Christ,
> Pax Christi.
>
> Though I have nothing particular at present to write about, yet I do so to satisfy the bearer of this letter and I can assure you that by the grace of God I am in very good health. I hope and pray that His Divine Majesty may grant you the same in body and soul. Today is the last of Carnival and on this day or shortly before, if I am not mistaken, I left you last year at Castiglione, with very good desires and resolutions, so I will not here remind you further, than to beg you now and hereafter to remember to put them into effect. I hope that *He who granted you to will, will give you grace to accomplish,* and earnestly entreating God by my prayers, such as they are, that He will bestow this grace upon you, I conclude by commending myself in the Lord and in my heart to your Lordship.
>
> Rome, February 26, 1591.
>
> Your most affectionate brother in our Lord,
>
> Aluigi Gonzaga, S.J.[5]

The conditions in which the scholastics and priests worked led to many becoming ill. Speaking of one of these, a friend, Brother Tiberius Bondi of Genoa, Aloysius said to a classmate, "How willingly I would change places with Tiberius and die in his stead, if our Dear Lord would but grant me the favor to do so." When pressed as to why he would say such a thing, he responded, "I say this because I have some reason to think that I am now in God's grace, whereas I do not know what may come in the future; so I would willingly die." Sometime later, he said to Robert Bellarmine, "I believe that my days are few", and when asked the reason, he replied, "Because I feel within me an extraordinary desire to labor and to serve God, and with such intense ardor that I do not think God would have given it to me if he had not meant to take me soon from this world."[6]

The obvious danger of contagion in the hospitals prompted the Jesuit superiors to prohibit certain of the young religious, including

---

[5] Aloysius Gonzaga to his brother Rudolfo, Feb. 26, 1591 (Letter XXXIV), in Cepari, *Life of Saint Aloysius,* 422.

[6] Cepari, *Life of Saint Aloysius,* 218.

Aloysius, from working with the sick. This was a real trial for Aloysius. In the end, he was not satisfied with simply being allowed to collect alms. Repeating his request to his superiors that he be allowed to serve in the hospitals, they grudgingly consented. A number of Aloysius' Jesuit confreres later testified to his courage and charity in seeking out and serving the sick.[7] Although he was prevented from working in any of the hospitals where the victims of the plague were housed, he was given permission to serve in the Hospital of Santa Maria della Consolazione, where ordinarily no patients were admitted who suffered from contagious diseases. Notwithstanding this fact, Aloysius was almost immediately struck down like his companions and was confined to his bed on March 3, 1591. Long-standing tradition relates that while on his way to the Consolazione, which was near the professed house, Aloysius found a man stricken with the pestilence, lying abandoned in the street. He approached the man without hesitation, took him on his shoulders, and carried him to the hospital where he attended to his needs. It has long been accepted that it was this act of selfless charity that led to his becoming a victim of the same pestilence.

In his account of the life of Saint Aloysius, Father Cepari relates the following anecdote of the service rendered by the young Jesuits:

It was a terrible thing to witness such a number of dying men going about the hospital half naked, with the loathsome and fetid disease, and to see them fall down dead in a corner on the stairs; but on the other hand, it was a very picture of the charity of Paradise to see Aloysius and his companions serving the sick with great gladness, undressing them, putting them to bed, washing their feet, and making their beds, bringing them their food, catechizing and preparing them for Confession, and exhorting them to patience. It was noticed by Father Fabrini[8] that Aloysius generally was engaged upon the most repugnant cases, and appeared not to know how to tear himself away from them.[9]

[7] Ibid., 218.

[8] Father Nicholas Fabrini, S.J., was minister of the Roman College. After serving as rector of the Jesuit college in Florence, he wrote an account of Aloysius' service in the hospitals in the spring of 1591.

[9] Cepari, *Life of Saint Aloysius*, 218.

From the first instant Aloysius began to feel ill, he believed (in accord with his premonition in Milan) that this was to be his final illness. Rather than being frightened or saddened by his approaching death, he was filled with joy that showed itself in his every action. So strong was Aloysius' desire to go to God that he asked his confessor if he were wrong to long for death so ardently. Bellarmine replied that the desire to die in order to be united with God was not wrong in itself, provided that there was appropriate resignation to God's Will and that many saints, ancient and modern, had shared the same desire. This response was a great consolation to the young cleric.

Aloysius' illness worsened so rapidly that within seven days those caring for him came to believe he had reached the end. Making his confession with great care, he received Holy Communion and the sacrament of the anointing of the sick from the hands of the rector, Father Bernardino Rossignoli, S.J. Aloysius was able to respond to all the prayers, while those of his Jesuit companions who were present for the rites wept because of the impending loss of so dear a brother. Although he was typically one who avoided drawing attention to himself, Aloysius asked the Father Rector to make a statement in his name to those confreres who were present. Several of them had often wondered if he would regret the severity of his penances as he lay on his deathbed just as Saint Bernard of Clairvaux is said to have done for having treated his body too roughly. He wanted to tell them he had no such scruple. Rather, his conscience reproved him for not having done more penance when he had had the opportunity. He found consolation in the fact that he had been obedient to his superiors in all things and in never having acted in accord with his own will. Finally, he added that he could remember having broken no rule and that he believed that no one would have been scandalized by having seen him at different times doing anything more than his confreres. Those present were very moved by his words.[10]

A short time later, Aloysius was visited by Father John Baptist Carminata, the Roman provincial. As soon as he saw the priest, Aloysius asked to be allowed to take the discipline. Obviously, this request was refused. He then asked to at least be allowed to die lying on the

[10] Ibid., 221.

ground, in imitation of the saints, hoping to unite his last moments with Christ's sufferings on the Cross. This, too, was denied.

God, in His wisdom, chose to prolong Aloysius' life for a time. After the seventh day, his fever broke, and, although he was weak, he recovered some of his strength. Sadly, a report had reached Castiglione and Aloysius' family that he had already died. When the news of his recovery came, Rudolfo was so overjoyed that he broke into pieces the gold chain he wore around his neck, distributing the fragments to those who were around him.

Although he was no longer in danger of death, Aloysius continued to suffer from a low-grade fever and showed signs of consumption (tuberculosis), a new stage in his illness that gradually robbed him of what little strength he had. When he fell ill, he had been taken to the infirmary where he was placed in a bed over which hung a curtain of rough and coarse fabric. Fearing that the bed curtains were some sign of distinction, he asked the superior for permission to have them taken away. When he was told, however, that the curtains had not been placed there for him, but rather for an old invalid, he was satisfied that he was in no way compromising his religious poverty. Instead of taking the candy and licorices offered by the infirmarian as a remedy for the disagreeable medicine given by the doctor, Aloysius chose instead to offer up the sacrifice of drinking the liquid slowly. He was eventually prevailed upon to take some of the licorices, saying that that was more appropriate for a poor man than the other sweets that had been offered.[11]

Even in his illness, Aloysius thought of others. Hearing that there was danger of the plague continuing through the summer, he asked for permission to make a vow that, should he get better, he would dedicate himself to serving the victims. Given the permission he desired, he made the vow with great fervor, to the edification of many who saw in it a great act of charity. The cardinals della Rovere and Gonzaga often came to visit Aloysius, and he found great delight in talking to them about the things of Heaven. When the Father Rector begged the cardinals not to trouble themselves by making such frequent visits, promising that he would send news to them of Aloysius' condition, the cardinals dismissed his concerns,

[11] Ibid., 222.

answering that they themselves obtained a great deal of good from their visits.

The visits of Scipione Cardinal Gonzaga were especially meaningful to Aloysius. The young man freely opened his heart to his kinsman and talked of his approaching death and desire for Heaven with a spirit of gratitude and hope. Aloysius said, among other things, that he considered the cardinal a father and his greatest benefactor, since it was through his assistance that Aloysius had been able to enter religious life. The cardinal was moved to tears by what was said and answered that it was he himself who was under an obligation to Aloysius and that, despite the differences in their ages, he had drawn great spiritual benefit from his words and example.

Aloysius became good friends with another infirmary resident, an elderly Jesuit, Father Luigi Corbinelli of Florence. As Father Corbinelli was dying, he and Aloysius often sent messages to one another via the infirmarian. Eventually, the old priest decided he wanted to see his young confrere and demanded to be carried to Aloysius' room. The two conversed for a long time, and, on taking his leave, he asked Aloysius for his blessing as they would probably not meet again in this life. Aloysius, himself only a cleric, would not even consider offering his blessing to a priest; on the contrary, he wished to receive the priest's blessing. The infirmarian, seeing the pain this brought to the old man, put an end to the dispute by telling Aloysius to give Corbinelli his blessing. Aloysius then had a happy inspiration: folding his hands, he said, "God bless us both and grant your Reverence's wish. We will pray for each other." After saying this, he sprinkled them both with holy water. Not long after this, the infirmarian came one morning to Aloysius and, while opening the window, asked how he had passed the night. Aloysius replied:

> I have had an extremely bad night, constantly troubled and annoyed
> by extravagant dreams, or apparitions, for I saw good Father Corbinelli three times in great distress. And the first time, he said to me:
> "Brother, you must pray to God for me this moment that He might
> grant me the patience and strength I need in the severe and perilous
> crisis I am enduring, for I don't have the courage I need, not without
> the help of God." I awoke and thought it was a dream, and I said to
> myself—You had better go to sleep and leave this nonsense alone.
> A very short time after, I had scarcely dozed off, when he appeared

to me again, and begged me more earnestly than before to help him by prayer, for his grievous pain was almost more than he could bear. Again I awoke, and again I blamed my imagination and made up my mind to ask for a penance in the morning for neglecting to do all I could to get some rest, as the doctors and superiors had ordered me. Just as I was falling asleep again, Father Corbinelli appeared a third time and said to me, "My very dear Brother, I am come to the final point of my life. Pray God that my passage may be a happy one and that in His mercy He will receive me in glory, where I shall not forget to pray for you in return." At this I woke up so thoroughly that I have not been able to close my eyes again.[12]

The infirmarian, hearing these words, hid his astonishment and, desiring that Aloysius get some rest, told him to disregard his dreams because Father Corbinelli was well and that he must not disturb himself. In truth, Corbinelli was dead. Aloysius showed that he knew for certain that the old priest had died and that he knew he was in Heaven. When Father Bellarmine asked him what he thought of the fate of Father Corbinelli's soul, Aloysius answered with great conviction: "He simply passed through Purgatory."[13]

During his illness, Aloysius wrote two letters to his mother. One was dictated near the beginning of his illness, after the first serious episode had abated.

Pax Christi.

For some time I have had reason and opportunity to comply with your Ladyship's desire and write you a few lines, and I do so now all the more willingly, since you give me occasion to afford you such consolation. I do not know what better advice I could give you than to exhort you to consider that Mother who suffered more than any other, and to see how she who took her example from her beloved Son Jesus Christ, Who took upon Himself all our cares, sufferings, and miseries, and even death itself, in order to exhort us to patience in suffering and to give us eternal life. Your Ladyship's sorrows are many and heavy, but they cannot last long; for if we receive everything with holy resignation from the hand of the Divine Majesty, we shall soon and certainly enter into the Land of Promise. Console yourself then

[12] Ibid., 225–26.
[13] Ibid., 226.

with the thought of the Blessed Virgin, and seek with her your rest. I see that I am also drawing near the end of my sufferings, and if it please the Divine Majesty, I hope to obtain from Our Lord the greatest grace that one can receive, that is, to die (as I hope) in His grace. I have already received the holy Viaticum and Extreme Unction, but it pleased God to defer this grace and to prepare me for it by a fever which still remains. The doctors, who do not know how it will end, are trying by their remedies to cure my body. I rejoice to think that God our Lord wills to give me a much better health than the doctors can do, and so I pass the time happily in the hope that in a few months I shall be called by the Lord God out of this land of the dead to that of the living, from the society of men here below to that of the angels and saints of Heaven; in short, from the sight of earthly and perishable things to the contemplation of God, Who is in Himself all that is good. This will be a ground for consolation to your Ladyship also, because you love me and wish for my good. I beg you to pray and to ask the Brothers of Christian Doctrine to pray for me, in order that during this short time I have still to voyage on the sea of this world God may deign, through the intercession of His Only-begotten Son, of the Blessed Virgin and of Saints Celsus and Nazarius, to drown my imperfections in the Red Sea of the most sacred Passion of Jesus; so that, freed from my enemies, I may enter into the Land of Promise to behold and enjoy God, Whom I beg to grant you His consolation. Amen.

Rome, April 5, 1591.[14]

The second and longer letter was written shortly before his death.

Most honored Lady and Mother in Christ.
Pax Christi.

May the grace and consolation of the Holy Ghost be with you always. Your letter found me still dwelling in these regions of death, but very soon to pass into the land of the living, to praise God forever. I thought to have made my last passage before now, but the violence of the fever, as I told you in my last letter, diminished somewhat, and so brought me to the glorious feast of the Ascension. Since that time it has again increased, by reason of the inflammation in my chest, so that now I shall soon enjoy the embraces of my heavenly Father, in

[14] Aloysius Gonzaga to his mother, Apr. 5, 1591, in *Lettere di S. Luigi Gonzaga*, ed. Oliviero Iozzi (Pisa, 1889), 69ff., quoted in Meschler, *St. Aloysius*, 243–44; translation adapted.

whose bosom I hope to rest safely and forever. And thus the accounts that have reached you from various quarters about me all agree, as the Marquis also has written to say.

Now if charity, as Saint Paul says, makes us weep with those who weep, and rejoice with those that rejoice, how great should be your joy, dear Mother, at the grace that God grants you in the bringing me to true joy and assuring me that I shall never lose it again. I confess to you, that I am quite confused and overwhelmed by the thoroughness of the Divine Goodness, that boundless and fathomless ocean that calls me to an eternal rest, after such short and trivial labor, which invites and calls me to Heaven to that Sovereign Good that I sought so negligently, and that promises the fruit of those tears which I sowed so sparingly. Beware, dearest mother, of wronging the Infinite Goodness, by weeping for one as dead, who is living before God to help you with his prayers far more than he could while here below. This separation will not be for long, for we shall meet again, and enjoy each other's society in the next life, never to be wearied of it, but be united together with our Redeemer, praising Him with all our strength, and singing His mercies forever. I do not doubt that you will put aside human considerations, and so will easily attain to that faith, to that pure and simple obedience that we owe to God, offering Him freely and promptly that which is His own, and all the more willingly the dearer it is to you; knowing for certain that all He does is good, and that He only takes back again what He had before given to you, for no other reason than to put it in a place of safety, and to give it what we all desire for ourselves.

I have said all this merely in order that you and all my family may acknowledge my departure as being an extreme gift and that you may follow and aid me with a mother's blessing to pass this gulf and gain the shore of all my hopes. And I have done it more willingly because I have nothing else left to prove the filial love and reverence which I owe to you. Once more humbly desiring your blessing, I conclude
Rome, June 10, 1591.
Your most obedient son in Christ,
Aloysius Gonzaga[15]

* * * * *

[15] Aloysius Gonzaga to his mother, June 10, 1591 (Letter XXXVII), in Cepari, *Life of Saint Aloysius*, 228–29; translation adapted.

Having now fulfilled the duty he owed to his mother and to his other relations, Aloysius set about preparing himself more immediately for his death. Throughout his final illness, during which he suffered greatly despite the care shown him by those working in the infirmary, he never showed any sign of impatience. He also never complained of anything or revealed any sort of unhappiness with those who took care of him. It is said that it is in illness that the best (or worst, as the case may be) in people comes to the surface. If that is in fact the case, then Aloysius revealed his true character to be one of patient endurance, gratitude, humility, and hope.

As always, he found great consolation in talking about the things of God and of the joys of Heaven, and those who came to visit him limited the subjects of their conversation to these topics. Father Cepari relates:

> If, by chance, anyone forgot himself, and began to talk of other things, Aloysius became abstracted and paid no attention; but when the conversation returned to spiritual matters he completely changed and showed not only pleasure but a sort of rapture. He gave as his reason for this that, although he did not consider that indifferent subjects, treated in ordinary conversation in a spiritual and prudent manner, were contrary to his religious life, nevertheless, in the state he was, it appeared to him more fitting (and God required it of him), that not only his discourse should be formally spiritual, by its being directed to the glory of God, but that even the matter itself should likewise be holy; and these last moments of his life appeared to him too precious not to spend on precious subjects.[16]

When he was feeling strong enough, Aloysius would sometimes ask for his clothes, and he would go very slowly through the infirmary and make a sort of pilgrimage, visiting the various pictures of the saints which lined the walls. When the infirmarian told Aloysius that he did have to get up to do this, that he would gladly bring the pictures to him, Aloysius replied very simply, "Brother, these are my stations." He also developed a short-lived habit that reminds us of the boy at prayer in Castiglione. Sometimes, during the day, when no one was about and the door was closed, he would get out of bed and

---

[16] Cepari, *Life of Saint Aloysius*, 230.

kneel on the floor to pray. When he would hear any noise, he would immediately get back in bed. When the infirmarian found him like this a number of times, he began to be suspicious, and having finally caught Aloysius still on his knees, he forbade him to do it anymore. Aloysius obeyed from then on.

Aloysius often spoke with his spiritual director, Father Bellarmine, during these weeks and months. One evening, Bellarmine recalled, Aloysius asked him if he believed that anyone could go straight to Heaven without having to pass through Purgatory. Bellarmine replied that he did, adding, "Indeed, I believe you will be one of those that will do so; for since God has given you all those graces and supernatural gifts that you have told me about, and, in particular, because you have never offended Him mortally, I am convinced that He will also grant you this further grace of passing directly to Heaven."[17] After Bellarmine left him, Aloysius was so filled with consolation that he fell into an ecstasy, in which he beheld the glories of the Heavenly Jerusalem. He later told Bellarmine that the night passed as a moment. It has long been held that it was during that night of rapture that Aloysius learned on what day he was to die, because afterward, he told several people that he would die on the Octave day of Corpus Christi.[18] This was in fact the day he was to die.

Shortly after this, one of his fellows from the scholasticate came to see him, and Aloysius greeted him saying, "*Frater, laetantes imus, laetantes imus*—we are going gladly!" These words, which made Aloysius so happy, caused those who were present to weep. During these final days, he was mindful of his other confreres and wanted to send letters to those three Jesuits who had been most important to him during his brief religious life: his former novice-master, Father Pescatore; Father Mutius de Angelis, who was then serving as professor of theology in Naples; and Father Bartholomew Recalcati, the rector of the college in Milan. Because he did not have the strength to sign the letters, he asked Father Guelfucci to hold his hand, and instead of his name, he made a cross with the pen.

Aloysius tried to spend the final week of his life performing those acts of devotion and piety that his strength would allow. When he

[17] Ibid., 231.
[18] Ibid., 232.

told Father Guelfucci, who was one of his close friends, that he was
going to die, he asked him to come to see him each day of the
Octave of Corpus Christi to recite with him the seven Penitential
Psalms. Guelfucci did so, and as he knelt by the bed reciting these
psalms that Aloysius loved so much, he would frequently stop to look
at his young confrere, who listened attentively, with eyes fixed on
the cross, showing such devotion and affection that the priest would
often weep. Cepari simply says of this, "Now and then, a tear fell
peacefully from the Saint's eyes."[19] At other times, Aloysius asked
him to read certain chapters of the writings of Saint Augustine and
Saint Bernard's *Sermons on the Song of Songs*. As news of his impending death spread, many sought to have some time alone with him,
hoping to recommend themselves to his prayers. Aloysius accepted
these requests with his typical graciousness. He spoke of death just as
others spoke of leaving one room to go to another. After one visit,
Father Jerome Piatti (who would, himself, die two months later, at
the age of forty-four) exclaimed to one of the Jesuits who was with
him, "I tell you, Aloysius is a saint, most certainly a saint, and so great
a saint that he might be canonized in our lifetime."[20] During these
last few days, Aloysius was often at prayer. As the customary rituals
prescribed, he often made acts of faith and other brief prayers such
as *Cupio dissolvi et esse cum Christo* (I wish to be dissolved and to be
with Christ).

[19] Ibid.
[20] Ibid., 233.

Chapter 18

His Death and Burial

When the Octave day of Corpus Christi (June 20, 1591) arrived, a certain Brother Mizetti, an assistant infirmarian, entered Aloysius' room early in the morning. Finding Aloysius still very much alive, he remarked, "See now, Aluigi, we are living and not dead, as you thought and as you were always telling us." Aloysius quietly observed that the Octave was not yet over. Going out, the brother said to the infirmarian, "Aloysius still holds firmly to his opinion that he is to die today, and yet it seems to me that he is better than he was on other days."[1] This scenario was repeated when another Jesuit priest came to see him. Aloysius' response was the same.

When the infirmarian came to check on him later that day, Aloysius asked, quite unexpectedly, to be buried in the same grave as the recently deceased Father Corbinelli. As the infirmarian observed that it was not the custom to bury together those who died near the same time, Aloysius explained that it was because the old priest had appeared to him three times that he made the request.

Spending the morning in prayer, he asked for Viaticum at midday. He had already made the request at dawn, but the infirmarian ignored him, believing him to be in no immediate danger. (The infirmarian observed that he had already received Viaticum once during the course of his illness, and he did not think it appropriate for him to do so again.) Aloysius replied, "Extreme Unction, no, but Viaticum, yes." Despite his insistence, the infirmarian did nothing.

Aloysius received a significant surprise that final day. It would seem that Pope Gregory XIV had learned from Scipione Cardinal Gonzaga

---

[1] Virgil Cepari, S.J., *Life of Saint Aloysius Gonzaga*, ed. Francis Goldie, S.J. (New York: Benziger Brothers, 1891), 234; see also Maurice Meschler, S.J., *St. Aloysius Gonzaga: Patron of Christian Youth* (Rockford, Ill.: TAN Books, 1985), 252.

that Aloysius was dying, and the pope, of his own accord, sent his special blessing and a plenary indulgence. When Father Nicolas Fabrini told him the news, Aloysius was so surprised and overwhelmed that he hid his face in his hands.

Around six o'clock that evening, Father Giovanni Lambertini, who had been in the novitiate with Aloysius, came to see his former classmate, and Aloysius begged him to seek out the rector and ask him to bring him Viaticum. Lambertini did so, and as they waited, the two recited the Litany of the Blessed Sacrament. The rector did finally concede to Aloysius' request, and he received the Eucharist with great devotion and with the firm conviction that he would soon be with God in Paradise. At the words, *"Accipe, Frater, Viaticum* ... (Receive, Brother, the Viaticum, the Body of Our Lord Jesus Christ, and may He preserve your soul to eternal life), none of those present were able to hold back their tears. After receiving Communion, Aloysius wished to embrace all those who were present in accord with a custom in the Society of Jesus, as when one arrives from or is going to any distant place.[2] As each approached to say his final good-byes, not one could restrain his grief. One of those present, Father Gaspar Alpieri, who had always been a close friend of Aloysius', held back and said to him privately that he hoped he was going to enjoy at once the Beatific Vision, and he asked his friend to remember him. Aloysius answered him with deep feeling that he trusted in God's mercy, in the Precious Blood of Christ, and in the intercession of the Virgin, promising that he would not forget his friend. Since he had loved him here on earth, how much more would he love him in Paradise, for love there is more perfect.

Because Aloysius had been so alert and able to converse so freely, few really believed that the end was imminent. Some hours later, when the provincial came to see him, he said, "What is Brother Aloysius doing?" To which Aloysius replied, "We are going, Father." "Where?" asked the provincial. "To Heaven, if my sins do not hinder me." The provincial whispered to someone standing near him, "Just listen to him—he talks of death as if it were a walk to Frascati."[3]

[2] Cepari, *Life of Saint Aloysius*, 236.
[3] Ibid., 237.

Around seven o'clock that evening, Father Cepari himself was with Aloysius. He remembers:

> I was by Aloysius, assisting him in bed, with my hand under his head, to relieve his fatigue, while he was gazing at and contemplating a small crucifix that had been placed for him upon the bed. He was praying before it to gain the plenary indulgence for the hour of death. While he was doing so, he raised his hand, and took off his linen nightcap. I thought it was the action of a dying man, and put it back on his head without saying anything. Very shortly after he removed it again, and while replacing it, I said to him, "Leave it alone, Brother Aloysius, for fear the evening air will harm your head." Directing me toward the crucifix with his eyes, he answered, "Christ had nothing on His head when He died." His words touched me and filled me with devotion and compunction, for then I perceived that even at that moment his whole thought was to imitate Christ on the cross. In the evening at the *Ave Maria* [8:15 P.M.], when we began to discuss in his presence who was to sit with him that night, though he was so fixed in contemplation, he said twice to Father Guelfucci who was near him, "Stop with me!" He had promised Father Francis Belmisseri, who was anxious to be with him at his death to warn him of its approach; and as if to keep that engagement he added, "Take care that you stay!"[4]

About a quarter past nine, the room was full, and the rector saw that Aloysius was speaking quite freely. Still feeling there was no immediate danger, he ordered everyone to leave and go to bed. Not believing Aloysius' prediction, he said that only Father Nicholas Fabrini and Father Guelfucci, should stay. Aloysius saw the grief of those being told to leave and promised to remember them in Heaven. He in turn asked for their prayers as he faced his last struggle.

Besides the two priests already mentioned, Father Bellarmine and Father Vitelleschi also remained behind. Bellarmine said to Aloysius that when he thought it was time, he should tell him so that he could pray the commendation for a departing soul. Shortly after, Aloysius simply said, "Now, Father, it is time." All knelt down and offered the prayers. When they were finished, believing themselves that he would survive until morning, Bellarmine was told by Father Fabrini,

[4] Ibid., 237–38.

who was Father Minister of the house, to retire for the night. Receiving the assurance of the infirmarian that Aloysius was not going to die immediately, he left.

The end soon came, however. The two priests had heard Aloysius repeating various lines from Scriptures at intervals during the night. Perceiving a change, Father Guelfucci went to check on him and seeing the change in his color asked him if he needed anything. Much to the priest's surprise and consternation, the dying man asked to be rolled onto his left side. Fearing that moving him would kill him, Guelfucci called for Fabrini and the infirmarian. The two came in and by the light of their candles saw the deathly pallor and cold sweat and knew the end was near. In response to Aloysius' request that he be moved (he had lain on his right side for nearly three days), they told him to be patient and to drink the last drop from the chalice of suffering.

When the priests saw that he could no longer speak or move, they offered him a blessed candle, after making the sign of the cross over him with it. Aloysius was able to grasp it and, with the candle still in his hand, tried to say the name of Jesus. He was able to merely move his lips, and between the hours of ten and eleven he went to his Creator in peace. Aloysius had obtained the grace he had desired, to die within the Octave of Corpus Christi, out of devotion for the Blessed Sacrament, or on a Friday, out of reverence for the Passion. In fact, he passed from this life at the close of the Octave of Corpus Christi, as Friday was about to begin, the night between June 20 and 21, 1591. He was twenty-three years, three months, and eleven days old.

* * * * *

Word of Aloysius' passing spread quickly among his Jesuit confreres. Rising from their beds, some recommended themselves to his prayers, believing him to be already in Heaven. Others offered prayers for the repose of his soul, keeping the promises they had made to him during his final illness. The two priests who had been with him at the end believed they had been granted a special privilege. Aloysius' friend Father Guelfucci was particularly moved by the young man's death and, desiring to have some keepsake, took away from the room where Aloysius had lived in his last months the strings from his shoes, the pens with which he wrote, and some other small trinkets.

Others of Aloysius' confreres were not so delicate in their quest for relics. Believing the young Jesuit to have been a saint, Cepari records that on the morning of June 21, the room was swarming with Jesuits who came to pay their respects and to seek a memento. Some of these took possession, by stealth, of his shoes, his shirt, his vest, and even went so far as to cut of small locks of hair, his fingernails, and even bits of flesh.[5]

As the infirmarian was cleaning Aloysius' body, he found on Aloysius' person the bronze crucifix to which the plenary indulgence had been attached. Stripping the body, they found great calloues on his knees, caused by years of kneeling in prayer on hard surfaces. The infirmarian also found two deep bedsores on Aloysius' right side. Aloysius had actually never uttered a word of complaint about the two wounds or about how the linen had sunk into his flesh. It was the pain of this wound that had prompted him to ask to be moved immediately before his death. Even that slight alleviation of suffering was not to be for him, and he did truly die as Christ on the Cross, quietly and full of resignation.

Later in the morning, the body was carried to the house chapel of the Roman College, where it was constantly surrounded by those who had known and loved the young cleric. That morning, every Mass said by Roman Jesuits was offered on his behalf, although, as Cepari recalls, many did this simply out of observance of the Rule rather than because of any belief that he stood in need of their prayers.[6] Stories were told about him, and those that knew him commented on his many virtues and endearing qualities.

In the evening, at fifteen minutes after six, the body was taken from the chapel to a large hall where all the priests and brothers were assembled. After receiving the body of their confrere with devotion, they carried his remains in procession to the Church of the Annunziata, the church of the Roman College, where they chanted the Office of the Dead. After the service, the extern students, as well as many others, came forward to venerate the body. The crowd became so large that the Fathers were obliged to shut the doors of the church. At some point during the push to get to the body,

[5] Ibid., 241.
[6] Ibid.

someone cut off two joints of the little finger of Aloysius' right hand, while another man was stopped just as he was about to cut off one of his ears. Mixed in among the crowd were nobles and prelates, one of whom Father Cepari saw quickly leaving the church with a large piece of Aloysius' habit.[7]

When the question of where to bury Aloysius had to be decided, it was the opinion of many in the college, especially of Father Bellarmine, that he should not be buried in the vault without a coffin (like the other Jesuits), but that his remains should be placed in a wooden casket. Since this was such a dramatic departure from custom, it was Claudio Aquaviva himself who gave permission for Aloysius to be buried in this way, thereby giving his own tacit testimony to the singular quality of the young Jesuit's life. That night, Aloysius' remains were placed in a wooden casket and interred in the Chapel of the Crucifix in the Church of the Annunziata.

For many days, the life and virtues of Aloysius were the main topic of conversation among those living and studying in the Roman College. Some began to show a certain reverence for Aloysius, visiting his tomb and frequently commending themselves to his prayers.

The body of Aloysius rested in the Chapel of the Crucifix until 1598, when an overflow of the Tiber River caused Father Aquaviva to order that the remains be exhumed out of fear that they might become mixed with the remains of other Jesuits buried in the chapel's vault. When the casket was opened, it was found that the body had undergone the natural process of decay, with all the flesh having decomposed. On this occasion, Father Bernardino Rossignoli, who was now provincial, distributed a number of fragments of bone as relics, and these made their way as far as Belgium, Poland, and India. On June 22, 1598, the remaining pieces of bone were enclosed in a new, smaller casket and placed in a niche higher up in the wall of the vault, where they would be more effectively protected from moisture.

As devotion to this dear soul began to spread and stories of miracles attributed to his intercession began to be circulated, Claudio Aquaviva ordered that the remains be moved to a more fitting resting place. On June 8, 1602, they were removed from the vault with

---

[7] Ibid., 242.

the greatest of secrecy. Then, on July 1, they were placed in a lead casket, which was then enclosed in another of wood, and laid under the predella (the platform on which the priest stands as he says Mass) of the altar of Saint Sebastian in the church of the Roman College. Although the translation was kept secret, the spot became known, and people began to throng to the altar of Saint Sebastian to venerate the remains.

Francis Gonzaga, the youngest brother of Aloysius, who had succeeded Rudolfo as Marquis of Castiglione and visited Rome as imperial ambassador, decided that his brother's remains should be moved to an even more noble resting place. In accordance with his request, Father Aquaviva ordered a third translation of Aloysius' relics on May 13, 1605. The body was placed in the Lady chapel of the same church, in a niche in the wall on the Gospel side of the altar. Don Francis was given a shinbone, which he took back to Castiglione as a venerated relic.[8] Aloysius' skull was given to the professed house of the Gesù, but this was soon given to Don Francis for the Jesuit church in Castiglione, where it is still venerated.

On June 15, 1620, Aloysius' relics were moved once again. The occasion was the dedication of a chapel in his honor in the Annunziata. Among those who served as an acolyte during the ceremony was a young Belgian Jesuit named John Berchmans, who was then studying philosophy at the Roman College.

Saint John Berchmans

Born Jan Berchmans in Diest, Belgium, in 1599, John Berchmans was the son of a master shoemaker and burgher of the city.[9] He was educated by Peter Emmerich, a Norbertine priest from Tongerloo Abbey, who taught him Latin and exposed him to a world beyond the confines of Diest. Although he preferred the company of those who were older than himself, he was also an enthusiastic actor and

---

[8] A short time later a large section of this bone was given to a church in Sasso in Valtellina, where Aloysius was said to have worked a number of miracles.

[9] For a fuller treatment of the life of Saint John Berchmans, see Paul Burns and John Cumming, eds., *Butler's Lives of the Saints: New Full Edition; August* (Collegeville, Minn.: Liturgical Press, 1998), 112–13.

enjoyed performing in mystery plays. When told that he would have to discontinue his studies and learn his father's trade to help support the family business, John replied that he wanted to be a priest. As a compromise, he was allowed to become a servant to one of the canons of the cathedral of Malines, and his time was divided between seminary studies and serving at the canon's table. The canon taught John how to train dogs as retrievers and even took the boy duck hunting.

In 1615, John became one of the first students at the new Jesuit college in Malines. Known for his piety, he continued to perform in sacred dramas and seems to have been well liked by his peers. Inspired by his reading of the life of Saint Aloysius, and despite his father's objections, he entered the Jesuit novitiate in 1616.[10] In his notes, we find evidence of a simple spirituality that seems to foreshadow that of Saint Thérèse of Lisieux; this was clearly expressed in John's maxim, "Prize little things best of all." Soon after John's investiture, his mother died, and his father was, somewhat surprisingly, ordained a priest a short time later. Unfortunately, John's father did not live to see his son's profession, dying the day before John professed his vows.

In the winter of 1617, John set out for Rome, arriving in the Eternal City on January 1, 1618. An enthusiastic student, John immersed himself in his studies. In May 1621, he completed his philosophy examinations and was chosen to participate in a public debate. The strain of preparations and the hot Roman summer, however, proved to be too much for the young man, and his health began to fail. In spite of this, he took part in another debate at the Greek College[11] on August 6, but was forced to enter the infirmary the following day. During his illness, he showed grace and good humor and even jokingly asked a priest who was present to say the grace after meals after John had had to take a particularly unpleasant medicine. John Berchmans died on August 13, 1621. His illness was never diagnosed.

Following John's death, a number of miracles were attributed to his intercession, and a cult quickly developed in his native Belgium. Despite the fact that the cause for his canonization was introduced

---

[10] Barbara Frances M. Courson, *The Jesuits: Their Foundations and History* (London: Burns and Oates, 1879), 1:320.

[11] The Pontifical Greek College of Saint Athanasius was established in Rome by Pope Gregory XIII in 1577.

the same year as his death, he was not beatified until 1865. He was canonized in 1888.[12] The Feast of Saint John Berchmans is celebrated on August 13.

* * * * *

In 1626, four years after the canonization of Saint Ignatius Loyola, Ludovico Cardinal Ludovisi laid the cornerstone of a new church in Rome. Built on the foundations of the Church of the Annunziata, this new Baroque edifice, dedicated to the Jesuit founder, would become the fifth resting place of the relics of Aloysius, the transfer of which took place on August 5, 1649. Originally placed in the chapel dedicated to Saint Joseph (which had been built on the site of the room where Aloysius died), his relics were placed in their current location, in a chapel dedicated to his honor, on December 20, 1699. The physical remains of the saint are housed in a lapis-lazuli urn placed resting beneath a magnificent marble altar depicting Aloysius being received in glory.

The numerous translations of Aloysius' remains allowed for an unusually large dissemination of his relics. In point of fact, Aloysius' remains have been so liberally distributed that no large relics are given away today.[13]

---

[12] Today, the relics of Saint John Berchmans, who has been long honored as a second Saint Aloysius, rest opposite those of Aloysius in the Church of Sant'Ignazio in Rome.

[13] Meschler, *St. Aloysius*, 262. See also Joan Carroll Cruz, *Relics* (Huntington, Ind.: Our Sunday Visitor, 1984), 209–10.

Chapter 19

The Miracles and Cult of Saint Aloysius

Although the first biographers go to great lengths to highlight Aloysius' many virtues, spirituality, and pious excesses, there are really no reports of any miracles worked by Aloysius during his life. Many who knew Aloysius were struck by this fact, but it would seem that God was waiting until the death of his faithful servant to glorify his name by many miracles.

It is striking to note that the first miracle attributed to Saint Aloysius was worked for the benefit of his mother, Donna Marta. Following the murder of Rudolfo, who was shot to death by a vassal on January 31, 1593, the family was plagued by political intrigue (Rudolfo had been accused of counterfeiting papal money and had been excommunicated) and other scandals. The peasants took Rudolfo's death as occasion to revolt, and they raided the Gonzaga castle. Added to this more public trial was the fact that Francis, who succeeded Rudolfo as marquis, treated his brother's widow with great harshness. All of this took a toll on Donna Marta, who became dangerously ill. Four years later, as the grieving mother was staying in Solferino with her youngest child, fourteen-year-old Diego, the castle was invaded by brigands, and Donna Marta and Diego were carried off to Castiglione. The raiders' intention was to overthrow the Gonzaga dynasty by murdering all its members at one time. Knowing their plan, Donna Marta refused to enter the gates of the castle in Castiglione. In response, the leader of the group ordered her to dismount the horse she was riding with Diego and commanded one of his men to shoot the boy. Diego ran to his mother and was shot to death as she received him into her arms. Donna Marta was repeatedly stabbed and left for dead on the ground. A citizen of Castiglione found her and took her into his house. Believing the end to be near, she received the last sacraments. The entire family was gathered around her bed

when, opening her eyes, her face brightened and a sweet smile trans-
figured her features and tears fell from her eyes for the first time in
years. She had been cured, and, to the amazement of all, she got up
a few days later, perfectly well. Aloysius, her beloved son, had stood
before her in celestial glory and cured her.

There were other miracles for Aloysius' relatives. Rudolfo's
daughter, Cynthia, was cured of heart disease in 1668 by touching
a picture of her saintly uncle, and another niece, Joan, a daughter
of Francis, was saved from death in a carriage accident in 1674. It
is further recorded in the family history that Aloysius appeared to
Rudolfo's widow, Helen Aliprandi, the week before her death, in
1608, to tell her that she would soon die. Others among Aloysius' kin
and former servants recalled times when Aloysius' intercession and
patronage were tangibly manifest in their lives.[1]

Aloysius' care extended to his brothers in the Society of Jesus
as well. In 1609, a Roman lay brother was stricken with a physical
disability that prevented him from kneeling. Bothered by his condition, the brother asked Aloysius to help him, promising to say an
Our Father and a Hail Mary in his honor every day. He was instantly
cured. A novice in Padua who was near death and who had received
the last sacraments was completely cured. A particularly striking miracle occurred in 1635, when a Jesuit scholastic, Aloysius Spinelli of
Palermo, was cured of complete paralysis. Even a general of the Society, Father Francis Retz (d. 1750), owed his life to Aloysius, when
he was cured of six abscesses in his abdomen in 1736. It was this
general who obtained permission for a special Mass and office to be
celebrated in Aloysius' honor and who promoted the devotion of the
Six Sundays of Saint Aloysius.[2]

While the hundreds of authenticated miracles related in the various lives of Saint Aloysius testify to the power and efficacy of his
intercession on behalf of those most in need, it is beyond the scope of
this present work to explore these in detail. There is one apparition
of Aloysius, however, that seems to be particularly relevant to our
purpose: it is the testimony of the glory of a saint by a saint.

---

[1] See Maurice Meschler, S.J., *St. Aloysius Gonzaga: Patron of Christian Youth* (Rockford, Ill.:
TAN Books, 1985), 264–66.

[2] For more on the Six Sundays devotion, see page 260 herein.

We may recall that in their youth, Aloysius and the future saint Mary Magdalen de' Pazzi both prayed in the Church of San Giovanni in Florence and may have even known one another by sight. The daughter of one of the wealthiest families of Florence, she is remembered today as having been an exceptional mystic and for her devotion to the Passion of Christ. The nuns of her community at Santa Maria degli Angeli had been given a manuscript copy of the life of Aloysius by Father Cepari, who was serving as their chaplain. Inspired by the life of the young Jesuit, a devotion to Aloysius grew up among the nuns, and Father Cepari went so far as to present Mary Magdalen de' Pazzi with a fragment of Aloysius' bone. On April 4, 1599, Saint Mary Magdalen was caught up in prayer, and she saw Saint Aloysius' glory. Taking down what was spoken during this revelation, the other nuns recorded her words:

> O! how great is the glory of Aloysius, the son of Saint Ignatius! Never would I have believed it, if You had not shown it to me, O Jesus!—It seems to me that I might say that there cannot be such great glory in Heaven, as I see Aloysius possesses. I assert that little Aloysius is a great saint.—We have Saints in the Church, who I believe do not possess such glory. I should like to go over the whole world and proclaim that Aloysius, the son of Ignatius, is a great Saint, and I should wish to show his glory to everyone, that God might be glorified—He has such glory because his life was hidden.—Whoever could tell the worth and power of interior acts? There is no comparison between those which are external and those which are internal.—Aloysius, who while on earth had his heart open to the Word, and that is why he is in such glory.—Aloysius, was an unknown martyr. For whoever loves You, my God, knows You to be so great and infinitely worthy of love, that it is a great martyrdom to see that You are not loved, as he would wish and desire to love You, and that You are not known by Your creatures, not known, offended.—He martyred himself, too.—Oh, how he loved when on earth! But now he possesses God in Heaven in the fullness of perfect love. During his mortal life his acts of love and of union were like a shower of arrows with which he pierced the heart of the Divine Word. Now these arrows are returning again into his own heart by those communications of love, which they have merited and which he is tasting and understanding in heaven. [Seeing Aloysius praying in heaven for all those who had been helpful to him, she went on to say:] I too will do my utmost to help souls, so that when they

get to Paradise they may pray for me, as Aloysius does for those who had been useful to him on earth.[3]

* * * * *

Although miracles and other signs worked, by God's grace, through the intercession of the Blessed Virgin and the saints can serve to enliven our faith, it is not in miracles and signs that we discover the true greatness of the saints. Rather, it is in the quality of their lives and in the witness they offered to those with whom they lived, worked, and prayed. In the case of Saint Aloysius, this certainly holds true. Although hundreds of miracles have been attributed to his intercession over the course of the past four centuries, it is not in these miracles that his glory lies.[4] Instead, it is in Aloysius' love for his family, for his Jesuit confreres, and for the sick and poor that we see what was best in the young Jesuit. His miracles are simply an extension of the love he manifested, very heroically, in his day-to-day life.

Following his death, his Jesuit confreres set about collecting remembrances and anecdotes about their departed brother; many remembered the life and deeds of this young man with fondness and with a sense of awe. Among the many tributes offered to Aloysius were those contained in letters of condolence written to Donna Marta. Father Claudio Aquaviva wrote from Rome that she would from then on have a dear and faithful intercessor in Heaven, where, there were good reasons to believe, at that very moment his happy soul was enjoying eternal glory; Aloysius would ever bestow his help upon her and his order. The rector of the Roman College wrote that Aloysius had died so peacefully that everyone envied his holy death. He went on to acknowledge that his death was in perfect keeping with the quality of his life. Donna Marta and her family had every reason to rejoice because they had sent a saint to Heaven.

Jerome Cardinal della Rovere wrote the following to Donna Marta:

---

[3] Quoted in Virgil Cepari. S.J., *Life of Saint Aloysius Gonzaga*, ed. Francis Goldie, S.J. (New York: Benziger Brothers, 1891), 274–75. All subsequent references, unless specified otherwise, are to the Goldie edition.

[4] The Holy See ultimately approved fifteen miracles in its investigation for the canonization of Saint Aloysius. According to the norms then in effect, only three were necessary.

On Thursday evening passed to a better life our good Frater Aloysius, leaving behind him such great regrets and so high an opinion of sanctity, that these Fathers have not less admired, than they have wept over his holy death. For they firmly hold the belief that, he has entered into Eternal Glory. You may console yourself for his loss with the thought that he will intercede with God for the peace of his brothers, and the happiness of his house. Again I pray you to take comfort at having a son in Heaven, where I hope he will pray for us all.[5]

Donna Eleanor of Austria, the Dowager Duchess of Mantua, also wrote to Aloysius' mother:

When I consider how bitter the grief you must suffer at the loss of your son, Don Aloysius, when still so young, and when I measure it by what I myself felt, though I was not his mother—true I have always loved him as a mother—I cannot but condole with you. And not merely with you, but with all your family, for the loss is common to us all, in our human nature. To this we cannot resist of our own strength, as long as we are in the flesh. Still if we choose to consider the matter more reasonably how that blessed soul has rent in two the dark veil of the body, and flown to eternal glory; if we think that now that he has arrived at the glorious end, towards which he was ever hurrying while in this valley of miseries, he can more quickly and expeditiously bear our prayers to his kind Lord, we shall praise and thank God for having taken him away in the flower of his age from this earthly slough, and made him citizen of the heavenly Jerusalem. For our own sakes we shall be consoled, when we see that from being a mortal man he has become a heavenly angel.[6]

Finally, Donna Marta received the following message from Thomas Mancini, the secretary of Cardinal della Rovere. Thomas had been present at the burial of Aloysius.

Most illustrious and excellent Lady.

I am still in doubt as to whether I should condole with or congratulate your Excellency on the holy death of the Blessed Frater Aloysius. I cannot be sure whether your maternal affection will take

[5] Quoted in Cepari, *Life of Saint Aloysius*, 250.
[6] Quoted in ibid., 250–51.

most into account your own loss or the inestimable gain of your son. I grieve for myself in that we are deprived of the presence of so great a personage. Your Excellency too will feel your grief all the more because you were unable to see him at least once in the course of his last illness. But I rejoice much on his behalf; by his holy life he has well deserved Heaven, and it is the general belief that he went there without delay, leaving behind him a reputation for sanctity in Rome and throughout the whole world. He could not have hoped to acquire a greater maturity, had he lived to the age of Noah, instead of being, as he was, a youth of but twenty-three. On Thursday evening at a quarter past ten o'clock, he gave up his soul to God, and yesterday evening, the twenty-first of June, he was buried in the church of the College of the *Gesù*, known as the *Annunziata*. I was present at the time. I must not omit to tell you that not only did the Fathers treasure as relics all that he left behind him on earth, but the people who were in the church took possession of his habit as of something holy and if I said much more than this I should say nothing but the truth; but I hope you will hear this from others, and especially from the Fathers themselves, who, better than me, will know how to relate to you what occurred.

No miracle is known to have been wrought by his intercession perhaps because there have not been any, or perhaps they keep it concealed. But as much devotion is shown to him publicly as would be shown to a Saint who had wrought miracles.

Today, Saturday the 22nd, I have just been told that many gentlemen have earnestly begged to be given something that has belonged to him, which are some of the reasons which make me hesitate to grieve on this occasion. Someone has already begun to write his life and a copy is promised my lord Cardinal as soon as it is finished. As the Cardinal was like one transfixed with grief at the news I gave him of the death, he is much consoled on hearing so much of him, and he also begs with much earnestness, but with greater reason, for something that has belonged to the blessed religious. I must not forget to tell you that last week when I went to visit him, he foretold his own death with great joy, and gave me his letters, and he begged me to take care that they should reach their destination, telling me they were the last he would write to your Excellency and to the Marquis, his brother.

I have written this little for the consolation of your Excellency who ought to be certainly consoled by it. I must now allow others to write who can do so with greater fullness than was possible to me.

I pray you to take comfort, and to offer up prayers to him for the peace and prosperity of your noble house, for his intercession will always be granted.

Rome, June 22, 1591.[7]

These letters, written at the time of his death, provide us with clear evidence of the high esteem in which Aloysius was held. This esteem continued unabated. In 1601, Aloysius' former spiritual director, Saint Robert Cardinal Bellarmine, offered the following statement, given as testimony to Father Cepari as he composed his biography of Aloysius.

My very Reverend Father,

It is with great pleasure, that I reply to what your Reverence asks of me, as it appears to me that it is conducive to the glory of our Lord God to make known the gifts of His Divine Majesty towards His servants. I was for a long time confessor of our gentle and holy Aloysius Gonzaga, and I once heard the general confession of all his life. He served my Mass and conversed freely with me, speaking often with me about the things of God. From these confessions and conversations it seems to me that I can with all truth confirm the following things.

Firstly, that he never committed a mortal sin; and this I know for certain as regards the period between his seventh year and the time of his death. As to the first seven years of his life, during which he did not live with the same knowledge of God, as he did later on, I hold it as to conjecture, for it is not likely that one whom God destined to such purity should in his infancy have committed a mortal sin.

Secondly, that from his seventh year, at which date he was converted to God as he himself told me, he lived a life of perfection.

Thirdly, that he never experienced any sting of the flesh.

Fourthly, that in his prayers and contemplations, during which he remained kneeling on the ground without support, as a rule, he was never troubled with distractions.

Fifthly, that he was a mirror of obedience, humility, mortification, abstinence, prudence, devotion, and purity.

During the last days of his life, he had one night such excessive consolation in representing to himself the glory of the Blessed, that though he thought it had lasted less than a quarter of an hour, it had really lasted nearly the whole night.

---

[7] Quoted in ibid., 252–53; translation adapted.

About this same time Father Luigi Corbinelli died; and I asked Aloysius what he believed to have been the fate of his soul. He confidently answered me in these words: "He has merely passed through Purgatory." And knowing as I did his disposition, how he was most careful in what he said, and reserved in stating positively what was doubtful, I hold it for certain that he must have known this by divine revelation: but I did not venture to ask further.

Finally, I believe that he went straight to Heaven, and I have always scrupled to pray to God for the repose of his soul for it seemed to me that this would be to undervalue the graces of God which I had seen in him. On the contrary, I have never scrupled to recommend myself to his prayers, and I have great confidence in them.

May your Reverence pray for me.

From my apartment in the palace, October 17, 1601.

Your Reverence's most affectionate brother in Christ

Roberto Cardinal Bellarmine[8]

* * * * *

As word of Aloysius' life and miracles spread, and devotion to him increased, he was almost universally honored by celebrations climaxing in his beatification and canonization. It was in 1603, during the reign of Pope Clement VIII, that Father Virgil Cepari began the ecclesiastical process of inquiry into the miracles that had taken place through the intercession of Aloysius. On May 12, 1604, the diocesan synod of the clergy of Mantua presented a petition to Pope Clement asking for the beatification of the young Jesuit on account of the general veneration he enjoyed and the miracles he had worked. The synod took this opportunity to distribute pictures of Aloysius bearing the title "Blessed", and votive tablets were sent to Rome in the hopes that someday they could be displayed on his tomb.[9] The Diocese of Brescia (of which he had been a native) celebrated two feasts in honor of Aloysius that year. The first of these consisted of a magnificent procession of students held on June 21. With the permission of the Bishop of Brescia, a picture of Aloysius was exposed for public veneration in the Church of Saints Celsus and Nazarius

[8] Robert Cardinal Bellarmine to Father Virgil Cepari, Oct. 17, 1601, quoted in Cepari, *Life of Saint Aloysius*, 254–56.

[9] Meschler, *St. Aloysius*, 278. It should be noted that these acts were in accord with the customs of the time. Such proclamations by a diocesan bishop or synod are no longer permissible.

in Castiglione. The second celebration was held on July 28. Among those in attendance was Donna Marta, who knelt before the image of her blessed child. Aloysius' mother died less than a year later, on April 3, 1605.

During the celebration in Castiglione, a Dominican born in that city, Sylvester Ugolotti, who had known Aloysius personally, preached a sermon in which he offered the following words to Donna Marta and the townsfolk:

> Happy Mother to have given to the world this noble scion, whose brow is now adorned in Heaven with a starry crown of inexpressible bright- ness. What Queen, what Empress, might not envy you? Mothers who today shed tears of joy at seeing their sons covered in glory, crowned with diadems of gold or with laurel wreaths and borne in triumphal chariots, will tomorrow weep other tears when they see them slain, covered with a pall, and carried to the sepulcher. But you behold his triumph in Heaven, his crown wrought of the pure gold of love, and inscribed with the name of Jesus. Your tears of joy can flow unchecked by any fear that they may some day be changed into tears of sorrow. For God will wipe away all tears from the eyes of the elect. O happy country of mine, which small as it is, can now compare in glory with noble provinces and even kingdoms like France. France had Saint Louis for its king . . . you have the Blessed Aloysius for your prince. What may you not expect from Heaven where you have so powerful an advocate? For who can suppose that Louis gazing on the Divine Essence as in a mirror can fail to look down upon his country, ever ready to cover those who need it with the shield of his protection? Open the eyes of your souls my countrymen to discern how highly favored you are. You have for your masters not tyrants or low-born upstarts, but lords of noble blood, not perverse and wayward, but lovers of the truth and of God—Saints, not men of the world. What more could you desire? And yet there is something to be added. Tell me what other people have ever possessed two princes of the same race and blood, one here on earth who represents you at the Court of the Vicar of Christ,[10] and the other, immortal in Heaven, who presents all your needs and wishes at the throne of God Himself?[11]

[10] Here Father Ugolotti is referring to Don Francis Gonzaga, who was serving as imperial ambassador to the Holy See.

[11] Quoted in Cepari, *Life of Saint Aloysius*, 281–82.

On August 5, 1604, Francis Gonzaga had an audience with the pope during which the pontiff ordered the new marquis to see that a proper vita of his brother was published. Father Cepari's *Life* was completed with the endorsement of Francis Gonzaga in fulfillment of the command of Pope Clement and Claudio Aquaviva. At this point, the canonization of Aloysius seemed like something that could be soon anticipated.

Pope Clement VIII died on March 5, 1605, and was succeeded by Pope Paul V. At Don Francis' first audience with the new pope, he requested that the canonical investigation of his brother's virtues be begun, hoping that the canonization could soon take place. Francis, along with Franz Seraph Cardinal von Dietrichstein (who as a student had been present at Aloysius' funeral), received permission to place a portrait of Aloysius over his tomb. The two men installed the portrait in the chapel of the Annunziata on May 21, 1605, only a few days after Aloysius' remains had been transferred from the altar of Saint Sebastian. During the Mass, which he himself celebrated, the cardinal announced that the pope had verbally bestowed on Aloysius the title "Blessed". This, then, was the public beatification of Aloysius Gonzaga.[12]

The pronouncement was celebrated in Rome for the next two weeks. Don Francis paid to have the chapel embellished, and Aloysius' former valet, Clement Ghisoni, hung up the first votive lamp over the tomb. The celebration in Rome was followed by festivals in Brescia, Parma, Cremona, Padua, Modena, and, of course, Castiglione. Votive offerings soon began to arrive from other parts of Europe, all intended as gifts to enhance the beauty of Aloysius' tomb.

The celebration of the Feast of Blessed Aloysius, June 21, 1605, saw the Church of the Annunziata adorned with hangings and tapestries, and a Latin inscription outside the church announced the festival: "To the Blessed Aloysius Gonzaga, of the Society of Jesus, Prince of the Holy Roman Empire and Marquis of Castiglione, who added to the nobility of his race by the glory of his merits, equaled the glory of the Saints by the sanctity of his life, and who surpassed the sanctity of many, by his incomparable innocence. The two classes of Humanities

---

[12] The ceremonies of beatification, as they have come to be celebrated, were not yet the custom. See Meschler, *St. Aloysius*, 280.

have affixed this, in the name of the Imperial Ambassador."[13] The chapel where Aloysius' remains were enshrined was resplendent with gold and silver, and a picture of Aloysius stood under a baldachin. Before the altar, a beautiful carpet was laid in which were worked the words: "Here rests the body of the Blessed Aloysius Gonzaga, of the Society of Jesus." The name of Jesus had been embroidered in gold, and below this was the coat of arms of the Gonzagas of Castiglione. On the day of the feast, Masses followed Masses, and the faithful flocked to the altar rail to receive Communion. The plan was for the festival to last for eight days, but the fervor of the crowds was such that the celebration was extended for another full week.

With the pope's consent, the formal investigations of Aloysius' life and miracles (with canonization as their end) were begun in earnest. Petitions for the canonization were sent to Rome from a number of noble personages, including the Grand Duke of Tuscany, the Duke of Parma, the Bishop of Mantua, the Duke of Mantua and his sister, the dukes of Savoy and Modena, the king and queen of France, the Archduke of Brussels, and the Holy Roman emperor. Don Francis asked the pope to ratify officially the title of "Blessed" that had been conferred on his brother, and this took place on September 21, 1605.[14] The celebrations of that year were concluded in Mantua when, on December 22, a solemn procession was held in Aloysius' honor, and his relics were exposed in the cathedral to the delight of more than thirteen thousand people. The Duke of Mantua ordered that a chapel be erected in Aloysius' honor in the court church of Saint Barbara.

Over the course of the next several years, the investigations of the life and miracles of Aloysius continued. The pope had the decisions of the Congregation of Rites concerning the general and special Processes (dating January 19, 1608, and November 19, 1612) examined by the Rota, and a final report was issued on January 3, 1618. At that time, the pontiff granted permission for a special Mass and Office of Blessed Aloysius to be used in all the states under Gonzaga rule and for the Jesuit houses in Rome. The permission to use the proper Mass and Office was extended to all houses of the Society of Jesus by Pope

---

[13] See Cepari, *Life of Saint Aloysius*, 283.

[14] Aloysius was beatified before Saint Ignatius Loyola, founder of the Society of Jesus, whose beatification did not take place until 1609.

Gregory XV in 1621. New petitions for the canonization (which could have taken place at any time) continued to arrive in Rome.[15]

While the canonization of Aloysius was delayed—prudently for fear of accusations that the pope acted under pressure from secular rulers—for several more decades, succeeding popes granted a number of privileges in the intervening years. Pope Alexander VII (1655–1667) extended the use of the special Office and Mass to the inhabitants of Valtellina, while Pope Clement X (1670–1676) included Aloysius in the *Roman Martyrology*, placing there a eulogy on his innocence of life and contempt of the world.[16] When Pope Clement XI (1700–1721) was requested by Father Michael Tamburini (d. 1730), the general of the Society, to proceed with the canonization, the pope, very surprisingly, replied that Aloysius was already so honored by the Church that he felt there was no need to canonize him.

The canonization of Aloysius was to be the work of Pope Benedict XIII, who had himself renounced the title of Prince Orsini so that he might enter the Order of Preachers. He had a great devotion to Aloysius and often preached on the *beati*'s virtues when he was Bishop of Benevento. Having named Aloysius patron of his diocesan clergy and obtained the right to use the proper Mass and Office of Aloysius in the cathedral of Benevento, it was only right that he should have the privilege of canonizing him. On June 21, 1725, Benedict named Aloysius patron of all the universities and colleges of the Society of Jesus. The following year, on April 26, 1726, he signed the decree of canonization for Aloysius Gonzaga and for Stanislaus Kostka. The solemn rites of canonization finally took place at Saint Peter's Basilica on December 31. The bull of canonization read, "On this day, which is dedicated to our predecessor, Saint Sylvester, Pope and Confessor, with indescribable joy and pomp, we are come to the Basilica of the Prince of the Apostles to enroll among the Saints the angelic youth Aloysius, the cleric who so triumphantly passed through the ordeal of religious life."[17]

---

[15] Pope Gregory XV desired the canonization of Aloysius but deemed it more appropriate that Saint Ignatius Loyola, Father of the Society, be honored as a saint before his spiritual son.

[16] The entry read: "Romae beati Aloysii Gonzagae S.J. principatus contemptu et innocentia vitae clarissimi" (At Rome, Blessed Aloysius Gonzaga, S.J., famous for the contempt of his kingdom and his innocence of life). See Cepari, *Life of Saint Aloysius*, 304.

[17] Pope Benedict XIII, Decree of Canonization, Apr. 26, 1726, quoted in ibid., 307.

In 1729, the year before his death, Pope Benedict placed all schools under the patronage of Saint Aloysius. Subsequent popes promoted devotion to the saint by extending various indulgences and privileges to those devoted to the holy patron of youth.

In 1873, during an audience granted to the students of the German College, Blessed Pope Pius IX (1846–1878), who had chosen Aloysius' feast day to be the day of his papal coronation, urged students to show their devotion to Saint Aloysius: "I still remember with what deep devotion I read in my youth the life of the angelic young man and how many tears I shed over it. Read, my sons, the life of this Saint, not only to rejoice in the sweet odor of his virtues, but to emulate them, and to grow like him in the perfect love of God."[18]

On January 1, 1891, Pope Leo XIII issued a brief marking the third centenary of Aloysius' death. Urging young people to grow in the virtues of the saint and to spread his devotion, the pope extended a plenary indulgence to any who made a pilgrimage to any of the places that were especially significant in the life and history of Aloysius.[19] Following Leo's example, Pope Pius XI issued the Apostolic Letter *Singulare Illud*, marking the second centenary of the canonization of Saints Aloysius and Stanislaus in 1926, in which he confirmed Aloysius as patron of youth. Most recently, Pope Benedict XVI (2005–2013), recognizing in his General Audience the memorial of Saint Aloysius on June 21, 2006, greeted the young, sick, and newlyweds, urging them, by invoking Aloysius' example, to appreciate the virtue of evangelical purity, to face suffering by finding comfort in the Crucified Christ, and to realize a deeper love for God and for one's spouse.[20]

* * * * *

In the centuries after his death, the cult of Saint Aloysius spread throughout the Christian world. Countless statues, paintings, mosaics, and stained glass windows depicting the "saint of youth" adorned

---

[18] Quoted in Cepari, *Life of Saint Aloysius*, 308.

[19] See Appendix A.

[20] Benedict XVI, General Audience, June 21, 2006, http://w2.vatican.va/content/benedict_xvi/audiences/2006/documents/hf_ben-xvi_aud_20060621_en.html.

churches, religious communities, and private homes around the globe. The proliferation of these images offers a very tangible proof of the extent of devotion to Aloysius. Hailed as a model of purity and contempt of the world, Aloysius became an important catechetical tool both within his Jesuit community and beyond. Together with Saint Stanislaus Kostka and Saint John Berchmans, Aloysius formed part of a holy triumvirate of virtue that can almost seem ridiculous when judged by the standards of our twenty-first-century sensibilities. As one biographer of Saint John Berchmans wrote:

> God has been pleased to raise up in the Society of Jesus three young saints, in rapid succession, each of whom is a model to youth and a powerful stimulus to those advanced in life: Stanislaus Kostka, Aloysius Gonzaga, and John Berchmans. They each represent different ways of divine guidance, all animated by the same spirit, embracing the same substantial virtues, tending to the same glorious end, and obtaining the same eternal reward.[21]

Aloysius became a particularly useful tool in the Jesuits' pedagogical and evangelical missions to form young men not only intellectually but in the life of virtue. Unlike Stanislaus (with whom he was canonized) or John (whose cult was confirmed much later), Aloysius was a noble of the Holy Roman Empire, and rather than having had the benefit of a Jesuit education early in his life, he made his decision to leave behind his title and status, choosing a life of evangelical poverty, chastity, and obedience in the Society of Jesus, against all odds. He had lived a life that many could only dream of and, in the end, chose to walk away from what he knew, into an unknown life of service and obscurity. Giving his all to the Society of Jesus and sacrificing his very life in the service of the poor made him useful in both promoting vocations to the Society as well as by providing a dramatic model of self-sacrifice and devotion, purity, and longing for Heaven.

Even beyond the bounds of Jesuit schools, Aloysius played a significant part in the work of his congregation. In the missions (both

---

[21] Giuseppe Boero, *The Life of Saint John Berchmans of the Society of Jesus*, trans. the Fathers of the Oratory (New York: P.J. Kennedy and Sons, 1910), x–xi.

urban and rural), he became the great model of chastity, as purity became the sign par excellence of sanctity.[22] Aloysius and Stanislaus became much-needed role models who could inspire young people to avoid sins of the flesh. Devotion to these two spread even to the smallest hamlets, and their respective feasts were often celebrated with great solemnity.[23]

One of the key elements of devotion to this saint was the practice known as the "Six Sundays of Saint Aloysius". Inspired by the six years Aloysius spent in the Society of Jesus, the devotion was granted papal approbation by Pope Clement XII (who on November 21, 1737, granted a plenary indulgence to any who visited a church, oratory, or altar dedicated to Aloysius on the saint's feast). In this particular devotion, a plenary indulgence was granted to the faithful on each of the six Sundays made "days of true repentance, by a worthy communion, by a serious application to vocal and mental prayer, and to other works of piety performed in honour of the saint, and directed to the greater glory of God".[24] Devotional works suggested a number of pious acts to be performed during the devotion, in addition to celebrating the sacrament of reconciliation and receiving the Eucharist; "taking for an advocate St. Aloysius"; hearing Masses celebrated in his honor; reciting six Paters, Aves, and the Gloria Patri before an image of Saint Aloysius along with particular hymns and prayers; spending time reading various reflections on Aloysius' virtues; or performing acts of charity.[25]

As opposed to many other saints (even of the modern era) whose cults were promoted and proliferated because of their reputations as

[22] Louis Châtellier, *The Religion of the Poor: Rural Missions in Europe and the Formation of Modern Catholicism, c. 1500–c. 1800*, trans. Brian Pearce (Cambridge, U.K.: Cambridge University Press, 1997), 172.

[23] Ibid., 173.

[24] Pasquale de Mattei, *The Angelic Youth Saint Aloysius of Gonzaga: Proposed as an Example of a Holy Life*, trans. Maria Elisa di Gonzaga-Mantua (London: Thomas Richardson and Sons, 1847), 11.

[25] Ibid., 12–13. For more on the Six Sundays of Saint Aloysius, see Sisters of Charity of Saint Vincent de Paul, *The St. Vincent's Manual: Containing a Selection of Prayers and Devotional Exercises* (Baltimore: John Murphy, 1856), 488–90. Devotions to Saint Aloysius were among the most popular in prayer books printed in the United States after 1840, with 63 percent including at least some prayers to the patron of youth. See Ann Taves, *The Household of Faith: Roman Catholic Devotions in Mid-Nineteenth-Century America* (Notre Dame, Ind.: University of Notre Dame, 1986), 25.

miracle-workers, Aloysius was emphasized for his virtues.[26] In being held up as a model for youth, he was, rather unfortunately, robbed of many of those humanizing qualities that endeared him to his Jesuit confreres. In the nineteenth-century, his inner fire and the dynamism of his personality were subsumed by enthusiastic preachers and hagiographers trying to highlight the saint's single-hearted devotion and his commitment to purity. Unfortunately, because of the way in which he was presented, with his scourge and lily, he became a sort of caricature of the very virtues he was supposed to epitomize.

As a means of furthering devotion to Aloysius and of encouraging young people to imitate him, pious unions and sodalities were established in various parts of the world. The intentions of these organizations, which were usually composed of young Catholic men, was the imitation of the saint's virtues (especially purity), to "take shelter under the glorious emblem of virtue and purity, celestially personified in the Most Holy Virgin and admirably imitated by the angelic young man ... St. Aloysius Gonzaga".[27] The *Manual* of the Saint Aloysius Society (which was printed with the approbation of the Bishop of Buffalo, New York, in 1885) states that the Society had "for its object the uniting in the bond of fraternal union those who have a desire to serve God faithfully, and acquire the virtues suited to their station in life, under the patronage of Saint Aloysius, the model of youth, the seraph of purity and charity".[28] The Society's members were expected to maintain a "gentlemanly decorum which should always and everywhere characterize those who have the high honor of being children of Saint Aloysius".[29]

In the conclusion of the *Life of Saint Aloysius Gonzaga* that was first published by Burns and Oates of London in 1867, the author makes the following observation: "Some may complain that we have begun by setting before them too perfect a saint: who (it may be said) can aspire to imitate Aloysius' heroic sanctity?"[30] This is a very good

---

[26] For a modern perspective on the virtues of Saint Aloysius, see David Paul Eich, *Desiderata: A Teenager's Journey to God* (San Francisco: Ignatius Press, 2001), 57–59.

[27] See Kathy Bacon, *Negotiating Sainthood: Distinction, Cursilería, and Saintliness in Spanish Novels* (London: Modern Humanities Research Association and Maney Publishing, 2007), 56.

[28] *Saint Aloysius Society Manual*, 6th ed. (New York: Fr. Pustet, 1889), 1.

[29] Ibid., 10.

[30] Virgilio Cepari, *The Life of St. Aloysius Gonzaga, of the Society of Jesus*, vol. 1 of Library of Religious Biography, ed. Edward Healy Thompson (London: Burns and Oates, 1867), 372.

question. In the making of Aloysius a model of all those virtues that seem to be most opposed to the values of contemporary culture and, arguably, human nature, his dynamism and the power of his witness have been lost to us.

* * * * *

In his novel *The Winter of Our Discontent*, Nobel-Prize-winning author John Steinbeck observes: "When two people meet, each one is changed by the other so you've got two new people."[31] Such is the nature of human relationships. Such can be our relationships with the saints. But how do you "write" another person, especially one who lived hundreds of years ago? This is the challenge faced by all biographers, historians, and hagiographers.

Having explored the life of Aloysius Gonzaga, prince, ascetic, religious, pilgrim, wonder-worker, saint, can we say that we know him better now than before? On the level of history, it seems we can. The events of his life, his letters, the impressions of those who knew him, provide a certain character portrait of this young man whom most everyone would acknowledge as having been heroic, zealous (albeit too much so at times), and maybe even holy. Yet, it seems that Aloysius remains largely ignored or forgotten today. Why does the Church, the world, need him when there are so many other models of holiness, ancient and modern, living and dead, to inspire, teach, and guide us? In order to answer that question, we must look beyond historical anecdotes or fragments of writing and try to see this beautiful and passionate man for who he really was. To reduce Aloysius to his lily and scourge or his life and legacy to two or three virtues (no matter how fundamental they may be) is to deny the possibility of a relationship.

As the writer Ethel Pochocki said of him:

> Aloysius was one of those holy-from-birth saints, those intense, passionate, driven, single-minded ones, rushing pell-mell into holiness,... So what did Aloysius do with his lovely light? From surface facts, he did not contribute to world peace or environmental causes.

---

[31] John Steinbeck, *The Winter of Our Discontent* (New York: Bantam Books, 1962), 66.

He did nothing to save the dolphins or the Lombardy poplar or promote democratic government. Aloysius' mission was in being rather
than doing, and in following God's will.[32]

Aloysius' way of being, grounded in a sincerity, a humility, and a
single-hearted devotion, all rooted in love, is the gospel he pro-
claims to us today. This young man knew that real nobility lies in
our capacity to love. He knew his true worth in light of God's love,
in understanding that, in spite of his unworthiness, he could place his
confidence in the reality of the gratuitous love of God. Aloysius' love
for all those around him was an expression of this truth.[33] Having
received God's love in all simplicity and humility, he was able to live
out his vocation in freedom.

Pope Saint John Paul II observed in his address to the bishop
and people of the Diocese of Mantua on the occasion of that local
church's twelfth centenary, "Still today, this ardent young man, follower of Christ, addresses a pressing exhortation to us of coherence
and fidelity to the Gospel, reminding us that God must have priority
in our lives."[34]

[32] Ethel Pochocki, "Aloysius: A Reluctant Admiration", in *Aloysius*, ed. Clifford Stevens
and William Hart McNichols (Huntington, Ind.: Our Sunday Visitor, 1993), 146.

[33] Thomas Merton, *No Man Is an Island* (San Diego: Harcourt Brace, 1983), 203.

[34] John Paul II, "Message of John Paul II to Bishop Egidio Caporello of Mantua on the
Occasion of the 12th Centenary of the Diocese of Mantua", from the Vatican, June 10, 2004,
http://www.vatican.va/holy_father/john_paul_ii/speeches/2004/june/documents/hf_jp-ii
_spe_20040619_bishop-mantua_en.html.

APPENDIX A

The Apostolic Brief of Pope Leo XIII of January 1, 1891*

To all Christian people who read this letter, health and Apostolic Benediction.

It is timely and auspicious that on the 21st day of June of this year, solemn festivities are to be held in honor of Saint Aloysius Gonzaga to commemorate the third centenary of his most blessed death. We have been informed that this happy recurrence has inflamed a remarkable love and desire of holiness in the minds of Christian youth, and that they have seen in this occasion an admirable opportunity to testify by a manifold demonstration their love and reverence to the patron of youth. It does not appear to be confined to the country which gave birth to Saint Aloysius, but his name and fame have gone abroad widely and in every land. We, who from our earliest years have been in the habit of showing the deepest devotion to the Angelic Youth, were filled with delight at the news.

With God's aid we trust these solemnities will not be without fruit for Christians, especially the young, who while they honor their patron and protector, will readily recall to mind the marvelous virtues of him who was a striking model while he lived. And as they reflect upon and wonder at his holiness, we may hope that with the help of God they will try to fashion their thoughts and minds after his, and strive to be better by imitating him. It would be impossible to put before Catholic youth a more striking example of one richer in those virtues which ought to be the chief glory of the young. For from the

* Quoted in Virgil Cepari, S.J., *Life of Saint Aloysius Gonzaga*, ed. Francis Goldie, S.J. (New York: Benziger Brothers, 1891), 308–11.

life and practice of Saint Aloysius there are many lessons they can learn, how by care and watchfulness to keep their innocence unsullied, with what constancy they are to chastise their bodies and put out the fires of unlawful desires, how to despise riches and scorn worldly honors, in what spirit and intention they should devote themselves to their studies and to all the other duties of their lives. Then, too, will they desire that teaching which is so especially needed in our day: with what faith and love they ought to cling to Mother Church and to the See of Saint Peter. For this angelic young man, whether he was living at home, or as a page in the Court of Madrid, or when, after his renunciation of his princedom, he was applying himself to the cultivation of his mind in holiness and learning within the Society of Jesus—where he had obtained what he desired, and rejoiced to see all approach to honors cut off, and his life entirely dedicated to the salvation of his neighbor—in all these walks of life he bore himself so that he not only far excelled everyone, but left behind him a splendid example of holiness.

It was then a wise idea for those who preside over the instruction and education of youth to put Saint Aloysius forward as a most noble pattern for imitation. In this they follow the counsel of our predecessor Benedict XIII, who chose Saint Aloysius as the chief heavenly patron of the young who are engaged in their studies. For this reason the societies of Catholic youth, which have been founded in Italy and elsewhere to keep with special honor the festival of Saint Aloysius are deserving of high praise. We are well aware what zeal and care they have brought to the work of preparing for this celebration in which the whole Catholic world is joining in honor of the Angelic Youth, and what trouble they are taking that the pious pilgrimages to the birthplace of the Saint and to this City, where his remains are preserved and honored, should be remarkable for the piety and the number of Catholics who take part in them.

We learn also that a method has been offered to boys and girls testifying the first fruits of pure love and devotion to Aloysius. Forms are being widely distributed, already made illustrious by some important names, in which they or their parents can inscribe themselves as his servants and clients. We trust and wish that this rare zeal, these holy resolutions and desires may through God's favor have an excellent and happy issue. Meanwhile since we have lately been implored to enrich and adorn this festival with the heavenly treasures of the Church so that it may produce still more bountiful fruit for souls, we have deemed it right to comply with these petitions.

Therefore, by the mercy of Almighty God, and with the authority of the blessed Apostles Peter and Paul, we grant in the Lord, a plenary indulgence and remission of all their sins to all the faithful who shall have attended each day of the *Triduos* or have been at least five times to the devotions of the Novenas to be held before the Solemnities that shall be ordered by the respective ordinaries. And on these conditions, that upon the day of the feast or on any of the days of the *Triduo* or Novena which they may choose, after a truly contrite confession and holy Communion, they devoutly visit any church or public oratory where the Feast of Saint Aloysius shall be celebrated, and there pour forth pious prayers for the peace of Christian princes, the uprooting of heresy, the conversion of sinners and the exaltation of our Holy Mother the Church.

To these we grant a plenary indulgence, and a remission of all their sins. To any who are contrite at least in heart and make the pilgrimages to these spots mentioned above, and also to children who as best they can and to their parents who sign their names in honor of Saint Aloysius, provided they have been to the *Triduos* or Novenas mentioned above, we grant an indulgence of seven years and of forty days in the usual form of the Church. And all these indulgences may, by way of suffrage, be applied to all who have died in a state of grace. They are to be available for this year only.

We wish also that to the copies and impressions of this letter, signed by a Notary Public and sealed by an ecclesiastical dignitary, the same credence be given as would be to these originals.

Given at Rome under the fisherman's ring at Saint Peter's, January 1, 1891, the 13th of our pontificate.

APPENDIX B

The Apostolic Letter *Singulare Illud* of Pope Pius XI on June 13, 1926*

To the Reverend Father Wlodimir Ledóchoski, Superior General of the Society of Jesus, on the occasion of the second centenary of the Canonization of St. Aloysius Gonzaga

Beloved Son, greetings and Apostolic Benediction.

Characteristic of the life of the Divine Master is a special love for young people. Indeed, he calls to himself the innocence of childhood (cf. Mk 10:13–16) and with terrifying words condemns those who corrupt them, threatening them with severe punishment (cf. Mt 18:6). He holds out to undefiled youth as reward and invitation the complete and perfect ideal of holiness (cf. Mk 10:21).

Since the Church has received this same spirit from its Founder, as heir of his divine mission and work, it has been involved and stirred with the same love toward young people and has taken to heart the protection of childhood. The Church is concerned with safeguarding their physical and moral welfare and has undertaken for her children primary education and then the higher disciplines, operating primary schools and universities. With this in mind, the Church has not only approved religious orders and congregations, but also promoted the foundation of universities, houses of study, schools open to the public, and societies for young people. At all times, the Church has claimed

* Pope Pius XI, *Singulare Illud*, June 13, 1926, http://w2.vatican.va/content/pius-xi/la/apost _letters/documents/hf_p-xi_apl_19260613_singulare-illud.html. Translated for this publication by Vincent Tobin, OSB.

as an inviolable right the education of the young, making known to all human society entrusted to her that she is the unique depository of authentic moral formation, the only and infallible teacher of that difficult art of the Christian formation of the human character. We heartily rejoice now in seeing everywhere so many young boys and girls of every social condition reaching out with great enthusiasm to their priests and pastors, longing to improve their knowledge of Christian life and doctrine, and to help the Church in its work of saving humanity.

Thinking back over the immense crowds of young people who came to Us from all parts of the world during the past Holy Year, We relive those happy feelings when We saw so many legions of them organized on a world scale, being able one day to form a peaceful army which the Apostolic See would utilize in reforming a world plunging into decay. We love them even more when We see the endless abhorrent traps laid to ensnare their faith and innocence. As a result, it often happens in the struggle of spiritual warfare that they are weakened and their youthful energy spent when they could have rendered outstanding service to Church and society.

And so the second centenary of Aloysius Gonzaga's canonization, which occurs next December 31st, brings in its wake so many advantages for the spiritual benefit of young people, that, while We are addressing you, beloved Son, We feel obliged to turn Our thoughts to all Our young people who everywhere represent the hope of the kingdom of Christ Jesus. Yes, since the young in their struggles and dangers should turn to this strong heavenly patron, so too should they follow him as an ideal guide of all the virtues. If they delve into his life, they will clearly understand the ways to follow toward Christian perfection. And what happy results they will be able to achieve in walking in the footsteps of this saint. Yes, if they contemplate him as he was and is—so different from the false picture by which the Church's enemies or even careless writers have deformed him— how will they not be able to find in him an outstanding example of youthful virtue, even among so many examples of holy virtues which recently have enriched the Church?

As we look back over the history of the Church, it is easy to discover that under the Holy Spirit young and old up to our own time have found themselves more worthy of wondering at the innocence of their life, since they have modeled their behavior in his school. To cite just a few examples, We recall John Berchmans, an alumnus of the Roman College who determined to follow Aloysius as a model; Nuntius Sulprizio, a young worker who from childhood imitated the Saint of Castiglione; Contardo Ferrini, called by his contemporaries the New Aloysius, who nurtured a tender devotion toward this Saint and took him as a guide and model of his own chastity; Bartolomea Capitanio, who in life and death copied the Saint and seemed to share in his glory since she was beatified in this centenary year. No one would hesitate to affirm that Aloysius heavily influenced Gabriel of the Sorrowful Mother, who when still young, showed himself flighty and fickle, nevertheless never stopped asking Gonzaga's help, having learned to venerate him as patron of the young. To mention one among the most recent educators and masters of the young, John Bosco was not only tenderly devoted to Aloysius, but passed on this devotion as an inheritance to his youthful sons and to all those under his care. Among them stands out the pure soul of Dominic Savio, who for so short a time God gave for the admiration of all.

Clearly the mysterious decision of Divine Providence was evident in that Aloysius in the prime of life was suddenly taken away, at the time when his outstanding qualities of mind and heart, his determination and astonishing prudence, his zeal for religion and for souls gave promise of a fertile apostolate. God indeed willed that adolescents should learn from this young lovable saint, their contemporary, what was the principal duty of their generation—to prepare themselves for the problems of life by practicing and cultivating the Christian virtues. Indeed, those who do not have and do not value those interior virtues which shone so brilliantly in Aloysius—We cannot consider them sufficiently suitable and armed against life's dangers and battles and capable of exercising the apostolate, but rather they are like "sounding brass and tinkling cymbal" (1 Cor 13:1). They gain nothing and may even harm the very cause that they pretend to foster and defend, something widely known and that has not infrequently occurred in the past. The celebration of the centenary of Saint Aloysius is indeed timely, a saint who by his example helps the young to understand that before thinking of others and of Catholic Action, they must especially make progress in their study and practice of virtue, even though they are looking forward to exterior things and are ready to throw themselves into action.

In the first place, this saint teaches the young that the substance of Christian education is founded on the spirit of a living faith. Men shining "like a lamp in a dark place" (2 Pet 1:19) come to know fully the importance of the moral life. And so Aloysius determined to spend his life on eternal and not temporal ways of thinking, the only ways in which he could consider himself a spiritual man. Hardly out of childhood, he kept meditating alone and for long periods on the Spiritual Exercises, and later, as a member of the Jesuits, he found here profound spiritual profit. We think it absolutely indispensable that our young people take to heart the example of this Saint and spend their lives not running after things that cannot last, but for the things that lead to blessedness. Adolescents will win this morally correct view of life if they imitate their heavenly patron and from time to time spend a few days with the Spiritual Exercises. Long experience shows how they win over and strengthen the sensitive young who are ready to learn.

Aloysius, guided by the light of eternal truths, determined to allow nothing to keep him from leading a life of innocence. From his earliest youth until his last breath, he kept himself clean from serious sin, so much so that his companions named him "Angel", a name Christians used from that time on. Blessed Robert Bellarmine, the saint's spiritual director, believed he was confirmed in grace. But Aloysius did not attain the divine gift of such perfection because he was exempt from those battles which often enough fight against nature fallen from original grace. If by a singular gift he was never tempted by lust, nevertheless in view of his high destiny, he was not completely free from outbreaks of anger or the excessive pride of vanity. Not only did he rein in such natural inclinations by his indomitable will, but he kept them under complete control through the power of reason. He was not unaware of human nature's weakness, did not trust in himself, and sought God's help in continual prayer. He was particularly devoted to the Virgin Mary. He realized that the source and support of the spiritual life was the Eucharist, and he received the Sacrament as often as was permitted in those days. To maintain his chaste life, always dependent on divine grace, he found refuge in the Holy Sacrament and in the intercession of the Mother of God, avoiding worldly things and mortifying himself. Others can admire, but they cannot equal him. It is scarcely believable that amid so much corruption he was so like the heavenly spirits. In the midst of pleasure-seeking, he distinguished himself by restraint and mortification. In a world competing for honors, he was so detached that he gladly gave up the vast estate that was his by hereditary right and sought entrance into that religious family where by vow he could not seek the dignity of high ecclesiastical office. In the midst of so much adulation of Greek and Roman antiquity, he gave himself to the study and practice of the holy, his soul fixed on God—so much so that when in contemplation, he did not experience distractions.

He reached the heights of sanctity scarcely available even to those of outstanding virtue. All this helps to show the young of our day how to preserve intact those gifts which are their glory, a pure and chaste way of life. We are not unaware that some educators, overwhelmed at the depravity of these days that can utterly ruin young lives, are engaged in planning new educational systems. But We ask that they concentrate on those skills and disciplines which drink deep of the tried and tested, centuries-old font of Christian wisdom: a living faith, flight from seduction, self-control, an active devotion toward God and the Blessed Virgin, and finally, a life strengthened and enlivened by frequent recourse to the Eucharist.

If young people would look to Aloysius as a perfect model of chastity, they would learn not only to control their passions, but also to avoid that kind of learning that scorns the teachings of Christ and the Church, learning which draws them into a false sense of freedom, intellectual pride, and undisciplined will. How different was Aloysius! Knowing full well that he was heir to a great fortune, he let himself be guided in his studies and piety by his future teachers. Later on, as a Jesuit, he submitted perfectly to his superiors, so much so that he in no way deviated from the rules of the Society. Such comportment is drastically different from the conduct of those young people who appear to be good, but are reckless and completely indifferent to the advice of the old.

Those who want to fight under the banners of Christ have to realize that if they wish to shake off the yoke of discipline, instead of triumphing, they will return only after happy defeat. Nature itself under Providence ordains that the young cannot achieve any profit of intellect or moral life, or make progress in understanding the Christian spirit, without being taught by others. What holds for the other disciplines is even more necessary when it comes to exercising the apostolate. These functions are entrusted by Christ to the Church and cannot achieve their holy purpose without deep respect for those whom the Holy Spirit "has appointed overseers to rule the church of God" (Acts 20:28). Just as in the earthly Paradise Satan promised our first parents incredible advantages as a reward for disobedience and thus seduced them into rebelling against God, so too in our days under the pretext of liberty Satan corrupts and drags down to ruin so many of the young, puffed up as they are with empty pride, unaware that their real dignity lies in obedience to lawful authority. Aloysius was exceptionally prudent and highly admired by his contemporaries, who based their fondest hopes on his expected vast wealth. His fellow Jesuits thought he would one day be the General of the Society, but he did not think highly of himself and obeyed humbly and with dignity all who were placed over him in the name of his eternal Lord and King.

Our saint profited mightily from the teachings of the faith, and in him, the gifts of grace and nature were so perfectly united that he serves as a model for the young. His native ability, mature judgment, nobility of thought—all make him an ideal model. A refined and unclouded intelligence led him to contemplate truth and right. His academic accomplishments and philosophical public debates were very well received. His writings, and especially his letters, few as they are, witness to his wise judgment, particularly evident in the difficult affairs entrusted to him by his father, after whose death Aloysius reconciled his brother with the Duke of Mantua. Everyone who knew him, high and low alike, praised him to the skies. His Jesuit superiors and companions were in admiration of him.

This heir to the vast estate of Castiglione, from the time he attained the use of reason, never wavered in his determination to lead a holy life. He is an ideal model to follow, especially for students who need to learn wisdom and avoid illusion and dissipation, not ruled by public opinion.

In his apostolic zeal, he never tired of helping others, always turning to the contemplation of the things of God, his life "hidden with

Christ in God" (Col 3:3). Hardly out of childhood, he edified others, urging them on to a virtuous life. As he grew older, he showed his zeal for souls and longed to work among heretics and pagans. This student of the Roman College was a familiar sight in the streets of Rome as he went about catechizing the young and the poor. Rome was witness to his heroic charity when he dedicated himself to helping those infected with the plague. As a result, he caught the disease himself and died a few months later at the age of 24. He left our young people a great example: a holy life, the teaching apostolate, zeal for the missions—in a word, the endless ways of charity. Adapted to today's needs, his work lives on.

Two hundred years ago, Our predecessor, Benedict XIII, proclaimed Aloysius a saint. Since that time, he has never ceased to shower his gifts on all devoted to him, especially the young. His example has encouraged so many to do penance and to lead a life of chastity. It is no surprise then that many popes chose him as a model and protector of the young.

So then, following the example of Benedict XIII and Leo XIII, We solemnly confirm and with Our own apostolic authority, proclaim Saint Aloysius Gonzaga heavenly patron of all Christian youth and, with paternal affection, earnestly ask them to honor him as their model and call on him with fitting devotions, such as the practice of the six Sundays, a devotion that has produced such happy results.

We are glad to learn that the Committee formed for the solemn commemoration of the centenary under the direction of Our Cardinal Vicar has suggested that, after some spiritual retreat, young people make a pact to lead a full and pure Christian life, inscribing their names which will be bound into a volume and deposited in the church where the saint is buried.

Saint Stanislaus Kostka was named a saint on the same day as Aloysius. This young Polish Jesuit was born of noble family and was known for his chaste life. He opposed the dissolute life of his brother and his companions and did not succumb to the wiles of the heretical family with whom he lived, ever drawing his strength from the Eucharist. He made long journeys on foot in obedience to God and to the Virgin Mary, who urged him to join the Jesuits, finally coming to Rome, but just as one in passing: he died shortly afterwards at 18 years of age, still a novice. It seems that God willed to reward his virtue so that he could offer his nation, and indeed all Christendom, protection against the incursions of the Turks. John Sobieski, who lifted the terrible siege of Vienna, maintained that his victories were due not so much to his army as to the patronage of Saint Stanislaus.

I pray God that these two saints obtain for the young the gift that is the only glory of Christians, a chaste and holy life.

As a pledge of heavenly blessings and of Our own fatherly affection, with all Our heart We impart to you, beloved Son and to all Jesuits and their students, the apostolic blessing.

Given at Rome, at Saint Peter's, on the 13th of June 1926, the fifth year of Our pontificate.

Pope Pius XI.

APPENDIX C

Prayers in Honor of Saint Aloysius

Litany of Saint Aloysius

(For Private Devotion Only)

Lord, have mercy.
Christ, have mercy.
Lord, have mercy. Christ, hear us.
Christ, graciously hear us.
God the Father of Heaven,
Have mercy on us.
God the Son, Redeemer of the world,
Have mercy on us.
God the Holy Spirit,
Have mercy on us.
Holy Trinity, one God,
Have mercy on us.
Holy Mary, Mother of God,
Pray for us.
Saint Aloysius, overwhelmed with the blessings of God,
And filled with the Holy Spirit, pray for us.
Saint Aloysius, worthy confessor of Jesus Christ,...
Saint Aloysius, devoted to the Blessed Sacrament,...
Saint Aloysius, faithful servant of the Blessed Virgin,...
Saint Aloysius, example of humility,...
Saint Aloysius, lover of poverty,...
Saint Aloysius, full of obedience,...
Saint Aloysius, admirable in your patience,...
Saint Aloysius, most powerful in Heaven,...

Saint Aloysius, honor and glory of youth, ...
Saint Aloysius, patron of schools, ...
Saint Aloysius, imitator of angelic life, ...
Saint Aloysius, bright light of the Church, ...
Saint Aloysius, comforter of all suffering with HIV/AIDS
    and of those who care for them, ...
    And filled with the Holy Spirit, pray for us.
Lamb of God, who takes away the sins of the world,
    Spare us, O Lord.
Lamb of God, who takes away the sins of the world,
    Graciously hear us, O Lord.
Lamb of God, who takes away the sins of the world,
    Have mercy on us.

Let us pray.

O God, the distributor of all heavenly gifts, you have given to Saint Aloysius the grace to join admirable innocence of life to the discipline of penance. Grant, by the merits of his prayers, that we who have not imitated him in his innocence may have the grace of imitating his penance. Through Christ our Lord. Amen.[1]

Chaplet of Saint Aloysius

The Chaplet of Saint Aloysius is composed of twenty-three blue beads (representing the years of the saint's life and his devotion to the Mother of God) and an additional single white or clear bead and a medal of the saint. On the medal are prayed the sign of the cross and the act of contrition, recalling Aloysius' penitential spirit. On the single bead, the Our Father is offered. The Hail Mary is prayed on each of the twenty-three beads. After each Hail Mary, the invocation "Saint Aloysius, pray for us" is added. The following prayer, taken from the Mass of the Memorial of Saint Aloysius, is recited at the end of the chaplet:

O God, giver of heavenly gifts,
who in Saint Aloysius Gonzaga

---

[1] Text adapted from traditional sources.

joined penitence to a wonderful innocence of life,
grant, through his merits and intercession,
that, though we have failed to follow him in innocence,
we may imitate him in penitence.
Through our Lord Jesus Christ, your Son,
who lives and reigns with you in the unity of the Holy Spirit,
one God, for ever and ever.
Amen.

Prayer of Pope John Paul II

Saint Aloysius, poor in spirit, we come to you with confidence, blessing the Heavenly Father for giving us in you an eloquent proof of
His merciful love. Humble and confident adorer of the plans of the
divine heart, as a young man you emptied yourself of every worldly
honor and fortune. You put on the hair shirt of perfect chastity, ran
the way of obedience, impoverished yourself to serve God, offering
everything to him out of love.

You are pure in heart; free us from all slavery to the world. Keep the
young from falling victim to hatred and violence; don't let them be
enticed by the flattery of easy, false, and selfish illusions. Help them
to free themselves from all foul thoughts, defend them from blinding
pride, save them from the power of the Evil One.

Let their lives be a witness to a pure heart. Heroic apostle of charity, obtain for us the gift of the Divine Mercy which rouses the heart
hardened by pride and strengthens the longing for holiness in each
of us.

Help today's generation to have the courage to swim against the
tide by spending their lives in building up the kingdom of Christ.
May this generation know how to share your own passion for people,
recognizing in each and every one the Divine Presence of Christ.
With you we call on Mary, Mother of the Redeemer. To her we
entrust body and soul, every misery and trouble, life and death, so
that everything in us, as happened in you, may be done for the glory
of God, who lives and reigns forever. Amen.[2]

---

[2] Pope John Paul II, "Preghiera del Santo Padre Giovanni Paolo II a San Luigi Gonzaga",
June 22, 1991, trans. Vincent Tobin, OSB, http://w2.vatican.va/content/john-paul-ii/it
/speeches/1991/june/documents/hf_jp-ii_spe_19910622_san-luigi-gonzaga.html.

Prayer of Carlo Maria Cardinal Martini

Lord Jesus, you showed Saint Aloysius the face of God who is love
and gave him the strength to follow you. In joy and simplicity of
heart, he renounced the world's prestige and wealth to spend his life
for others. Through his intercession, give us the grace to accept your
plan for our life and to share with everyone the joy of the Gospel and
the smile of your loving presence. As it was for him, so too let your
cross be our consolation, our hope, the answer to life's dark troubles,
the light of all our nights and trials.

Mary, you inspired the young Aloysius Gonzaga to live a life of
virginity. Strengthen in us a longing for purity and chastity, and
obtain for us the gift of contemplating the mystery of God through
the Words of the Gospel in which Jesus speaks to us, calls us, and stirs
us to answer.

All of this, Father, we ask through Jesus Christ our Lord, in the
grace of the Holy Spirit. Amen.[3]

Novena in Honor of Saint Aloysius

O Glorious Saint Aloysius! Wonderful example of the power of grace!
In your early years you attained the summit of Christian perfection;
receive my most ardent devotion, and join me in giving thanks to
the Almighty for the graces bestowed on you. O perfect victim of
divine charity! Fervent follower of a crucified God, whose spotless
innocence did not exclude you from the trials of penance, you know
well all that is necessary to meet the penetrating eye of infinite holiness. Look with compassion on me, consider my misery, and, above
all, the cold insensibility of my heart, which, like yours, should live
only for love. O blessed Saint! By your glowing zeal, which con-
sumed your soul for love of Jesus, by the ineffable delights which
now come from the unending contemplation of his adorable and
unending perfections, take me under your protection, and ask for me
the intentions of this novena (mention your request here). Obtain for
me, that from this moment, I may work to become truly humble,
fervent, and contrite; that detached from all which is not God, I may

[3] Carlo Maria Cardinal Martini, *Preghiera del Card. Carlo Maria Martini*, trans. Vincent
Tobin, OSB, http://www.santuariosanluigi.it/san_luigi.html#preghiere, accessed November 10, 2016.

advance daily in divine love, purity of heart, ardent devotion to the wondrous mystery of the altar, and tender and filial trust in the Holy Mother of God.

And you, O Virgin of Virgins! Immaculate Queen of Angels, and dear mother of angelic Saint Aloysius! You whose glowing charity and spotless charity is reflected in the saints, remember the maternal tenderness with which you loved Saint Aloysius, and obtain for me the grace to imitate all that endeared him to the Sacred Heart. Unite your prayers with mine, for the intentions of this novena; receive me into your arms during this life, and be my powerful protector at the hour of death. Amen.[4]

Prayer to Obtain the Virtues of Saint Aloysius

Antiphon: He was filled with goodness and sweetness, modest in his looks, simple and pure in life, and versed from his infancy in the practice of all virtues.

V. Remember, amiable saint, the days of your exile.

R. Pray to the Lord for us and recommend to Him our greatest needs.

Let us pray.

Loving Saint, who watches over the young and whose angelic virtues are placed before me for my imitation, help those who make an effort to reach God by imitating thee. Help me, I beg of you, to acquire thy humility, meekness, obedience, purity, compassion for the unfortunate, and thy tender and solid piety toward Jesus. Grant that under your protection I may have the happiness of preserving here below the precious gift of innocence, so as to receive, as you did, an immortal crown in Heaven. Amen.[5]

Prayer to Saint Aloysius for Purity

O Blessed Aloysius, adorned with angelic graces, I, your most unworthy client, commend to you the chastity of my soul and body,

[4] Adapted from *The Life of St. Stanislaus Kostka of the Society of Jesus, Patron of Novices* (Baltimore: Kelly, Piet, 1870), 133–34. This prayer was written such that it could be addressed either to Saint Aloysius or to Saint Stanislaus.

[5] Based on prayer found in Maurice Meschler, S.J., *St. Aloysius Gonzaga: Patron of Christian Youth* (Rockford, Ill.: TAN Books, 1985), 346–47; translation adapted.

praying that you, by your angelic purity, will plead for me to Jesus Christ, the Immaculate Lamb, and His most holy Mother, the Virgin of virgins, that they would keep me from all grievous sin. Let me never be defiled with any stain of impurity, but when you see me in temptation, or in danger of falling, remove from my heart all bad thoughts and unclean desires, and awaken in me the memory of eternity to come, and of Jesus crucified; impress deeply in my heart a sense of the holy fear of God; and so, stirring up in my heart the fire of divine love, enable me to follow in your footsteps here on earth, so that, in Heaven with you, I may be worthy to enjoy the vision of God forever. Amen.

Our Father.
Hail Mary.

Prayer to Saint Aloysius for Young People

Dear Christian youth, you were a faithful follower of Christ in the Society of Jesus. You steadily strove for perfection while generously serving the plague-stricken.

Help our youth today who are faced with a plague of false cults and false gods. Show them how to harness their energies and to use them for their own and others' fulfillment—which will be for the greater glory of God. Amen.

A Traditional Young Person's Consecration to Saint Aloysius

O glorious Saint Aloysius, honored by the Church with the title of "angelic youth" for the purity of your life while on earth, I offer myself to you this day with all the devotion of my mind and heart, and to you I consecrate myself entirely. O perfect example, O kind and powerful protector of youth, how much I have need of you. The world and the devil lay snares for me; I feel the fire of my passions; I know the weakness and immaturity of my age. Who can protect me if not you, O angelic saint, the glory, ornament, love, and mainstay of the young? To you, then, with all my mind and heart I have recourse; in thee I confide; to thee I consecrate myself. Therefore, I firmly resolve to be especially devoted to you, to glorify you for your sublime virtues, and especially for your angelic purity;

to imitate your example, to promote devotion to you among my friends and companions; and to invoke and bless, to the end of my life, your dear and holy name. To you I consecrate my soul, my senses, my heart, and all my being. O dear Saint Aloysius, today I am all yours, and yours I wish to remain forever. Protect, defend, and preserve me as your possession, so that through honoring you, I may be better able to serve and honor Jesus and Mary, and come one day with you to see and bless my God forever in Paradise. Amen.[6]

[6] Based on prayer found in ibid., 348; translation adapted.

INDEX